Tim Cawkwell's

CRICKET ON

THE EDGE

SFORZINDA BOOKS

Published by Sforzinda Books
30 Eaton Road
Norwich NR4 6PZ, UK

Text set in Book Antiqua 10 point

CONTENTS

This book is dedicated to all the cricketing heroes of times past, in every country under the sun; to all Old Aficionados of the game; to my grandsons; to all the not-yet-born who come to love cricket.

GLOSSARY

If you are a long-time cricket fan, you can skip this page, but if you are a cricket virgin, the following explanatory notes might prove helpful.

red ball   The traditional cricket ball, good for swing, seam and spin. Harder to see for batsmen and fielders.

white ball   Used in One-day games (e.g. World Cup and County One-day Cup). England batsman Jonny Bairstow: "We know the new balls, being white, only swing for an over or so, max." England batting coach Mark Ramprakash: "In one-day cricket the ball really doesn't swing, seam or spin too much."

four-day cricket   The county championship in two divisions in 2019: 8 teams in Division One, 10 teams in Division Two. Strictly the Specsavers County Championship. Fixtures scheduled for 4 days each game, hence **slow cricket**.

one-day cricket   The ECB 50-over competition. Strictly, the Royal London One-Day Cup. An **ODI** is a One-Day International.

T20   Played in Leagues around the globe, notably the Indian Premier League (IPL) and the Big Bash in Australia. In England and Wales, see 'Blast'. A **T20I** is an International T20.

Blast   The ECB T20 competition. Strictly, the Vitality Blast. Generically, 'blast cricket' as a description of **fast cricket**.

The Hundred   The ECB's new short-form format of 100 balls each side (less than the 120 balls in T20 matches), i.e. fifteen 6-ball overs (equals 90 balls) plus one 10-ball over (making a total of 100 balls). There will be 8 teams of 11 players, each drawing from a 15-man squad. To speed things up, there will be 9 changes of end in an innings, not the 19 changes in a T20 innings. A women's tournament with the same teams is to run alongside.
*

bowling figures   Traditionally these give overs bowled, the number of maidens, runs scored, wickets taken. For example 10-4-14-3.

Dot balls/ maidens   Maidens used to be the chief way of assessing a bowler's miserliness in giving away runs. 'Dot balls', i.e. balls off which no runs or extras are scored, are another and perhaps better way of expressing the same idea.

runs per over   Statistic used to assess performance, whether that of a batsman or a bowler. Also to assess performance in short-form cricket. See also 'run rate'.

run rate/required run rate/rrr   Crucial figure in engaging with a run chase in short-form cricket.

economy rate   Applied to bowlers: the average number of runs per over bowled.

strike rate   The 'batting strike rate' measures how quickly a batsman achieves the primary goal of batting, namely scoring runs, calculated from the average number of runs scored per 100 balls faced. The 'bowling strike rate' measures how quickly a bowler achieves the primary goal of bowling, namely taking wickets, calculated from the number of balls bowled per wicket. Both batsmen and bowlers can have other goals. A batsman may wish to staunch the flow of wickets before scoring runs; a bowler may aim to slow the rate of scoring as much as take wickets.

powerplay   A rule for restricting field placings in T20 and one-day cricket. It is called 'powerplay' since the rule encourages batsmen to hit over the top of fielders. Rules differ for both forms but share an intention to prevent the bowling side restricting runs by pushing fielders beyond a 30-yard circle.

ramp shot, scoop shot   A new development in batting whereby the batsman deliberately steers the ball over the heads of the wicket-keeper and fielders with a view to scoring a boundary, whether a four or a six.

*

WC	World Cup
CC	County Championship
ECB	The England and Wales Cricket Board
ICC	International Cricket Council, the global governing body for the game
TMS	Test Match Special
Cricinfo	A sports news website devoted to cricket. It is owned by ESPN which is itself owned by the Walt Disney Company and the Hearst Corporation. Mickey Mouse it is not.

*

DRS   The Decision Review System that uses technology to assist decisions taken on the field of play.

'sandpapergate'   On tour in South Africa in March 2018, Australia resorted in the Third Test to using a piece of sandpaper to rough up the ball in order to affect its performance in their favour. The culprits were Steve Smith (captain at the time), David Warner and Cameron Bancroft. Naturally it was all caught on camera, and punishments meted out by Cricket Australia to the three players, including a ban from domestic and international cricket for a period. Smith was stripped of the captaincy. For a full account of the grisly details, search the '2018 Australian ball-tampering scandal' on Wikipedia.

'mankad'   The verb used to describe a bowler 'running out' the non-striking batsman by removing the bails when the batsman is out of his crease in their eagerness to back up the batsman on strike in scoring runs. Named after the Indian bowler Vinoo Mankad.

The **Duckworth–Lewis or Duckworth-Lewis-Stern method** is a mathematical formula designed to calculate the target score for the team batting second in a one-day or T20 game match interrupted by weather or other circumstances.

TIMELINE

27 Dec. 2018	Third day of New Zealand v Sri Lanka second Test at Christ Church, NZ
Jan. to Mar. 2019	England tour of West Indies: 3 Tests, 5 ODIs, 3 T20Is
13 to 16 Feb.	South Africa v Sri Lanka first Test, Durban
5 April	County championship (CC) Round 1
11 April	CC Round 2
17 April to 7 May	Group stages of One-Day Cup
10 May	One-Day Cup play-offs
12 May	One-Day Cup semi-finals
14 May	CC Round 3
20 May	CC Round 4
25 May	One-Day Cup Final at Lord's: Hampshire v Somerset
30 May to 6 July	Group stages (45 games) of World Cup (WC)
3 June	CC Round 5
9 June	CC Round 6
24 June	CC Round 7
30 June	CC Round 8
2 to 31 July	Women's Ashes: 3 ODIs, 1 Test, 3 T20Is
7 July	CC Round 9
9 to 10 July	WC first semi-final at Old Trafford: New Zealand v India
11 July	WC second semi-final at Edgbaston: England v Australia
13 July	CC Round 10
14 July	WC Final at Lord's: England v New Zealand
18 July to 30 Aug.	T20 Blast group stages
24-26 July	England v Ireland Test at Lord's
1-5 Aug.	1st Ashes Test at Edgbaston
14-18 Aug.	2nd Ashes Test at Old Trafford
18 Aug.	CC Round 11
22-25 Aug.	3rd Ashes Test at Headingley

4-8 Sept.	4th Ashes Test at Old Trafford
4-7 Sept.	Quarter-finals in T20 Blast
10 Sept.	CC Round 12
12-16 Sept.	5th Ashes Test at the Oval
16 Sept.	CC Round 13
21 Sept.	T20 Blast Finals Day at Edgbaston
23 Sept.	CC Round 14
Nov. to Dec.	England tour of New Zealand: 2 Tests, 5 T20Is

FOREWORD

Cricket on the edge, yes, but of what? Of a precipice? A plunge from on high into the abyss? From greatness to abasement?

The edge of revolution? Of an unknown future, possibly, perhaps probably, turning the cricket world upside down?

The edge of extinction? Of being unfit to survive as the supreme sport? Of being swamped by marketeers?

The edge of the end of an era? Of never being the same again? Of exiting its golden age and finding it irrecoverable?

It has been possible to experience all these ideas and their emotional impact in recent years, especially after the announcement of 'The Hundred' in 2018. Yet, by some paradox, 2019 was one of the sport's best years ever and this book tries to convey some of that excitement. Admittedly it is England-centred, and whether it looks so exciting in other cricket-playing countries is open to question. On the other hand, there is an answer of sorts since other countries had their own rewards and disappointments: Australia won the Ashes in England for the first time in 18 years, India felt they had had their hands on the World Cup and then they got off to a flyer in the new World Test Championship, New Zealand were as close to putting their hands on the World Cup as is conceivable, only to have it snatched from them – and then beat England 1-0 in a home Test series. Afghanistan beat Pakistan in a Test match. West Indies beat England 2-1 in a home Test series. This is before any of the players of 2019 are mentioned: Kohli, Smith, Cummins, Williamson, Sharma, Rashid Khan, Holder, K Perera., among others.

On the other hand, fate decreed it would be England's year, not just because it was England that wrestled the World Cup from New Zealand, and it all climaxed at Lord's. England witnessed an Ashes series that was as pulsating as I could have wished. I even got to have an affair with Blast cricket. All the while, four-day county cricket played on.

But then anxiety breaks in. Was that form of cricket playing on like the band on the Titanic? Does an iceberg await it? Or a massive mine that will blow it out of the water? Metaphors race through the mind, but Blake is most apt, the William Blake who wrote 'Jerusalem', the England cricketing anthem par excellence. He also wrote this poem:

O rose, thou art sick!
The invisible worm
that flies in the night
in the howling storm,
has found out thy bed
of crimson joy:
and his dark secret love
does thy life destroy.

The rose is an English summer's day of slow cricket, lovely and temperate. The worm is 'The Hundred'. The howling storm comes from the marketing department. The dark, secret love is the protestation of a golden future.

I exaggerate. The future is different from what is imagined, and not just different but even better. We move from foreboding to being pleasantly surprised. Blake was articulating, in magnificent simplicity, a great theme of how innocence can be corrupted. Cricket is not like that: it has already been corrupted by time, by money, by human incompetence, by other ailments of an unspecified kind, so how can it be corrupted again? Nevertheless it can be, because by some process which I am tempted to call not just mysterious but mystical, it retains the pleasures of slowness no matter how fast-wired humans become, of repetitions that are not repetitions since minute variation makes each repetition different, of a team game that makes use of individual genius; it requires superlative athletic ability, although ability feels inadequate to describe the elegance, the violence, the subtlety – of bowler to batsman, of batsman to boundary, of guided missile to slip fielder, of the lightning run out, of captain plotting with bowler, of the theatre of it in front of a crowd in suspense. Where would the human race be without slow suspense?

Prelude   KINDLING

1   Cricket's ambitions

It is a theme of this book that by some happy contradiction cricket both entertains the ambition in great seriousness to be a global game, and yet draws strength from its national roots and national characteristics, in England certainly, but in all the Test-playing countries. Playing to a common set of rules, they allow cricket to express a national character – Indian flamboyance, Australian self-confidence, West Indian calypso cricket, New Zealand understatement – and yet to dispense with, to overthrow even, such stereotypical views by fostering individual expression and complexity.

Yet the ruling bodies want to change the old order – hence for example the momentum behind developing the women's game – and want the game to be global – hence the World Cup, hence the emergence of Ireland and Afghanistan, hence teams in unexpected places, Papua New Guinea for example, hence even the idea of a Euro T20 Slam. The latter in fact has not materialised so far but the ambition has been articulated, and the will to realise it has been formed.

In all this, at least in this country, at least among cricket aficionados, the plans for The Hundred, a 200-ball companion to set alongside the 240-ball T20 competition (maybe replace it even) and the 600-ball one-day competition, and Test cricket of uncounted duration, have been marked, learnt, inwardly digested, and largely spat out. But by the end of 2019 the juggernaut could no longer be halted. Its trump card was that it was for a new cricket audience, not the old one, which could rage, but in doing so only miss the point. This was the public narrative at least; the underlying, truer one was that money was driving the decisions. This is understandable, even if one's reaction is a rueful one, since money earned can sustain slow forms of cricket. Far more troubling is the impression sometimes given that the minds of cricket boards are infected with the notion that slow cricket is a dinosaur headed for distinction.

It was an unlikely place to find an analysis of how cricket has evolved from a slow-moving game into 'three very different ones', but on 15 June 'The Economist', much addicted to using statistics to understanding what is going on in the world, and entering into the spirit of the World Cup, used average boundary rates to show graphically how much cricket has changed in the past 20 years. In 2000, batsmen scored boundaries nearly as often in Tests as in ODIs. Then along came T20 cricket so that in 2004 to 2007 batsmen learnt to take more risks in shorter formats. From 2008-11, in the average T20 match, 15% of balls were being hit to the boundary (i.e. in 240 balls, 36 of them were going to the boundary). In 2012-15, in some T20 matches the boundary rate was 3 times higher than in Tests. In 2016-19, batsmen had brought these aggressive tactics from T20 matches to ODIs, although they still played more safely in Tests. The same point was made non-statistically by the former Essex stalwart, James Foster, now 39 and therefore a professional cricketer all through this period: "The way the game has evolved from when I started playing professionally is [remarkable]. The ball-striking ability is off the scale. But then you see how often players are practising it now. . . [When I started] you were either able to hit a long ball . . . or you couldn't. Now everybody can do it." Cricket feels on the edge of evolving into something else, which is why it may be called 'on the edge'.

Significant changes in culture and power often occur undetected, but in 2019, global change was markedly visible, and uncomfortable. It was not possible to write a commentary on the cricket free of all reference to Brexit, the negotiations by the UK to be free of the rules of the European Union and commit itself to an uncertain future, to turn away from the known towards the less known. In the New Year, I meditated glumly on the process being no World War One but startlingly similar at certain points. Prime Minister Cameron calling the referendum in 2016 on whether the UK should remain in the European Union, or leave it, was like the assassination at Sarajevo: a pretext for upheaval if not an underlying cause of it. Then when the referendum was won by the Leave vote, a clear voice would have echoed the sentiment of Foreign Secretary Edward Grey in 1914 that the lights were going out. I did not think the negotiations would be over by Christmas 2016, but I did think they would be largely concluded by Christmas 2017. And when that did not happen then it would be over by Christmas 2018. Instead trench warfare developed: the UK fighting the EU, the Leave party fighting the Remain party in Parliament. By Christmas 2018 we seemed hardly any further forward. In January 2019 that it would be over by Christmas was a forlorn expression of hope rather than of expectation.

At the beginning of the year, as the England cricket team entered their own trenches to play three tests against the West Indies, Prime Minister Teresa May battled to get her deal with the EU through a hung Parliament. "Three times she tried, three times she was driven back," like some flawed hero in a fairy tale. The votes against her deal were 202 in favour and 432 opposed on 15 January; 242 for and 391 against on 12 March; 286 for and 344 against on 29 March. Not a great strike rate, and on 24 May she resigned to take on a caretaker role as PM. On that day Somerset were top of Division One in the county championship, and six days later the World Cup started. Salvation would come in turning the eyes from Parliament to the cricket.

And cricket did come in abundance, yet when it all came finally to an end in September, after Boris Johnson had replaced May as Prime Minister in July, a Parliamentary Passchendaele was in full swing, leading to a General Election by the end of the year. Cricket proved a diversion from these important events, at least for the UK, while for other countries it was just a sideshow with all the contemptuous connotations of that word. And yet for the English spectator as a diversion it proved a blessed one.

2 From New Zealand to the West Indies

When should a cricketing year start? Should it be in an armchair on the last Monday in January when something you know in theory you see in practice, namely it dawns on you that the daylight is beginning to lengthen? 'Dawn' is not the right word, since it is more a question of the darkness being held back rather than dispelled. This is the slow revolution of the seasons that we experience each year, with a glimmer of pleasure at the prospect of the unimaginable summer.

Full pleasures withheld, only a glimmer.
One lengthening day does not make summer.

But it helps. It was around then that I read an article somewhere about The Hundred, the new cricket competition to be introduced in 2020. So, it is only a cricket season away, and suddenly the days feel like they are shortening again, inducing not just twilight but an occluded sky: not even moonlight may be visible, for the moon is hidden in the overcast making all black.

Again I exaggerate. "The more things change, the more they stay the same," I tell myself the next morning. However the morning after that, I tell myself something else: cricket change is real, and I can feel my own cricket extinction rebellion. So it feels to me that cricket might be on some sort of precipice.

So, I come back to the question of where I should start this spe-

cial year? Less airy-fairy and more attractive is to choose Christmas Day 2018, when I was on holiday with my daughter's family in New Zealand, that country of the future, staying in Wanaka, a chic lakeside resort in the South Island. Her three boys, then aged 12, 10 and 8, were just awakening to the pleasures of cricket. On Christmas Day we found a meadow and played quick cricket in the blazing sunshine with snow on the mountains in the distance. This was a novel experience for Christmas Day, and it was oddly exhilarating.

Also on Christmas Day, New Zealand embarked on a second Test against Sri Lanka at Christ Church and the game was live on television, not in the house we were staying in, but at the Speight's Ale House on Wanaka waterfront. It turned out to be one of those surprising games: Sri Lanka won the toss and chose to bowl, a decision that paid off when New Zealand were all out for 178. But then it had gone wrong for them when Southee (3 wickets) and Boult (6 wickets) ran through the Sri Lanka batsmen for 104 all out. Having got on the front foot, New Zealand then charged ahead in the second innings. All the batsmen chipped in, but 176 from Tom Latham and 162 from Henry Nicholls were the outstanding contributions. The total had something old-fashioned about it when New Zealand declared on 585-4. Looking at this, one would conclude that the pitch was a benign one, except that in the first innings, 20 wickets had fallen for 282 runs.

Conscious of this going on in the background to our holiday, when on 27 December I had some responsibility for the two younger boys (the eldest being out with his parents hiking Roy's Peak), what better than to take them to the ale house to watch Test cricket? 'Pub' evokes the wrong picture: the ale house is modern, not 300 years old, spacious not pokey, furnished in chrome and veneer not stocked with brown furniture, more wine bar than beer bar. We found a table for the three of us, got a drink, and watched while we drunk it all up, both beverages and cricket. By this stage we were into the New Zealand second innings in which they relentlessly stretched out their score. I had hoped for a clatter of wickets to keep us engaged, but this was not necessary, nor was the cricket dull. I did some explaining, but the boys certainly understood the essence of it: the bowler was striving to take a wicket, the batter to hit runs, some ritual performance of an age-old contest, bat versus ball. What is more, in Test cricket there is always a game plan to talk about: what is each side trying to achieve over several days?

So this seems to be my starting point – will The Hundred reinvent this contest in unpredictable and exciting ways? Or not?

*

2018 had ended well for the England Test team, not least because they had won a Test series overseas, beating Sri Lanka in three Test matches in November. They had done so by the bold move of including 3 spinners in the team: Moeen Ali, Adil Rashid and Jack Leach, plus the secret weapon of Joe Root. In the second Test, 38 wickets out of the 40 taken had fallen to spin: Ali took 6, Rashid took 4, Leach 8, while Root snaffled one.

When 2019 arrives, the bounce from the series in Sri Lanka put a spring in the step of England supporters for the New Year only for that spring to stumble badly in the West Indies. Three Tests were scheduled in January and February against a West Indies team dismissed by many as Test minnows, since it did not match up to the country's illustrious history. Or at any rate dismissed as medium-pounders in a pond in which larger fish were swimming. When a friend commented in a way that suggested he thought this was true, I counselled caution. In my own mind, I have felt that when West Indies cricket does badly, cricket as a whole does badly. Part of me wanted them to do well.

In dispelling these fears, I fell into new ones when the matches took place. In the first Test, England were bowled out for 77 in their first innings, a signpost to later in the year, and West Indies in their second innings then hammered them further by scoring 415-6 declared. England had to score 627 to win. What do they say to themselves? Can we spin out a draw? We're going to lose but we must get some batting practice? In particular we need to get familiar with their bowling. Even if they said this to themselves, they could only manage 246 all out, still less than the 289 the West Indies scored in their first innings. This was chastening and worse was to come. England batted first in the second Test but could only manage 187 runs, and West Indies went on to take a 119-run lead. A big effort was needed to give the bowlers something to bowl at, and a score of at least 300 would help. Something was wrong, as they were all out for 132, leaving the West Indies 13 runs to win, which they knocked off joyously.

The commentators were critical: why was X not selected? Y should be dropped! That Root fellow should not be captain . . . None of these thoughts went through my head. Big disappointment naturally but a West Indies Test team competing at the highest level could only be good. On the other hand, the third Test loomed in importance. The rubber may have been dead, but England's honour needed restoring, which was what happened: it was played at the enchanting-sounding Gros Islet on 9 to 12 February. England were 277 all out, including a Stokes-Buttler partnership of 125 runs; West Indies were then 154 all out, thanks to Wood's 41-5 and Ali's 38-4; in their second innings England were 361-5 (Root 122), and dismissed West Indies for 252 all out (Chase 102). England won by 232 runs.

The standout performance was Joe Root's 122 in the second innings. Some truism was restored: he is a batsman of considerable quality, and his motivation to lead the side to success was authentically and triumphantly on display. The first two Tests were an aberration: a re-encounter, after that success in Sri Lanka, with the difficulties overseas teams face; and possibly a failure to recognise West Indies aplomb and steeliness when it began to show itself, especially under Jason Holder's captaincy. The series served as a reminder that England needed to raise its game if it was to contend successfully with the heavyweight Australians in the summer.

When England tour, I get very involved with the red-ball games, and can only summon up mild interest in the white-ball one. Yet the ODI series in the West Indies was part of England's preparation for the World Cup starting at the end of May, so if I was going to enjoy that I needed to pay attention. England momentum in the one-day game needed maintaining. Somehow a 2-2 draw in the five-match series, one game being rained off, did not dent that momentum, but it did serve notice that if the pitches were right, West Indies calypso cricket might topple teams. In the fourth game, England made 418-6 off their 50 overs (Buttler 150 off 77 balls). Unattainable one would think. Inevitably un-beatable. But when the West Indies got to 389 all out from 48 overs, they were only 29 runs short of turning England's 'inevitable' victory into defeat.

3   February: crossing the Styx

The Third Test against the West Indies had finished on 12 February. Five days later my father died around midnight on Sunday 17 February. He was 99 and in his own words 'done for', having lived a very fulfilling life. He was a New Zealander by birth and upbringing, coming to Britain just after the war. Since it was the New Zealand 'national religion', he had played rugby football at a high level, including one game for Scotland in January 1947, but in later life he maintained that cricket was the game he loved. After his death I found a photograph of him in cricket whites and blazer in his teenage prime (left), with bat poised to

strike, a much milder version of FS Jackson's pose for George Beldam's camera (right).

I like the photograph in itself, but like it doubly when I juxtapose it in my mind with the photo of his great-grandson bowling to his grand daughter in New Zealand (page 19), not just a return to the King Country, but the persistence of the genes across four generations. In inventing The Hundred, the ECB wants a keenness for cricket to be implanted in a very young generation and thus counter an imagined – perhaps real even – fall-off in interest that has occurred in the past 20 years.

In that time I had talked a lot about cricket with my father, and I regretted he had to be a victim of the removal of Test cricket from free-to-air television after 2005. I realised by now that there might have been ways around this digitally, but the will in him was not there. In other words I might have got him the necessary hardware, but he would not have liked mastering the software, especially with the memory of just turning on the television and there it was. In retrospect, being in his house in September 2005 and able to watch England peg back Australia on the Sunday, the fourth day of the final Ashes Test, one of a number of Andrew Flintoff's finest hours, was a valediction: we would not be able to do so again in the new broadcasting landscape. Knowing his liking for Tennyson, I quoted to him: "The old order changeth yielding place to new . . . lest one good custom should corrupt the world." However, I never received his assent to this piece of Tennysonian wisdom.

Still, he watched highlights at the end of the day and picked up snippets of cricket news on television. He knew that England's performance in the West Indies had caused disappointment, not of great concern in itself, but he felt for Joe Root coming under pressure.

When I went to Oxford on Friday, 15 February he was fading, and his pain was being controlled by serious pain-killers. That evening, I had what turned out to be my last conversation with him. He had come round from sleep and his eyes were open. I took the opportunity to tell him that England had won the Third Test against the West Indies, to encourage myself, and to encourage him. As proof that sharpness of mind had not quite deserted him, he said in a slurred but comprehensible voice, "And how did Joe Root do?" As last words go, I am inclined to rate these quite highly, and I was elated to be able to reply that he had made 122. The next day he had embarked on his passage across the Styx, the river in Greek mythology that separated the world of the living from the land of the dead in Hades, and 48 hours later he arrived, while the Styx flowed on separating the two of us in irrevocable fashion.

George Cawkwell had been a tutor in Ancient History at the University of Oxford from around 1950, so his memorial service in University College (where he had been a Fellow for 7 decades) was well attended. A number of stories emerged that I had not heard before, and the one I thought the best brought together Roman History and cricket.

It is both witty and arcane, and either the former trumps the latter (as I think) or it does not. However, I set it down here so that, like a classical text that moulders secretly in a monastery before the triumph of redis- covery, it does not exist solely in some oral tradition, likely to decay, but in written form.

In his histories of the Roman Empire in the first century AD the historian Tacitus (c.56 AD to c.120) made one of his most lapidary judgements on the Emperor Galba who met his end at the hands of an armed mob in the Roman Forum in 69 AD. the so-called Year of the Four Emperors. *Capax imperii nisi imperasset*, Tacitus wrote. Translation has to be mealy-mouthed: 'He seemed capable of ruling until he actual- ly did so' – ten words to translate four. Galba seemed up to it but proved not to be.

The contrast is an arresting one. My father admired the verbal wit, and its quotable quality. In the 1950s, when he still played club cricket, he captained the Emeriti, a team of Oxford dons. One fixture was a game against a team of Cambridge dons, and one year they suf- fered a defeat which, in the eyes of the Oxford team, was the result of a series of poor decisions by an umpire supplied by the Cambridge team. Nothing of course rankles like a poor umpiring decision, whether objec- tively poor or subjectively so. As the Emeriti left the field defeated, George, in a loud voice, pronounced: *Capax umpirii nisi umpirasset*. This was 'caviare to the general' admittedly, but in the context of a Varsity match, albeit between dons, the remark was memorable enough to be remembered. So, may it continue to be remembered as long as Roman history is taught and cricket is played, i.e. forever. And yet: nothing is forever until it happens.

At George's memorial service at the end of March the concluding lines of Tennyson's 'Ulysses' were read:

> . . . that which we are, we are;
> One equal temper of heroic hearts,
> Made weak by time and fate, but strong in will
> To strive, to seek, to find, and not to yield.

These words echoed in my head, especially the last line, at various points of the long cricketing summer that was about to begin.

Part 1 BLAZING

4 April to May: slow (red ball)

I am lucky, I have time on my side. I am 71, and have the time to give attention to the four-day game in county cricket. Its virtues are well regarded and well trumpeted by cricket journalists and of course the devoted band of spectators at county games. I have to remind myself frequently that these pleasures are largely denied to those going to work each day. The idea of taking time to engage with slow cricket is out of the question. Whatever reservations I have about quick cricket, I have to lay them aside in recognition of the fact that, for many people, at least it means a chance to enjoy a whole game of cricket.

However, I am not a regular spectator at county grounds. Living in Norwich, this is not easy, and beside the cost of the ticket, which in general is reasonable considering that one gets, weather permitting, a full day's spectacle, to my mind of a high quality, there is also the cost of transport to and from the ground.

The games were scheduled between the beginning of April and the end of September, providing some 64 playing days in all, some of which would be affected by weather and early finishes. The biggest regret was the lack of games to watch in high summer, but this year that fact would be compensated for by the scheduling of five Test matches against Australia, starting right at the beginning of August and running through to the middle of September. The overlap therefore was with the Blast games that are part of the T20 tournament, giving a straightforward choice between slow cricket and fast cricket.

However, the first two rounds of the championship were scheduled for Friday 5 April and Thursday 11 April. It has to start sometime, and pleasant April weather is not unknown. However conditions can test both players and spectators. I almost wish that the first round was a trial one to get both parties in the mood, but this would not work – it would only be devalued even further as teams did not take it as seriously as they should.

There is plenty to relish anyway. In Division One, it gives an opportunity for a number of Test players to play for their county, including Root for Yorkshire, Overton and Leach for Somerset, Broad for Nottinghamshire, Burns for Surrey, plus a number of players who have played for England and been discarded, although that adjective seems hardly the right word to use for the 43-year-old Marcus Trescothick and the 34-year-old Alastair Cook. In committing himself to Somerset after an illustrious career for England, Trescothick had become a cricketing treasure, while Cook having retired from Test cricket made an admirable commitment to slow cricket by continuing to play for his county Essex with the laudable motivation that he wanted to help them win the Championship again. In Division Two, England's finest bowler of our time, James Anderson, was playing for Lancashire. If star players are the essence that encourage spectators to watch county cricket, then there are plenty of fine England players to watch.
*

The **two opening CC rounds** of Division One saw Somerset win at Taunton and then beat Nottinghamshire at Trent Bridge by an innings. This was a pointer to the season ahead: Somerset would be strong contenders to be champions, while Notts would have a dismal time. Essex on the other hand lost by an innings against Hampshire who declared in their first innings on 525-8. What happened to the flaccid Essex attack, later to become so fearsome? This: Porter 112-1 / S Cook 105-0 / Quinn 104-3 / Bopara 54-2 / Harmer 13-2 / Lawrence 6-0. Essex's next game against Surrey at the Oval was a draw, so they only got 14 points from their first two games. What sort of prognosis was this?

When two fancied contenders met at Southampton in the second round, Yorkshire trounced Hampshire by an innings, even while Hampshire had done the same to Essex the week before. On this basis, Hampshire would end higher than Essex, and Yorkshire higher than both. In hindsight this is mockery.

Surely Kent, newly promoted, would struggle? Yet in their first game against Somerset they only lost by 84 runs, and in their second game, their first innings came to 504-9 declared, and they won by eight wickets. On this basis they would survive, and perhaps flourish.

In May, the weather began to improve and to stir a few juices. In the **third CC round** Essex were playing Notts at Chelmsford and at the end of Day One Notts had been bowled out for 187 while Essex were 68-0, Alastair Cook on 29 not out. I felt strongly the pull of a contest between Cook and Broad, but needed to be there for the start of play at 11 o'clock. The train timetable should have let me do this, but the train was delayed and my friend and I did not reach the ground until 11.20, only to be told at the ticket gate that Cook had just been dismissed off the bowling of Broad for 31. Here was disappointment. Looking later at the clip of this wicket, the left-handed Cook had edged a ball angled across him to Mullaney in the slips. Bad judgement more than bad luck (I write this in the comfort of my chair), but the cloud had a silver lining: Broad's drive to keep bowling skilful balls to the left-hander pointed to August when the Australia left-hander, David Warner, kept succumbing to Broad's superb bowling.

While I had expected Broad to be devastating he felt only re-spectable, his figures for the innings being 20-2-50-2. It was Luke Fletcher (50-5) and the spinner Matt Carter (68-3) who took the wickets

So, Notts only conceded a 54-run lead on the first innings, but then their troubles started. They began their second innings reasonably with Duckett and Nash seeing off the opening bowlers, Porter and Sam Cook, but they then succumbed to the spin of Harmer, seen in this photo warming up while Duckett adjusts his armour.

At the end of the day they were 90-6, only 36 runs ahead. Nash was still at the crease on 13 not out as a number 3 batsman battling to stiffen the Notts resistance. On Day Three they found no respite: they were all out for 158 and Harmer's figures were 60-6. This was the swallow that made Essex's summer: Harmer was to rampage through county cricket teams in the coming months, especially at Chelmsford.

We were able to watch Harmer wheeling away in late afternoon sunshine.

The ground at Chelmsford is pleasantly understated: you would never guess in this boastful age that this was the home of county champions. The support, like I imagine it is at many county grounds, has the same understated quality. The murmur is barely audible, the day punctuated by ripples rather than gasps. I calculated that perhaps one in three of the seats was occupied, about one in twenty of the spectators being female, but virtually everybody was over sixty years of age. As my friend remarked, county cricket is a social service to the community and worth valuing on these grounds alone. That argument would not appeal much to the ECB, but there is now another dimension, livestreaming by the counties, and the brisk highlights of the day on YouTube. These latter are no substitute for the visual memory of being at the ground, but they are a reminder of the day, and indeed give a better view of how wickets fall than when they are seen square on from the boundary with imperfect eyesight.

Cricket thrives on statistics so I gathered some figures. The highlights on YouTube on Day One had gathered 548 views, on Day Two 699 views, and on Day Three 424 views. The Essex Cricket TV livestream had 3,100 subscribers. Very moderate figures, I felt, and Essex has plenty of scope to build this. Compare the 30,000 who subscribe to each of Somerset and Surrey, and here are viewing figures of their highlights (assuming they are reliable!):

Day One   1,256 views (Surrey 330-6)

Day Two   30,802 views (Surrey 380 all out, Somerset 243-5)

Day Three   50,254 views (Somerset 398 all out, Surrey 152-5)

Day Four   7,977 views (Surrey 255-8, no Somerset second innings, match drawn and spoilt by rain on the last day)

Yorkshire's figures on the other hand were more like Essex's. Highlights of Yorkshire versus Kent were:

Day One   1,300 views (Yorks 210, Kent 130-4)

Day Two   1,400 views (Kent 296, Yorks 166-3)

Day Three   1,300 views (Yorks 469, Kent 34-3)

Day Four   228 views (Kent 211 all out, Yorks win by 172 runs)

To round out the Division One picture, Hampshire Cricket had 2,200 subscribers and Kent 5,600. Warwickshire on the other hand had no livestream that I could find. In Division Two Worcestershire had 3000 subscribers. There must be room for improvement here. You can see a real audience at the ground, but there is a virtual one as well shadowing the game in the privacy of their own homes, atomised but still engaged in their way, and still benefiting from the social service.

At the end of this **third CC round** of games, Somerset (54 points), Yorkshire (52) and Hampshire (50) were out front with Essex (34) and Kent (33) in mid-table. Unexpectedly Surrey (23 points, but only two games) and Notts (19) were struggling. Was Warwickshire (7 points, also only two games but both defeats) doomed?

5 April to May: fast (white ball)

I had resolved to make this the year in which I engaged properly with one-day cricket, that is to say the 50-over game, 50-50 cricket perhaps, 300 balls maximum each side, fast but could be a good deal faster.

The county one-day game has an illustrious history in England, county aficionados retaining strong memories of when their side had triumphed, and in what manner. In my case all those games had merged into a blur. So why should this year be special? The World Cup being played in this country was the reason. It was being strongly marketed, and since England was rated as one of the favourites to win, I realised that I should watch it or listen to it, so that I could say I was there – if we did win it. I realised too the risks involved: if we did not win it, knocked out by generally perceived incompetence rather than by some quirk of ill fortune (as happens in sport and such as in fact afflicted New Zealand), I would suffer a serious deflation of morale – at least for a day or two and then life would resume.

The county one-day game, known as the Royal London One-Day Cup (thunderously or ponderously, according to your point of view), began on 17 April, virtually off my radar. Teams were split into a northern group and a southern group, each playing each other in their group, from which quarter-finalists emerged (10 May), and then the semifinalists (12 May), leading to a grand final at Lord's on 25 May. This is too early in the season, but it was quite understandable that the ECB wanted to complete the tournament before the first game in the World Cup on 30 May. What was more rebarbative was the simultaneous scheduling of a five-match series against Pakistan through May on the 8th, the 11th, the 14th, the 17th and the 19th. This was to warm up the two teams, although the results were fairly meaningless, and proved to be so in the World Cup itself when England played Pakistan on 3 June. The focus of attention was on England chasing the 500-run innings, i.e. 10 runs an over, on how much the one-day game belonged to batsmen (as exemplified in the ODI England played against the West Indies on 27 February when Buttler scored 150 with 12 sixes) and on the question of whether the repeated boundary lost its oomph when it is too frequent, or not: could one become a connoisseur of boundaries, as of dot balls? England won 4-nil, and reached 340 on three successive occasions, i.e. scoring at a rate of 6.8 an over, and this reinforced the view that the World Cup would be a high-scoring tournament, full of sixes to the delight of those wanting a simple, crude set of facts with which to trumpet the event. Again, it turned out to be much more interesting than that.

Preparations for the World Cup also meant that certain players in the England white-ball squad would not be allowed to play for their county in the domestic 50-over cup. This was viewed by some supporters as devaluing the county competition. However, power resides at the top in life, and the ECB is only keen on the counties provided they know their place. I can see this point of view, but it did preclude James Vince and Liam Dawson playing for Hampshire in the final. Although we shall never know, this might have mattered, and in any case it took a slight gloss off the final. In such a game spectators want to see the best players playing. It was remarked by a spectator that before a ball had been bowled Hampshire were two wickets down already, since Vince and Dawson were not allowed to play. This grumble hardened into a grievance during the day, being issued periodically through the match.

The absence of Vince and Dawson was as a result of their playing for England against Australia in a warm-up match for the World Cup. What is more, this took place at Hampshire's home ground in Southampton. Such supporters had a choice: watch England at the Ageas Bowl – and, as it turned out, see their own man Vince hit 64 – or Hampshire at Lord's. The crowds were respectively 12,000 at Southampton and 20,000 (about two-thirds full according to my estimate) at Lord's. Healthy enough, but Lord's on a finals day needed to be packed. However one advantage of this spare capacity was that I easily got two tickets for the final at Lord's, and in my quest to understand white-ball cricket better, I did so.

Expectation was tempered by reality when, coming down on the train to the final, I read Theresa May's announcement that she would be standing down as Prime Minister. She had become another casualty of Brexit being all over by Christmas.

The weather for the day was billowing cloud, which blue sky and sun came to dominate, seeing off the opposition as it were. We had caught the 7.40 train, and were in our seats at Lord's by 10.45. I had regained my sense of anticipation and I was immediately struck by the white ball: I could see this pretty well! Who cares if it doesn't do as much as a red one? Lord's was full-ish, but at first glance you notice the empty seats before the occupied ones. Nor were they just stragglers, Hampshire or Somerset supporters arriving late, the seats were just never occupied all day.

There was a big pleasure in the white ball being visible. While the shots may be a blur I can see it flying in my mind's eye. Elizabeth Ammons in the Sunday Times the next day reminded me that "[Banton] nonchalantly pulled a good ball from Fidel Edwards through deep square leg for six." He hit nine more boundaries. He stands at the crease ready to receive like a warrior, or rather like a warrior statue, stiff and imposing (see over page).

And here is the stuff of evil daydreams: you are watching cricket and the red ball is hit high in the air, and you don't track it, and in your bewilderment at where it is it comes down on your head, an irrevocable moment, you're in the ferry on the Styx. Well, with Hampshire on 231-8, in the 50th over, second ball and wanting to pump up the total, James Fuller smashes Jamie Overton squarish to the leg side boundary. It's coming my way! But this time I am without fear, for the white ball is highly visible, and indeed I'll catch it if necessary – camera in my hands or no camera! But it's coming for Phil. "Catch it!" all his mates shout. Phil moves sharpish to avoid it, losing his beer in the process. Phil shouts in reply to the batsman: "You owe me a pint!" I was grateful I didn't have to shout, "You owe me a camera!"

In the event, as can happen in all forms of cricket although the shorter forms seem to exacerbate the effect, the game itself never quite caught fire. Somerset ran out winners, and since I knew more about them than Hampshire I could not help noticing Josh Davey. From side on he seemed to bowl up and down at no great pace, but his figures were 8-0-28-2 with an economy rate of 3.50. Half an hour into the game he had Tom Alsop dropped in the slips by James Hildreth, but immediately repeated the ball, the batsman immediately repeated the

One-day Cup: final
between Hants and
Somerset. Tom Banton
in full flow.

stroke, and this time Hildreth held the catch. I noticed too that the drinks were being carried by Dominic Bess, a player with two Test matches to his name (against Pakistan in 2018), and when he came on as a substitute fielder he was still biting his nails. And not just one Overton, Craig (4 Test appearances), was bowling but his brother Jamie as well. Craig's economy rate was 5.20 with no wickets, but Jamie's was better at 4.80 and 3 wickets. For Hampshire Sam Northeast made 56 workmanlike runs but with 28 off 17 balls until he got out it was Rilee Rossouw who looked destructive. They needed more of that destructiveness which James Fuller, a name completely new to me, endeavoured to supply with 55 off 48 balls.

When Somerset batted, I realised I had seen Fidel Edwards' slingshot action before but it seemed to me, side on admittedly, to lack control. Results for the batsman were juicy if you could lay a bat on it. Kyle Abbott (9-0-43-0, economy rate 4.78) felt anonymous, something he was going to rectify spectacularly in the red-ball game between these two teams in September. We did have a starry performance from the opening bat Tom Banton. His scores in the games leading up to the finals indicated a batsmen who could be destructive once he got in – provided he got in. These were: 107 (off 79 balls), 14 (29), 7 (26), 1 (3), 11 (29), 3 (10), 18 (18), 53 (61), 112 (103) and 59 (55). Here he scored 69 off 67 balls. I could finally see for myself, close-up, how thrilling the conjuring of boundaries at the expense of the attritional game could be, plus the sight of that remarkable batting skill of being able to pierce the field with precision. Banton's wicket fell on 112 with Somerset still needing 133 to win, but Banton made his statement in a final in a way which must have contributed to his inclusion in the England white-ball touring team for the autumn.

Somerset cruised really: Hildreth stepped forward and despite being dropped progressed smoothly to his 50 and thence to victory. They were only 4 wickets down when they got the necessary 245 runs.

Why should Somerset have been the winners? What was the difference between the two teams? Was it the bowling? I thought this was about the same, with its particular strengths: Edwards' and Abbott's pace for Hampshire, the two Overtons for Somerset. Davey's opening spell of 8 overs on the trot for Somerset felt good. For Hampshire Mason

Crane (1 Test appearance) did 10 overs and seemed to be turning it, although perhaps his length was giving the batsmen too much time, because his economy rate was 6.20 an over.

With the batting, Somerset drew ahead. Rossouw for Hampshire felt dangerous, but when he fell for 28, bowled by Jamie Overton, Somerset had Hampshire in check, and stayed on top. By contrast Banton's 69 for Somerset, whacking Edwards and Abbott, felt more like the necessary firestorm. When he was finally caught behind off Edwards the game had moved firmly in Somerset's favour. The supporting cast of batsmen ensured victory, none more so than Hildreth. He is very classy in slow cricket, so I wondered whether fast cricket was his game. Decisively yes, since it was the way he anchored the innings by nudging runs, interspersing those nudges with boundaries, that did it.

The final factor was Somerset's confidence. They radiated energy in the field, while Hampshire's felt lacking, as if the loss of the two key players of Vince and Dawson had got to them even before they took the field. Even if that was true, they should not have risked showing it to the opposition. Momentum in the Somerset innings caused Hampshire to slow up, not helped by Edwards' and Abbott's long run-ups. Somehow they emanated a lack of mental urgency.

One comment I heard on the forthcoming Hundred, coming to a cricket ground not near you, but on the other hand to a television that is: "Ridiculous. They are still keeping the T20 matches." It is striking how hostile the vocal cricket-going public is to this plan. What is more, all the energy seems to be with them. Anyone speaking up for The Hundred sounds a bit shy, at any rate unconvincing. I have a notion that the history of cricket is an organic one. Slow cricket has evolved to its glories such as the West Indies sides of the 1970s and 1980s, the Ashes 2005, India passim. And yet in fact this evolution has experienced disruption that is far from organic. First came the Packer revolution of the 1970s. And then with the arrival of the IPL in 2008, power shifted to India so that they now dictate to England and the other countries how cricket should be done. These revolutions succeeded because, as I was slow to learn, people love razzmatazz and celebrity sportsmen. Triumphs and humiliation are real, not impostors. Vanity rules okay. From my watch tower I could see all that was happening, and accept it while still harbouring the notion that not all that glitters is silverware.

In the final, Hampshire's 244 was obviously not enough. But 300 might have been. In the WC warm-up game Australia mustered 297, which might have felt insufficient until England only got 285. In the other warm-up game India could only muster 179, still feeling the chill, and New Zealand, much warmer, were 184 in the 38th over. The talk in the press remained of a team scoring 500 in an innings, but I asked myself whether this was a marketing ploy, the wish being father to the thought. Still, the interest in the World Cup was certainly on the rise. There may have been only 12,000 at Southampton with the locals distracted by the Lord's event, but the game between India and New Zealand at the Oval (capacity 25,000) was a sell-out.

However, the Lord's one-day final did have a melancholic note to it: in 2020, the 50-over cup is to be a 'development' competition, i.e. pushed into the realms of the imprecise, and the final moved to Trent Bridge. That feels like a downgrade.
*

On Thursday 30 May, five days after the One-Day Final, the World Cup officially started at the Oval with the game between England and South Africa. No doubt many cricketing eyes were trained on this, but perhaps not all. On Friday 31 May Pakistan was due to play the West Indies at Trent Bridge, which to quite a number of people in this country would be felt to be a priority, and in any case 30 May was the fourth day of the next round of the county championship, which would also divert some people's minds. It was therefore possible, if you had the time, to track England's progress against South Africa, and also be stimulated by the prospect of a tense conclusion to at least three county games in the **fourth CC round** in Division One.

At 4.50 p.m., Essex, with 17 overs remaining in the match, were trying to dislodge an obdurate Daniel Bell-Drummond of Kent, who was 81 not out, in order to win. Essex had got to this position with scores of 313 and 206-7 declared in each of their innings, thanks to Alastair Cook playing what might now be called the Steve Smith role: 125 in the first innings, and 90 in the second, making a total of 215 out of all the Essex runs of 519, that is to say over a third of them. In saying he wanted to help Essex win the county championship again, this must have been what he meant. The other half of the Essex formula for success was the way their bowlers worked as a team. In the first innings, the 10 wickets had been spread between Jamie Porter, Sam Cook, Peter Siddle and Simon Harmer, the latter taking 3 for 72 off 35 overs. Now, with Kent 8 wickets down, Harmer had already taken 6 of them. The chances of Bell-Drummond seeing out the remaining 17 overs with the last two Kent batsmen felt slim. However, nothing is impossible.

Over at Edgbaston Surrey were 8 wickets down in their second innings needing 149 runs to win and, in their case, 21 overs remained. Another tall order for them. The situation was not quite so critical at Headingley where Hampshire needed 196 runs to win against Yorkshire with 7 wickets in hand and again 21 overs remaining. In the main event at the Oval, played with a different ball of course, at about this time South Africa were 5 for 167 off 31.4 overs, chasing England's 311. Possible, one might think. However their current run rate was 5.27 an over against a required run rate of 7.9 an over, and as I followed on Cricinfo ('watched' gives the wrong idea but it was what I was doing), Rassie Van der Dussen was out for 50 runs making South Africa 6 for 167. Their chances of victory were moving from the possible to the improbable.

And at 4.56 in another part of the land (Chelmsford) Kent were 9 for 224, and a minute later, 224 all out, giving Essex a convincing victory. Harmer had bowled almost 33 overs and taken 8 for 98. Their quartet of bowlers had moved, no doubt with their full consent, to a singleton bowler. Harmer was continuing to make his mark at Chelmsford.

Half an hour later South Africa were 7 for 186 and the required run rate had gone up to 9.74 an over, while at Edgbaston Surrey were clinging on at 9 for 141 with 12.2 overs remaining, their hopes resting on Rikki Clarke at 51 not out. But soon after that Warwickshire had seized victory when Surrey were 141 all out, and at the Oval England had done the same by bowling South Africa all out for 207.

Whether one's taste was for red-ball or white-ball cricket, or for both, this was a rewarding day in which to follow games, unless you were a South African watching your team underperform, and with a sense of chagrin that your fellow countryman Simon Harmer was flourishing in England rather than at home. For England what the game will be remembered for before everything else was an extraordinary sporting moment contributed by Ben Stokes. Andile Phehlukwayo had clonked Rashid in the air to the legside boundary where Stokes was fielding. Had he fluffed it by coming in too far off the rope? If so, how might this error be rectified, even if it could be? The answer was to twist his arm up above his head and trust in an extraordinary piece of hand-brain co-ordination to claw the ball out of the air – outside his vision. So that was what he did. The World Cup was off to a good start with an England victory but that catch got it off to a flyer, and its fame will last beyond that particular time and place: by 14 October it had received 2.1million views on YouTube (search 'Stokes catch'). Naturally it thrilled the crowd, especially spectators close to where he was fielding, but one attractive feature of this incident was the evident boyish pleasure it gave to Stokes.

Little Jack Horner
stood in his corner
tracking the ball in the sky.
With his bucket-size mitt
He clawed it . . . he's pouched it!
And grinned, "What a good boy am I!"
*

The next day allowed for further reflections on the round of county games. Harmer's spinning genius (8-68 in one innings) was trumped at Edgbaston by Gareth Batty for Surrey, 41 years old, who had taken 8 for 64, including a hat-trick. Both were trumped by Warwickshire captain, Jeetan Patel, 39 years old, who had taken 12 wickets in the match, with 8 of them for 36 runs in the second innings. Warwickshire had set Surrey a competitive target in the knowledge that victory would keep them on the front foot in the championship table. This confidence paid off when 5 wickets fell in 4 overs for 12 runs.

The match at Headingley ended in a draw, but Yorkshire had done well against the lead team, Hampshire. Gary Ballance had scored his fourth century in six innings, and his total runs so far for 2019 came to 538 at an average of 89.66. Could that sort of weight propel Yorkshire to the top?

In bald terms, the table on 31 May now looked like this:

Hampshire	5 matches	3 won-1 lost-1 drawn	81 points
Somerset	4	3-0-1	74
Yorkshire	4	2-0-2	60
Essex	4	2-1-1	56
Kent	5	1-3-1	46
Surrey	4	0-1-3	39
Warwickshire	4	1-3-0	31
Nottinghamshire	4	0-3-1	23

In contrast to the bare statistics, Rory Burns, captain of Surrey, gave an eloquent defence of county cricket. While conceding that Surrey would have difficulty defending the title they won in 2018, he felt that was not so much a reflection of any shortcomings on their part as of the high quality of English domestic cricket at top level. He went on: "I think it just shows . . . that our first-class system in England is the best in the world. Division One cricket it is as good as you get and as tough as you get. . . We played at Taunton against Somerset the other week and Marcus Trescothick said it was as close to international cricket as he has witnessed in his career. I think we need to cherish our game and respect it. I think it is a wonderful product . . . The quality of players is as good as it has ever been, if not getting a bit stronger. I feel like we need to champion some of the good stuff we do in the English game rather than trying to concoct reasons as to why we need to change things." This was an arresting statement to make just as the World Cup was about to begin, although Burns was not directing his comments at that since he was looking forward to the Ashes series in August. Was the gap between Test cricket and four-day cricket impossibly large or not? An answer to this will be important to the future of red-ball cricket at least in this country. At the least it was encouraging that such an unspun endorsement of the longer form of the game was coming from someone like Burns who had played at both levels.

6   June: getting to the WC semis

It was an England defeat that brought their World Cup campaign fully to life. On Monday 3 June they lost to Pakistan who made a very good score of 348-8, while England's reply was 15 runs short of victory. This made 682 runs in all, more in line with expectations of a high-scoring competition. This was not expected, England having trounced Pakistan in the five-game series in May. England were apparently guilty of 13 misfields. Particularly forgettable (except it can be searched for and found on YouTube), in contrast to Stokes's catch in the first game, was when Muhammad Hafeez, with only 14 runs to his name, hit a skyer straight down the ground to Jason Roy fielding in the deep. Having seen it dropped he went on to make 84 runs off 62 balls, was a significant contributor to Pakistan's victory and won the Man of the Match award. Hafeez from zero to hero, Roy in the opposite direction, although he had ample chance to make up for it later in the competition, and did so. Cricket, like all great sport, has elements of the circus in it, including public humiliation.

On Wednesday 5 June Bangladesh (244) played New Zealand (248), with only 492 runs scored in a very tight contest. Perhaps, as one journalist commented, this made for a better game. Tight bowling could itself make for a tense finish.

The next day, Thursday 6 June, the 75th anniversary of D-Day, Surrey played Somerset at the Guildford outground in the **fifth CC round**. At the end of the first day, Somerset were 344 all out, having been 3 for 35, and would have been 4 for 35, if George Bartlett had not been dropped on nought. He went on to make 137. Banton went in at number four and made 44 runs off 87 balls, 36 of them in boundaries. After lunch, he went 24 balls without scoring before getting out. Despite the modest total, this was a valuable contribution to stabilising Somerset's innings. Is he of the most desirable breed, that he can play both red-ball and white-ball cricket?

The third day of the game saw the fall of 17 wickets. In their second innings Somerset had collapsed to 153 all out, while at the end of the day Surrey were 2 for 99, chasing a target of 267 runs, and entitled to be confident of a win. Was Somerset faltering? In the second innings Trescothick had been caught behind off the bowling of Morkel for 11 runs. Do all sporting careers end in a whimper? Trescothick, now 43 years old, just could not get his batting going in 2019 when he needed to as much as he has ever needed to if he was to help Somerset win their first county championship ever. Yet Somerset character still prevailed, Surrey character again failed: Surrey suffered a middle-order collapse, wickets falling on 118, 118, 120, 127 and 131, all out 164, 102 runs short of victory.

At Headingley, Yorkshire had scored 390 runs and Essex having looked as if they might not, had not only avoided the follow-on but reached a respectable 309 thanks to 60 from Siddle batting at number 9, so a draw looked likely. One unexpected presence in the Yorkshire side was Dominic Bess, brought in to provide them with a spin bowler. This was proving a good move because his figures in Essex's first innings were 22-10-39-3, but he had also made 91 not out in the Yorkshire first innings. Also in the Yorkshire armoury was the South African Duane Olivier, capable of 90 mph bouncers so that batsmen kept getting hit on the helmet. He is the 43rd Kolpak player to enter county cricket since the Kolpak regulation came into force in 2004. As the journalist David Hopps observed, "The collapse of the South African Rand enabl[ed] him to earn three times as much."

Listening on the radio, I heard the question raised of Surrey being in a relegation fight. This was hard to believe, especially as only one team was going down from Division One, and even at this stage it looked as if it was probably going to be Nottinghamshire. Last year Surrey had looked set to dominate the county championship for a few years to come, but they were now second from bottom. This raised comparisons in my mind with Middlesex. Having been champions in 2016, they had been relegated in 2017 to Division Two; now they had just been thumped by Sussex who had scored 481-9 declared and Middlesex had then collapsed to 138. On the fourth day, if Middlesex could battle it out, the game would be a draw, but in fact they were all out for 293 in the final hour with only 12.4 overs left.

On 9 June, after the **fifth CC round**, the county championship table read:

Somerset	96 points (4 wins)
Hampshire	81 (3 wins, 1 defeat)
Yorkshire	71 (2 wins)
Essex	65 (2 wins, 1 defeat)
Kent	46 (1 win, 3 defeats)
Surrey	43 (2 defeats)
Warwickshire	40 (1 win, 3 defeats)
Nottinghamshire	29 (3 defeats)

*

From Friday 7 June to Saturday 22 June, I was away from home, first on a walking holiday in South Uist in the Outer Hebrides, a break from cricket and a blessed relief from febrile UK politics, and then in the Dee Valley. But even in the Hebrides I could still connect with the cricket when I wished to. On Saturday 8 June England felt well back on track in the World Cup when they beat Bangladesh by 106 runs at Cardiff, courtesy of a massive 153 from 121 balls from Jason Roy. Yet distance did make a difference. When England beat West Indies on 14 June, I was on Benbecula and the event quite passed me by, and the same happened with their thumping of Afghanistan by 150 runs on 18 June. What I did catch sitting in a hotel room in Inverness was the highlights of a very big game on Sunday 16 June. This was between India and Pakistan, which India won by 89 runs by the Duckworth-Lewis method. India got their 50 overs in and scored 336 runs. In reply when the match ended Pakistan were 212-6 off 40 overs when their target was 302, not enough to give them victory. This needle match was very inadequately covered by the Channel 4 highlights. It was only one hour long, which was a pity considering the political background which should have had more attention, and was crammed with masses of short edits showing boundaries, wickets with replays in frenetic succession punctuated regularly, too regularly, by shots of fans waving flags. Reputedly 1 billion people watched the game itself on television. Since India won easily, it became mere lame spectacle in the end. To the neutral observer this was a pity.

On the other hand the seriousness of the game was given respect in the press, sometimes in unexpected places. Cricinfo had a piece on the India-Pakistan rivalry, while 'The Economist' linked the game to the political background and the 'Times Literary Supplement' had an essay entitled 'High Spirits '. Together, these articles gave a very positive account of the match and the way it bought cricket fans together. This was a particular merit of the World Cup although there were some awkward incidents when Pakistan played Afghanistan on 29 June.

Engaging with cricket in its various forms this year brought home the extent of cricket's worldwide links to this country, from overseas players in county cricket extending their skills – and their CV -- by learning the nature of English conditions, not to mention the pleasures of slow cricket, to overseas mercenaries in the Blast, coming for the money, and for the fun of it. Yet nothing exemplified that global quality like the World Cup. The fact that it featured only ten countries obscured the number of upwardly mobile ones eliminated in the qualifying rounds. It turned out that Sundar Pichai, the CEO of a truly global American company, Google, is a cricket aficionado, having been born in Tamil Naidu and brought up in Chennai before becoming an Indian American. He attended some games and hoped for an India-England final.

The atmosphere throughout the tournament was not just cordial, it was raucously benevolent. It only got malicious in one game, that between Pakistan and Afghanistan on 29 June, not on the field but in the stands where some fans exchanged punches and threw rubbish at each other; two spectators had to be evicted early in the match. Fractious relations over the border between the two countries seem to have fuelled this, yet this does not quite explain it considering the good-natured partisanship at the India-Pakistan game on 22 June, when the festering sore of who owns and who governs Jammu and Kashmir might have been expected to disturb it. Earlier in the year there had been a terrorist bombing followed by Indian air strikes, and the capture by Pakistan of an Indian pilot who had been shot down. To complicate matters, Indian cricket is getting richer, while Pakistani cricket is not.

In these circumstances, can cricket be healing? One can start with the idea that the India-Pakistan game in England was maybe

watched by a billion (that's 1,000 million) people on the sub-continent, sporting pleasure trumping politics. The thoughtful piece in the 'Times Literary Supplement' (5 July 2019) by an Indian MP, Shashi Taroor, drew some comfort at the harmonious presence of partisan spectators side-by-side in one stadium. "I found myself, as an Indian Member of Parliament, posing for selfies with cricket fans, but was surprised to discover as many Pakistanis wanting a photograph with me as Indians." He referred to the UN "values of co-existence transcending political differences". Wisely he stopped there, refraining from any hyperbolic and unrealistic conclusion that cricket could be a substitute for geopolitics in that part of the world. In similar fashion I drew encouragement from the way England could host a tournament played in such a successful and hopeful spirit, without tipping over into a conclusion that it would be easy for the UK to flourish on its own in a global world. It was soft power of a sort, which is a long way from hard power.
*

I learnt subsequently that in beating Afghanistan, England had almost reached the 400-run mark thanks to 148 from Eoin Morgan, including 17 sixes, which was a record for an ODI innings. Was this exciting to watch? I daresay, especially if you were at the ground, but I do not have the mental equipment to make subtle distinctions between sixes. It is either a good six or a poor six, even though I have never seen the latter. There is the question of how far they go – a spectacular six – but there is a certain elegance in a six that just clears the fielder and the boundary rope – as we were to witness later at Headingley from the bat of Stokes. There is also the matter of how they are struck: straight down the ground – impressive; or by a ramp shot – clever, sly even; or by a sweep of some kind - audacious. At the other end of the scale are dot balls. Are these boring in themselves or just perceived to be boring? They should not be, because there is a great art in bowling a ball in any kind of cricket off which the batsmen cannot score. In white-ball cricket it is necessary that scorecards do not just record overs, runs and wickets, but also the number of dot balls the bowler bowls.

Unfortunately, coming back south again on Saturday 22 June I was not able to experience two of the most exciting games in the whole World Cup when New Zealand beat West Indies by 5 runs at Old Trafford, West Indies looking dead and buried until Brathwaite (101 off 82 balls) hauled them tantalisingly close to victory, only to fall short. I heard about this from my niece since her family had gone to watch the game. It was a day-night match, and finished about 9:45 pm. Their elder son was riveted, listening to the TMS commentary on his earpiece, while his younger brother was asleep in his mother's arms.

At Southampton, at the other end of the country, Afghanistan, who were obliged to bowl first, restricted India to 224 runs but then almost brought off the coup of the tournament by beating India, falling short by only 11 runs. Both these games must have provided a large dose of suspense.

*

While I was away the county championship moved on beyond my ken, except that in the **sixth CC round** there was an ominous result for all the other teams when Essex (214) beat Hampshire (118 and 88) at Chelmsford inside two days (16 and 17 June). The match winner was Harmer, with 12 wickets for 61 runs. Just before the start of the important Essex v Somerset game on Monday 24 June, both sides had played 6 games each and were on 85 and 115 points respectively. Separating them was Hampshire on 91, but they had played 7 games, as had Yorkshire behind the top three teams on 84 points.

Having just returned from holiday with things to do, and having an appointment for an echocardiogram on 25 June, both took my attention off the needle match in Chelmsford starting Monday 24 June in the **seventh CC round,** the first encounter between Essex and Somerset, the two leading contenders for the title. I had hoped that it would come to a climax on the fourth day, 26 June, when I would have time to engage at Chelmsford, but it turned out to be straightforward in Essex's favour. By the time their second innings finished on the Wednesday they were 268 runs ahead, and then ran through Somerset for 117 runs in 32.2 overs. Without knowing anything of the conditions I thought that it might be a Harmer-Leach battle to see who could bowl most lethally. But it turned out that pace was king, Porter taking 7 for 73 in the match off 28.5 overs and Beard 7 for 45 in 9.2 overs, building on the fact that Cook had contributed 127 out of the 399 runs in total scored by Essex. The team won, but so did three members of it. While the result was not necessarily ominous for Somerset, it felt like a shift in power was taking place, even if at this stage they must have had their eye on the return match at Taunton at the end of September.

*

Cricket is not what it used to be, but what it is going to be. On Wednesday 26 June, in mid-morning, I discovered on Cricinfo that Germany Women were playing Scotland Women in an ICC Women's T20 World Cup Europe Region Qualifier. Germany were 37-8 at the end of 20 overs at a run rate of 1.85. The batswomen's scores were five, four, zero, three, zero, zero, three, two, five, two. One of the German players was called Suzanne Renée McAnanama-Brereton, 34 years old and born in New York. When Scotland replied, after one over, they were 9-1, needing 29 runs for victory: would they do it? Opener Bryce and Glen at number four took them to 36-2 after 5.4 overs, and after six overs they were 38-2 winners! I felt very warmly to this event, because the scores brought back remembrance of things past for myself during my own cricketing days. It was played at Cartagena in Spain, so the weather was good: a pleasant 26° with a light easterly breeze. One of the contributory factors to Germany's defeat was bowling 8 wides in allowing Scotland to reach 38-2.

Similarly on the edge in my mental universe were events at Kuala Lumpur, where Thailand (130-7) were beaten by the Maldives (131-8). The Maldives needed 2 runs to win with 2 balls left when Hassan was run out on the fifth ball of the over. A tricky task just got trickier. But then Malinda scored a two off the last ball to give the Maldives victory. This was the third match in the Malaysia Tri-Nation T20I series, and it would have been enticing to be able to watch those last two balls on a livestream.

*

Deprived of a fourth day in the Essex versus Somerset game, I tuned in to what was happening at the Oval. Surrey's two innings had been 194 and 325, giving a total of 519 runs and in reply Warwickshire had been 230 and were now 171-4 requiring 119 runs to win with 6 wickets remaining. Sibley was 69 not out and there were plenty of overs left (80 at 11.49 am). Things were on Warwickshire's side, I felt, but did they have the necessary patience quotient? Dominic Sibley was 69 not out and certainly had. At 11.50 I tuned into the Surrey livestream to find they had replays, which was an advance. Sam Curran was bowling to Sibley, and went past the edge twice. Then just after midday we were given a view of the field from high up at the opposite side to the gas holder. This was even more of an advance, to give the spectator on livestream a view of the whole field.

Shortly after noon, Adam Hose fell to Curran, bringing the promising Sibley-Hose partnership of 41 runs to an end. Three balls later I was able to see Curran bowling Matthew Lamb, sending the off stump flying out of the ground. This was good to watch but not good for Warwickshire because they needed someone to stay with Sibley. It got worse, suggesting the impatience quotient was on the rise. Batty came on to bowl, and Tim Ambrose was run out exuberantly by Ben Foakes taking a very good throw by Scott Borthwick and demolishing the stumps. This image was going to repeat itself on a big stage shortly. The livestream replayed this run out from the aerial advantage point, which gave an excellent view of how well Borthwick had done with his throw (see opposite).

Hose, Lamb and Ambrose had all departed with the score on 190, and the game had turned dramatically in Surrey's favour. Next they brought back on one of their main strike forces in 2018, Morné Morkel, tall and hostile, and offering no quarter for the tailenders – nor for the obdurate Sibley. Morkel removed Surrey's main threat by getting down on his follow-through to pick up a catch down by his boots. Sibley had been proving his mettle for Test consideration, with 73 off 165 balls, but his departure meant the end. The Warwickshire captain, Jeetan Patel, was not in 'they shall not pass' mood. He lofted the ball high into the deep, where Jordan Clark almost took a catch but "had to run among the pigeons which put him off", as the radio commentary put it. I was enjoying the livestream but it could not last. Patel took the wildest of cross-batting swipes at Batty and was stumped for 17 runs. After 74 overs Hannon-Dalby was caught and bowled Batty and the innings was over. Batty ended with figures of 34 -4. This was a much-needed Surrey win lifting them to fourth from bottom and putting Warwickshire down at second from bottom, albeit with 26 points more than Nottinghamshire.

Borthwick throws, right of picture

Foakes breaks stumps

Nor was the excitement over for the day. At around 5 pm in the afternoon I saw that Gloucestershire and Glamorgan were fighting a close contest in Division Two. Gloucestershire had scored 474 runs over their two innings, leaving Glamorgan, who had scored 287 in their first innings, a target of 188 to win. The game was on livestream and when I looked Marnus Labuschagne and Billy Root, brother of the more famous Joe, seemed to be cruising, as there were enough wickets in hand, and probably enough overs to get the runs, with not even a difficult run rate. But they lost Root on 147, and Labuschagne on 153. Soon after they lost Dan Douthwaite on 179, still 9 runs short. Gloucestershire were seeking to apply the screws, but the pressure was completely released to an unintended six from a bouncer scored by AO Morgan – Owen Morgan, no relation of the more famous Eoin. Glamorgan reached their target, leaving Gloucestershire to reflect ruefully that a score of 200 to 220 in their second innings might have meant that the run chase would have eluded Glamorgan. They would have had an over or two less to get those runs, and yet they would have been eager to win and thus maintain their hopes for promotion.

Glamorgan had 114 points, one above Lancashire, but having played one game more. Gloucestershire had 80 points with a good chance, despite the defeat, of pushing strongly for a promotion place; they too had a game in hand. Sussex stood in their way with 96 points but they had needed 437 runs to defeat Durham batting last. Durham I had discovered was being captained by Cameron Bancroft, an Australian name of ill omen since he had been involved in 'sandpapergate'. Over a hundred years ago Hilaire Belloc's Cautionary Verses about Lord Lundy (who was too freely moved to tears, and thereby ruined his political career) ended with his crushing humiliation at the hands of his grandsire: "But as it is . . . My language fails! Go out and govern New South Wales!" Australia was now returning the compliment. Penal servitude was served on Bancroft by sending him to captain Durham in Division Two, where as I observed his progress he excelled himself. He had patiently scored 158 runs off 305 balls in the first innings and consigned Sussex to defeat courtesy of Ben Raine's 27-6.

So, were Lancashire, Glamorgan and Sussex to go up at the end of the season?

*

At the end of the **seventh CC round** Essex were coming up on the rails:

Somerset	118 points (5 wins, 1 defeat)
Essex	105 (4 wins, 1 defeat)
Hampshire	92 (3 wins, 1 defeat)
Yorkshire	84 (2 wins, 1 defeat)
Surrey	73 (1 win, 2 defeats)
Kent	71 (2 wins, 4 defeats)
Warwickshire	65 (2 wins, 4 defeats)
Nottinghamshire	39 (0 wins, 4 defeats)

That is the statistical story. The human one was of Trescothick announcing his retirement at the end of the season, having scored only 86 runs in 8 innings.

*

During my absence in Scotland, I had learnt that Sri Lanka had beaten England on Friday 21 June by 20 runs. This should not have happened, and reflecting afterwards, Chris Woakes said, "We got our tactics wrong. It wasn't complacency, we just got stuck. It was completely out of character for us as a team. For four years we have been about taking the positive option, and here we just didn't do that . . . We dug ourselves into a hole by blocking. There wasn't that intent that we normally have." Although England in red-ball cricket often does not, to my mind, block enough, this was a moment of illumination for me: Woakes was saying that he who dares wins, but that England didn't dare.

Four days later, at Lord's, Australia beat England by 64 runs. I did not think this was woeful, but it was sobering. Having thrown two games away against Pakistan and against Sri Lanka, could they show the necessary mettle against Australia? No was the flat, unadorned answer. It raised the prospect that England might not qualify for the knockouts, and someone made the comment (radio or online I cannot recall) that they did not deserve to. This seemed to me an odd view to take. Sporting results often do not seem to me to do with deserts as much as to do with being in the right place at the right time in the right mood. In any case, if they were to get through to the knock-outs, they would have to pull victories from the games against India (30 June) and New Zealand (3 July). Were they to do that, they would surely deserve to go through. The author of the comment might, I hoped, have to eat their words. For his part, Michael Vaughan, in his insouciant laddish manner, commented, "When do the Ashes start?" I thought of striving, seeking, finding, and not yielding. This was what England had to do and that they were capable of it.

Worse was to come in a way from the commentariat, when Kevin Pietersen suggested that Morgan looked 'scared' during England's loss to Australia. This raised my eyebrows, since I think it is difficult to interpret emotions from the way people look, especially under a helmet. Jonny Bairstow came out fighting: "It's just showbiz. They [the critics] are paid to have an opinion and if they don't have an opinion they get sacked." The press seized on this outburst with glee at the notion that someone should criticise their collective wisdom and methods. For my part, I thought this honesty was welcome, since in assessing what someone says it is often necessary to unpick any hidden or unspoken motive they might have for saying it. Morgan's considered response however struck a wise note: "You have critics being critics. But they need to do that; that's their job. So let them be."

The World Cup was beginning to heat up. Returning from London on Friday 28 June, I had an hour to kill at Liverpool Street before boarding my train. I idly wandered into the Broadgate piazza to find it filled with City workers having their Friday evening alcohol in the warm evening sun, and the soft evening light drawing a veil over the travails of the week – "and God saw it, and it was good." In the background was a very large outdoor TV screen, showing the highlights of the South Africa-Sri Lanka game, won by South Africa by 9 wickets. (England had well beaten South Africa in the opening game, and a week earlier had succumbed to Sri Lanka by 20 runs. Could this result have been predicted?) Actually the result was immaterial in a way, as the highlights were just a biffed six, then four, then out, then six, then zap caught in the deep, then kerrang and so on. There were a lot of people milling around, but as far as I could tell no one was watching. It was a game without significance to those there, so they reduced it to wallpaper. Humiliating for cricket in a way, even if it was atmospheric.

The crowd felt alienated, not even turning its back on the game, but instead seeing it without watching it, present but not involved.

On Thursday evening, 27 June, the England women's football team had beaten Norway 3-0, and was progressing to the semi-finals of the Women's World Cup. "We can go all the way," was the tenor of the headlines. This seemed in stark contrast to the resentment that had arisen at the possibility that the England's men's cricket team would not go all the way in the World Cup. We are hard taskmasters of ourselves.

On Saturday, Australia beat New Zealand by 86 runs, a game in which Trent Boult took a hat-trick in the final over of the Australia innings. This was good bowling at the death, but I especially liked the understated way he celebrated what he had done.

*

Life carried on, so did the World Cup. Sunday 30 June was day 38 of a 48-day contest. England were due to play India, with a win crucial for both of them, even more so for England if they were to stay in the World Cup by their own efforts. "To strive, to seek, to find, and not to yield."

After the Cathedral service, I looked in at the Murderers pub in Norwich to see how England were doing against India, in a certain amount of trepidation as I approached, but when I got there I found England motoring very strongly in the shape of Roy and Bairstow. I almost gasped audibly with the pleasure of it, in particular at the way Bairstow was backing up his words against the pile of negative punditry with deeds. And then Roy's front foot, or perhaps his bat, was not perfectly aligned with the trajectory of the ball, and he holed out to a very good running catch at long off by Ravi Jadeja, fielding as a substitute. Joe Root came in and lost no time in maintaining the momentum of the innings in a quite different way by nurdling the ball around the field in his brilliant manner. At 12.45 I left, well pleased really. England had negotiated the first half of the innings well, could they negotiate the second? And could they bowl sufficiently cleverly in the third and fourth parts of the game to win it? However, by the time I had cycled home, Bairstow and Morgan had both gone. England were 224-3 with 12 overs to go. Stokes was now at the crease with Root and consolidation would be needed, I guessed, before making another assault. Stokes took on the role of kingpin and scored 79 runs off 54 balls in the last 16 overs of the innings. When he was out, there was some doubt whether Bumrah had bowled a no ball. Even if everyone else was interested, Stokes was not, and was back in the pavilion before it was finally ruled legitimate. This was theatre, which must have been even better at the ground with replays on the big screens. At 1.30 the innings ended on 337-7: this felt very competitive, but would India now consign it to the dustbin?

The TMS commentary felt particularly good-humoured, and generous too. It conveyed well how excellently Jaspit Bumrah had bowled, and they speculated on whether Stokes's innings would prove to be a matchwinner. Vaughan pointed to Kohli as the man to win – or lose – the match for India.

In the afternoon I had to work in the garden, but clocked into the radio to find India were one wicket down with Kohli and Sharma at the crease. If anyone was going to win it for India, these two could. However there was a problem for them: Woakes had opened the bowling, and started with three maidens. I completely missed the moment when in the second over Root had dropped Sharma in the slips. If he had gone then, it would have saved England a bit of trouble, although the game might have been a lot less entertaining for both sets of spectators. After 18 overs they were 1 wicket for 71 runs, and the win predictor was for England who at the same stage in their innings were on 130 runs. The Indian required run rate was therefore 8 per over for the rest of the innings. Dan Norcross commented to the effect that if England were to lose, and thus be dumped out of the World Cup, this would be a blow to plans to reconnect cricket with a larger audience. This seemed dramatic, hyperbolic, distasteful even, but probably contained a kernel of truth. In support of Norcross, I learnt that the fanzone in Birmingham's Victoria Square was absolutely packed, which suggested the crowd there was taking it very seriously and properly reconnected - except was it mainly India supporters? After 24 overs, India were 1 wicket for 112 runs and picking up the pace, trying to make England panic. Rashid came on, and the two batsmen went after him to good effect. Make England panic. Stokes was leaking runs with a lack-of-economy rate of 8.5 an over. India were now 133 for the loss of only 1 wicket, and Rohit Sharma was on 75 off 79 balls. They had got the required run rate down to 8.5 an over, when Jofra Archer came back on, and then Liam Plunkett. Which team could hold its nerve? The ice-cold part of me was thinking, "What nerves?" But it proved a good way of conveying the volatility of the mood: India can do it, no they can't. England can do it, no they won't.

In the event, maybe not India. At 4.45 Kohli drove to point and was caught by James Vince fielding as a substitute, out for 66 runs off 76 balls, succumbing to Plunkett's leg cutter. This made one 'cautiously less nervous'. Rishabh Pant came to the crease for his first World Cup one-day international. The match situation caused him much excitement, probably as a result of nerves as much as anything. Vaughan commented, "Pant's causing chaos," as he tried to get off the mark, get runs, get panicking. One measure of the strength of England's arm-wrestling may be gauged from Archer's 29th over: dot dot dot dot 1 (Sharma) 3 (Pant). India were now 152-2 off 30 overs which, following a crude formula, would convert to 300 off 50 overs, leaving them the losers. The required run rate was now 9.5 an over and creeping upwards.

Then in the 37th over the third wicket fell, the crucial one of Sharma caught behind off Woakes. Pant and Hardik needed to build an aggressive partnership, and Hardik dented Woakes's figures by hitting him for 3 fours, and taking 16 off the 39th over. Strong chants of 'India' were coming from the crowd. Official confirmation then came through that 95% of the fans in the fanzone were Indian. But then things turned again in England's favour when Woakes in the outfield took a brilliant catch running along the boundary at deep backward square and diving to hold onto the ball. Did he turn to the crowd to celebrate, as Stokes had done in the first match? Woakes commented afterwards: "Where I was fielding there were lots of India fans and there wasn't much of a roar from that part of the ground, so I kept it quite low-key, but inside I was thrilled. We were back on track." Indeed he barely smiled as he got up from the turf. This was something to look forward to watching on the highlights.

India were now 4 for 226 when M(aster) S(triker) Dhoni came in, their knight on horseback on past occasions. The England fielders were showing massive commitment, none more so than Bairstow, and Morgan was changing the field for every ball. In the 40th over 104 runs were still needed, a required run rate of 10.4 an over. Dhoni would have thought that was achievable by scoring at just under 8 an over and getting to the last two overs needing some two dozen runs and then blasting them off. 9 runs were scored off the 41st over – good – but in the 42nd, bowled cannily by Adil Rashid, 5 were scored – not good enough. Dhoni needed to panic – but wouldn't. India needed to hit sixes – but couldn't. Woakes was on at the other end, and every dot ball was getting clapped by the England fans. Archer was similarly miserly so that off the last 7 overs, or 42 balls, 83 was still needed at 11.85 an over. Plunkett then came on for the 45th over. It was remarked that so far India had not hit a six, and what is more on the fifth ball the substitute fielder, Vince, caught Pandya to make it 5 wickets for 267, the wicket falling just after Pandya had changed his bat. It made one wonder whether this had been a mistake. The new batsman was Jadhav and Mark Wood came on to bowl the 46th over. The game was seriously slipping away from India since they now needed 71 runs off 30 balls. The tension was draining away, and rather than England fans having to hold their breath they could now breathe much more gently and easily. In the 47th over, bowled by Archer, only 5 runs were scored. "Come on

MS" was coming from the Indian stands, a sentiment with which I agreed entirely since he needed to get a move on to take his side to victory. In fact his studied coolness was almost disconcerting it felt so out of place. 3 overs left, 57 runs needed. Wood bowled the 48th, and they took seven off the 49th over, taking them to 294. At this point, with the game quite out of reach, Dhoni hit the first six of the innings, taking them finally to 306, 31 runs short of victory.

In the last 20 minutes, the tension leaked away as a result of Dhoni being unable to take the game by the scruff of the neck and prove the Master Finisher his team and their fans wanted. The last 31 balls produced 7 dot balls, 20 singles, 3 fours and 1 six. Less obvious than India's failure to blast itself out of trouble was the impressive way the England bowlers strangled the batting by delivering 133 dot balls out of the 300 bowled.

That was not the end of the day since Channel 4 was showing highlights at 10 pm, or rather titbits from the Sky Sports feast, free but emphatically second-class. The programme was not entirely without its rewards, but in a way it was the shoddiest sort of television. The game had ended over three hours previously, which was time enough to put something together more thoughtful than wham-blast. Its shortcomings were, in no particular order: too much time devoted to adverts, including one for a Channel 4 cricket programme they were trying to promote, and to frenetic credits at the beginning, which they felt obliged to repeat after every ad break; all the helpful stats on Sky such as scores, number of overs bowled, run rate etc, could not be digested as they moved so fast. None of that counts for much but this does: a cricket match has a shape, a beginning, a middle and an end, and its pace is never uniform. Making a late programme is a chance to recollect the emotion in tranquillity. Not a hope. It would not have been difficult to show a bar chart of England's and India's runs per over, which would have been so instructive in revealing the pace of the game. There was nothing about the runs Bairstow had saved. They should have found a way to show Woakes's opening three overs which produced one wicket (this was shown) but also three maidens, which were not even mentioned. The deflation of the India innings was suggested but no explanation was given of how it unfolded. This was disappointing since quality in this case was not to do with money, just visual intelligence – which does not cost.

*

Despite this victory, England still had to win against New Zealand on Wednesday 3 July to guarantee a place in the quarter-finals. In fact they won by 119 runs in a markedly different game from the one the two teams would play in the final. I joined a friend at the Murderers to observe England's progress. England had started well by scoring 86 runs off 13 overs at a rate of 6.6 an over, but when I got to the pub I found that the cricket had become attritional. New Zealand had started to strangle England in their middle order, but England had broken free sufficiently to score a flurry of runs at the end of the innings. They ended with 8 wickets for 305 after 50 overs, maintaining that 6-an-over run rate. This did not feel match winning, but the pitch was slowing up, and the ball was getting softer, with New Zealand making good use of the conditions.

The turning point in the New Zealand innings, in the game really, was the dismissal of the star New Zealand batsmen, Kane Williamson, for 27 (off 40 balls, so the pitch was definitely slowing up) when Mark Wood got his fingertips to a ball hit straight down the ground by Ross Taylor and onto the stumps, an act of fortune more than will that meant running out Williamson at the non-striker's end. To what extent could such a run out be deemed premeditated? Hardly at all: it was the moment Williamson's number came up. At a moment like that, England must have thought that it was going to be their day, and New Zealand the opposite. And so it proved, since 9 balls later Ross Taylor was run out intentionally by Rashid's quick-witted exercise of his free will: he ran round from deep square leg, and threw to Buttler so that the ball reached him on one bounce allowing him to do the rest. In hindsight, Taylor should never have gone for the second run, but in real-time, a risk had to be taken in order for New Zealand to keep in the game. England's 100 had come in the fifteenth over; when Taylor went in the seventeenth over New Zealand had only scored 69 runs.

So it transpired that England would get a second chance against Australia in the second semi-final on Thursday 11 July.

7   30 June to 13 July including Super Wednesday on 3 July

On Sunday 30 June, there was another important set of games in the **seventh CC round**: Somerset v Hampshire, Kent v Warwickshire, Notts v Essex, Yorkshire v Surrey in Division One. In Division Two Derbyshire v Middlesex, Glamorgan v Worcestershire, Lancashire v Durham, Northants v Sussex.

Yorkshire's game against Surrey was played at Scarborough, which I had visited for the first time in 2018. The Yorkshire crowd appreciated Bairstow's century in the World Cup. I would have liked to have recorded their views on whether Bairstow's public comments ("It's just showbiz . . ." See p. 52) were considered as petulance or as honesty.

For Somerset, as leaders, every game was important. On the radio, Anthony Gibson remarked that it was a pivotal game for Somerset in their whole season. The crowd at Taunton on the first day, the Sunday, was given as 3000 and on the Monday, as 2000. I noted with pleasure that the Somerset livestream was doing replays.

Somerset kept their campaign well on track: they made 408 in the first innings, with scores by Abell, Hildreth, Banton and Bartlett, with their only nemesis in the Hampshire bowling being Kyle Abbott whose figures were 17.5-4-84-6. Hampshire replied with 349, Rahane and Northeast contributing runs, and Jamie Overton having figures of 23-4-70-5. Somerset were 59 runs ahead, and then when they made 358 in the second innings that gave Hampshire a target of 418 runs to win. At the close of play, they were 1 wicket for 12 runs off 4 overs which left them with 406 runs to get and 9 wickets in hand. The situation was classically difficult for them: getting the necessary runs would be extremely hard, but almost as hard would be batting out the whole day for a draw, especially with two good spinners in the Somerset team. And so it proved: Hampshire caved in to 104 all out. Leach's figures were 10-4-14-3, while Bess's (now back with Somerset) were 4.2-1-12-2. At 4 for 28 around 11.30, after half an hour of play, I noted that Hampshire seemed to have thrown in the towel.

It was later that afternoon that I found that Somerset had trounced Hampshire. Essex had also trounced Nottinghamshire who had only made 230 in their first innings, in reply to which Essex had scored 519, of which Nick Browne hit 163, and Ravi Bopara 135. This was despite two fine bowlers being in action against them, Stuart Broad and Ravi Ashwin, each taking three wickets. To make Essex bat again Nottinghamshire had to score 306 runs, but, perhaps finding as Hampshire had done that motivation eluded them as well as the necessary skill, they had collapsed to 183 all out. Inevitably Harmer had had a hand in their destruction, his figures being 40-24-35-4. Essex won by an innings and 123 runs.

With these games finishing early, I needed a game to watch. Fortunately Yorkshire v Surrey was turning into a cliffhanger. Yorkshire had made 327, to which Surrey had replied with 362 runs, nominally a lead of 35 but really equal on first innings. For their second innings Yorkshire had then scored 352 runs, putting them 317 ahead. When I engaged with the game Surrey were 2 wickets for 149, with 169 runs needed for the win. 48 overs had gone, and 35 remained. That made a required run rate of 4.82 runs an over, demanding but not impossible. Should they go for that target, which would make for very good entertainment, or should they bat out a draw if possible? This would provide entertainment of a more subtle quality, and in a short-attention era might be felt to be dull although perhaps not to a knowledgeable Yorkshire crowd – except of course they would want Yorkshire to roll over Surrey. As I watched on the livestream Dean Elgar, as a result of a muddled call by Ryan Patel, was run out speedily and cleverly by David Willey, but unfortunately there was no replay. The departure of Surrey's best batsman opened the door for Yorkshire. The game swung importantly their way when Ben Foakes was bowled first ball by Ben Coad, leaving them 4 wickets for 157. In the event Surrey were all out but with only ten balls to spare. While Coad's ball to Foakes was so good as almost to make his wicket inevitable, there were two avoidable run outs. First of all Patel the Surrey batsman had run out Elgar, and then this happened: Jamie Smith was batting at number seven for Surrey, and resisting stoutly in preserving his wicket at the tender age of 18. Yorkshire's demon spinner was Keshav Maharaj, and when Smith batted Maharaj away, he kept his eye on it and made no call. Morkel, backing up, started to come, then turned back, slipped up and ended flat on his back while Kohler-Cadmore's throw allowed Maharaj to remove the bails at the bowler's end. Morkel was out, but this did not stop him holding the pose flat on his back with his arms out, as if crucified.

He lifted his head as if to say to Smith, "What have you done?" In truth Smith should have been looking at Morkel and asking, "What on earth were you doing?" It was seriously irresponsible from the senior player, who needed not to take risks in order to bat out the game, and instead trust his younger partner who had the measure of the Yorkshire bowling. Was there a sort of arrogance here? Surrey were now 9 for 180 with some dozen overs remaining, so it had been vital that Morkel stayed in. As it was, with 2 overs to go, Smith was still there on 24 runs from 93 balls. Gareth Batty was keeping him company but fell on the second ball of the 81st over. They were all out and done for.

Were Surrey unlucky? You could say that, but they engineered their own downfall with Patel running out Elgar, and Morkel running himself out. They made their own bad luck. In effect it was Morkel who had succumbed to nerves, while Smith had been steely on coming to the wicket. I wondered whether Morkel had said to Smith that he wanted to face the bowling because he could manage it, implying that Smith was less able. And then I wondered about the scene in the dressing room afterwards: I guessed that a bit of truth and reconciliation would be needed.

Oh to be in Scarborough when the World Cup synthetic razzmatazz is here. England versus New Zealand was a good victory for England, but had meandered to a close, while events at Scarborough were the compelling climax to a four-day game. That World Cup game had been played at the Riverside Stadium at Chester-le-Street, turfing Durham out. Where did they go? Sedbergh in the north of England. And so I longed to be at Sedbergh where Durham helped see off Lancashire for a draw. Their main bowling opponent was Graham Onions, an ex-Durham player. The Cameron Bancroft redemption continues.

So this was good news for Durham. And what is more the England-New Zealand game at the Riverside had been attended by a full crowd, and what with the two other games at this ground (Sri Lanka v South Africa and Sri Lanka v West Indies), the club had netted about £1 million.

*

11 counties made use of outgrounds in 2019 so that first-class slow cricket was played on 17 of them during the season. This helps such cricket to find new audiences, and they can prove an attraction to young spectators, perhaps because their curiosity is piqued. Paul Edwards wrote in 'The Cricketer' most eloquently about the Hants-Notts game at Newclose on the Isle of Wight, and on Lancs-Durham at Sedbergh, both venues hosting county championship cricket for the first time, and both capturing that original village environment out of which the modern high-speed, big-city game evolved.

The Newclose ground was created *ex nihilo* – well, pasture – by Brian Gardener and his family who had money but also the vision to create a ground good enough to host a county match. The Isle of Wight, with plenty of retired people, is a perfect place for slow cricket. The game was played on 20 to 23 May and the result was a Hampshire win which saw 332 overs bowled over the 4 days, one champagne moment occurring when a swarm of bees crossed the field during the first day. Edwards' story was headlined 'Outground Heaven'.

He found transcendence too at Sedbergh, which is currently in Cumbria's border country but which up to 1974 was in Yorkshire – and perhaps because of this blemish chosen by Durham as the venue for their home game with Lancashire. Their home of Chester-le-Street was denied to them by the World Cup, and they were seduced into coming by sporty Sedbergh School. The ground has a setting of perfection surrounded by trees, a fine church dating from around 1130, stone houses and cottages, and a complete set of school buildings, all overlooked by the Howgill Fells. England not gone yet.

The result was a draw, but close: Lancashire were 4 wickets short of victory in a game of 375 overs, and spectators were witness to the sight of James Anderson bowling Cameron Bancroft well set on 77, and then having Graham Clarke lbw in the next over, his 950th first-class wicket. They then witnessed this green valley poisoned by a black cloud when he had to leave the field, and the game, with a calf strain. So a touch of mortality. Yet Edwards found too a touch of immortality in the scene at the end of the first day. To paraphrase:

Trees in shadow.

Fells in late sun.

Cricket at the close.

For this a lifetime.

It was Briggflatts, just a mile out of Sedbergh, that moved the poet Basil Bunting to write one of the most imposing English poems of the twentieth century, to which in 1975 he added three chiselled quatrains under the title 'Briggflatts Meeting House', which opens with the words: "Boasts time." What is true of the meeting house is true of cricket too.

*

All in all 3 July was a version of **Super Wednesday**: Yorkshire v Surrey, Lancashire v Durham, Somerset v Hants, Notts v Essex, plus England's first meeting with New Zealand in the World Cup.

With the emphatic wins for Somerset and Essex, the Division One points table, at the end of the **eighth CC round**, was Somerset 142 points, Essex 127. Yorkshire were just hanging in there with 106 points, and for Notts things continued to look bleak and getting bleaker: they only had 41 points. Really it did look as if it was down to a race between Somerset and Essex, and commentators were pointing to the showdown between the two teams at Taunton in the last match of the season. There were still six rounds to go before the finish, but there was the prospect of a really delicious climax to the whole Division One season.

In Division Two emphatic results were less forthcoming. Northamptonshire did beat Sussex but the other three games (Derbyshire v Middlesex, Glamorgan v Worcestershire, Lancashire v Durham) were all draws. Over the four days, between them, these six teams had scored 3522 runs, averaging 320 per innings, or 880 runs per day over the 3 matches - thanks perhaps to long midsummer days.

*

On Thursday 4 July, England women played Australia women in their second ODI as part of the Women's Ashes. This series was not going well for England, who had lost the first ODI if only by 2 wickets. In the second ODI Australia's victory by 4 wickets was more pronounced. As it turned out the whole series ended brilliantly for Australia – and badly for England. Having won the first two ODIs, Australia's victory in the third ODI by 194 runs when they bowled out England for 75, with Ellysse Perry taking 22-7, was even more emphatic. England eked out a draw in the four-day Test at Taunton but were really clinging on: Australia were 420-8 declared in their first innings (Perry 116) and 230-7 (Perry 76*) in their second. England were 275-9 declared on their first innings and were spared a second. There were then three T20Is, the first two of which were firmly won by Australia, although England managed a consolation victory by 17 runs in the third one. This led to much soul-searching for England, and the inevitable departure of the coach. What was really striking was the fact that Australia have set the women's team up so that they can select from a substantial pool of 100 professionals, in contrast to England who could only draw on 21 players, despite the fact that the population of Australia is under half that of England and Wales.

Meanwhile there was a cliff-hanger at the Civil Service Cricket Club at Stormont in Belfast where Ireland had scored 242 runs for 9 wickets. Although they had been 150 off 196 balls, in their reply Zimbabwe had taken 187 balls to score 150 so they seemed to be on track for a win, but could only end their 50 overs on 237 runs, 6 runs short. Tim Murtagh's figures were 5 for 21 with an economy rate of 2.10. He was getting in practice for when Ireland played England in a Test match in July.

*

Sunday 7 July was the first day of the **ninth CC round** of championship games, Yorkshire v Essex, Somerset v Nottinghamshire, Surrey v Kent and Hampshire v Warwickshire. At 4 pm Essex had bowled Yorkshire out for 208, and were on 1 for 42. Harmer had taken 5 wickets for 76 runs. However, I could not find a livestream, and concluded that this was not operated on a Sunday as a way of encouraging people to come to the ground. There was a livestream for the Hampshire v Warwickshire game but it was too letterbox in format so players were a bit squashed and the camera was not necessarily behind the bowler's arm. This made for an unsatisfactory viewing experience.

The next day the Essex livestream was operating with cameras at both ends. Similarly at Taunton where Somerset were playing Notts and this was providing replays as well. Surrey were playing Kent at the Oval and had their normal livestream going at both ends. Even Division Two clubs were getting in on the act with livestreams at Leicester and at Northampton, but the two games being played at outgrounds (Gloucestershire v Middlesex at Northwood and Worcestershire v Derbyshire at Kidderminster) understandably did not have it. Progress has been made this summer, but there is still some way to go to improve the experience.

In Division One, Essex were looking in a stronger position than Somerset. Would Harmer nail Yorkshire again? Would Ravi Ashwin help to keep Notts in contention against Somerset?

The gas holder at the Oval, for the Surrey battle with Warwickshire, had a banner put up (for the World Cup, naturally) saying 'World's Greatest Cricket Celebration'. I thought this was fractionally hyperbolic for the county championship but a nice touch, all the same.

On Monday 8 July I had had an angiogram to check the state of my coronary arteries, but returning home and engaging with, and ruminating on, the championship scores was as therapeutic as I could wish. Somerset and Essex had started their arm-wrestling contest, and Yorkshire were still saying, "We want to wrestle too." Even Notts were doing so. Somerset had started their second innings near the end of the day. Ravi Ashwin, the right-arm spinner, had taken the first over and on his fifth ball had Tim Groenewald caught at the wicket. The captain Tom Abell came to the crease: it was important that he and Azhar Ali survived the day. The second over by Luke Wood was a maiden, and so was the third. Somerset then took 4 runs off the fourth. So, in the last over of the day, the fifth of the Somerset second innings, Ashwin bowled to Abell on strike, with Ali at the other end. Could they survive the last over? Yes, just: dot dot dot dot 1 2. The figures seem as dull as clouded glass, but cannot convey the intense illumination provided by this brief passage of play, a pleasure to watch from afar. Once again I felt that it was possible to find in county cricket a very high standard of play, provided one had the time to give it attention. Ashwin had played over 60 games for India in red-ball cricket, Ali over 70 games for Pakistan. Abell had not played for England, and I suspect will never do so, but he is turning into a fine county cricketer, his skills enhanced by facing Ashwin.

*

To be a great cricketer, you need a dose of decency. Steve Smith and Virat Kohli are the two greatest contemporary batsmen. After sandpapergate, Smith cannot be a great cricketer, even while remaining a great batsman. Kohli still can, and indeed is trying to do so: in the India-Australia World Cup match, he signalled to the crowd to stop getting on Smith's back. This was a statesmanlike intervention. Smith has been judged by Cricket Australia, he is being judged by his conscience, and will be judged by the cricket historians. It is not the crowd's job to judge him.

*

Around 10 July, at the end of the **ninth CC round**, Division One results had a predictable look. Essex had beaten Yorkshire by 8 wickets, effectively putting them out of the title race. Somerset had beaten Notts by 132 runs. (This game had elicited poetic musings from Paul Edwards on Cricinfo, turning his report on the second day, 8 July, into a cod-Shakespearean drama.) Surrey continued to struggle in getting their season started, losing to Kent by 5 wickets at the Oval. Kent were proving their deserved membership of Division One. The most exciting game was between Hampshire and Warwickshire at Southampton, the excitement being provided, in cricket's perverse manner, by Warwickshire managing to draw with Hampshire. Warwickshire were chasing 404 runs in the fourth innings and at six wickets for 103 runs looked largely dead, but then Sam Hain made 104, having made 129 in the first innings, and the sixth-wicket partnership with Ben Mike put on 120 runs. After they had both departed, the Warwickshire captain, Jeetan Patel, made 70 with Harry Brookes at the other end and saved the match for them.

The Division One table showed Somerset still in the lead with a healthy 164 points, and Essex still well in touch with 149. Surrey and Warwickshire were on 85 and 83 points respectively, but the risk for them of going down was small in view of Notts only having 45 points. Division Two was looking positively lively. Lancashire were reasonably strongly in the lead with 134 points, but there were several contenders for the other two promotion places, including Gloucestershire who were second from the bottom with 84 points, but a game in hand. A win would certainly put them in the mix for promotion at the end of the season.

On Friday 12 July I had a postcard from one of my grandchildren, taken from 'Cricket: batting and bowling' in 'Outdoor Sports: a complete guide', published in 1913. It showed a series of poses such as the forward play, playing back, forcing the ball off the legs, overhand bowling, lob bowling, i.e. underarm! etc. Not a slog sweep in sight, nor a reverse sweep, ramp, scoop, dowsra and so on. It offered the immense attraction of the quaint, from cricket's archaic era. It was to be overtaken by a classical period in the middle of the 20th century, and we are now in a post-classical period where anything goes. However, this is progress of a kind, and there is a fascination in trying to determine what the game will look like 50 years from now. Will there be four-day county cricket for example? The pessimists rule, so, they claim, there won't be. Optimism on this score might seem foolish, but shrugging off inevitability, ways can be found of maintaining it, provided the will is there from both players and administrators.

So to the **tenth CC round**, starting on Saturday 13 July, notably Essex against Warwickshire at Fortress Chelmsford, and Yorkshire against Somerset at Headingley. These were two key matches, offering Essex the chance to catch up with Somerset. At the end of the first day things did not look too good for either team.

At Headingley, no toss had been made, so Yorkshire batted first. At the end of the day they were 3 wickets for 282 runs, and the next day proceeded to a total of 520 runs, with centuries from Ballance, Kohler-Cadmore and Harry Brook. At Chelmsford, Will Rhodes had taken 5 wickets for 17 runs, to help dismiss Essex for 245, the innings propped up by 84 from Alastair Cook. The Warwickshire choice of bowling first seemed to have paid off handsomely. The games were now being affected by international duties: Leach and Gregory from Somerset were on Lions' duty, and Warwickshire's Sibley and Hain were involved, as was Essex's Jamie Porter.

How would things pan out for both teams? There was no way of concentrating on an answer since the 48th match of the World Cup was due to be played at Lord's between England and New Zealand, a final no less. England had made it! Cricket eyes turned in that direction, provided they were not distracted by the men's tennis final at Wimbledon, nor the British Grand Prix at Silverstone. In theory all three events could be watched on television, laptop and mobile but I felt that the sum of these to be much less than the whole experience of concentrating on one of them. Common sense and magnanimity had prevailed, and for once major cricket was to be on free-to-air television. I could be there! Anticipation was in the air, and at 10.47 I heard the crowd singing 'Jerusalem' which was becoming cricket's unofficial anthem, an upmarket version of 'It's coming home'.

The sentence "I like 'Jerusalem'" does not quite convey the attachment I have to it. I am uplifted hearing it at a cricket match. The

Cricket Society bulletin had published a disparagement of 'Jerusalem' from one of its members. Reading it I spluttered into my muesli and immediately took up my pen to write to the Society on these lines:

"I was encouraged to learn the poem at a young age and it has been plumbed into me ever since, unaffected by breakdowns or the corrosions of the decades . . . The meaning is clear: Blake is articulating a vision of the heavenly city in England. The potency of this idea is why Hubert Parry set it to music in 1916, why the Women's Institutes chose it as their anthem, and why it bats high up the order at the Last Night of the Proms. We need visions to sustain us.

"In August 1999 I was at the Oval for the Fourth Test between England and New Zealand. As the crowd got tanked up, chants broke out: 'If you hate Man U, stand up' (a category mistake on two grounds: i) poor manners, ii) wrong game), 'There's only one Philip Tufnell' (better). The mood then ascended to a higher plane: 'Swing Low Sweet Chariot' – fine, even if it is really a rugby anthem. Then 'Jerusalem'. What more apt accompaniment to high-intensity cricket before a full crowd on a lovely afternoon? Truly, I tell you, here was the heavenly city. For a brief moment you could believe God liked the English. Hats off to William Blake."

It kept being sung through the summer but unlike with some anthems I never got bored with it. I also purred on learning in September that it was the United Kingdom's favourite hymn in a poll by the BBC's Songs of Praise. Had its singing at big cricket matches contributed to it being catapulted into the charts?

Part 2   EXPLODING

8   World Cup: the two semi-finals

After the forty-fifth game of the World Cup, the last of the group stage, the points table looked like this, listed in alphabetical order:

Afghanistan (won 0-9 lost)		0 pts
Australia	(7-2)	14 pts
Bangladesh	(3-5)	7 pts
England	(6-3)	12 pts
India	(7-1)	15 pts
New Zealand	(5-3)	11 pts (nrr 0.175)
Pakistan	(5-3)	11 pts (nrr -0.43)
South Africa	(3-5)	7 pts
Sri Lanka	(3-4)	8 pts
West Indies	(2-6)	5 pts

In noting that the top four teams were India, Australia, England and New Zealand, spare a thought for Afghanistan. They lost all their games but they gave India a shock on 22 June. India only reached 224-8 in their innings, and Afghanistan then battled to 166-6, needing 59 runs with 8.3 overs to go, i.e. 51 balls. This was about 7 an over, which would be very manageable. When Rashid Khan fell in the 46th over, with 26 balls to go and 35 runs needed, not surprisingly the Afghan tail could not make it, but it would have been a delicious victory for them if they had.

As an incidental point, New Zealand only pipped Pakistan to the semis by virtue of net run rate (nrr). It sounds simple and definitive, but it is certainly not simple. Learn and mark the Wikipedia definition: "The NRR in a tournament is the average runs per over that a team scores across the whole tournament, minus the average runs per over that is scored against them across the whole tournament. This is the same as the weighted average of the run rates scored in each match (weighted by the lengths of the innings batted compared to the other innings batted), minus the weighted average of the run rates conceded in each match (weighted by the lengths of the innings bowled compared to the other innings bowled)." I cannot digest this, and conclude that because it is not simple, it is unlikely to be definitive.

The two semi-finals were therefore to be India versus New Zealand on 9 July and England versus Australia on 11 July. They hardly seemed worth turning up for, since the Final was surely going to be Australia versus India. However, my mind was not on cricketing matters following the angiogram on Monday 8 July and a visit to Oxford on business on 9 July. Subconsciously I was not turning up.

But in fact I did attend to the England-Australia semi-final, out of patriotic duty more than pleasure. As it turned out it was a stroll in the Edgbaston Park for, surprisingly, England. Australia, having won the toss, chose to bat, and collapsed to 223 all out in 49 overs. Steve Smith alerted England fans to his forthcoming obduracy and chutzpah by scoring 85 off 119 balls, about 40% of all the balls bowled at Australia: he had gone to the crease in the second over and was run out in the 48th. But apart from him, three others got scores over 20 (Carey, Maxwell and Starc) and seven scores under 10, including the two openers, Warner and Finch. Honours instead went to the England bowlers. There were 3 wickets each for Woakes (economy rate 2.50) and Rashid (5.40) and 2 for Archer (3.20) of whom the Australians got a first sighting, a skirmish in bigger battles to come.

England then knocked the runs off in 32.1 overs for only 2 wickets with scores of 85 (Roy), 34 (Bairstow), 49*(Root), 45*(Morgan). The key to victory and defeat was in how the two opening pairs performed, and theirs did not, ours did. Indeed Roy's 85 came off only 65 balls, and the Australian bowler's economy rates were mixed, Behrendorff (4.65 an over) and Cummins (4.86) being the best. So, an early finish of the game meant I could get on with things with a certain lightness of spirit: I discovered victory had mattered after all.

The first semi-final on the other hand was a different story. Rain on 9 July stopped play with New Zealand on 211-5, which meant that the game went into a second day, and by a stroke of felicity we drove home to Norwich from Oxford able to listen to the India innings on the radio. This is yet another way of experiencing cricket, especially if it is at all stretched out. The experience of listening can transform a dull journey to the point where you would not wish to be anywhere else but tootling along in a car transfixed by what is happening miles away.

This game was another switching-on of lights for me. I had learnt that the 50-over game could be exciting in theory but here it was riveting in reality. Which team deserved to win? You could have loyalty, e.g. the vast majority of the crowd at Old Trafford were India supporters so that it was virtually a home game for them. For my part, my parents had come from New Zealand so I had a residual loyalty to the team, topped up by admiration for their low-key monosyllabic quality to which players allied terrific skill without flaunting it, none more so than their captain Kane Williamson. Also, it was a test of character not to let the 'home' crowd intimidate them, or put them off their game.

What especially struck me was how a low-scoring game could so capture the cricketing mind. This was a dot-balls match: 338 of them, a contest won by New Zealand's 180 against India's 158. There were 28 boundaries in all with only 6 sixes, 4 of them hit by Jadeja in cranking up the Indian innings to try and overtake the New Zealand score. The pitch was in fact dry and cracked, and runs were elusive. New Zealand's masterstroke was to have India 3 wickets down for 5 runs in the fourth over, including that of captain and icon Kohli. Karthik at number four then took 22 balls to get off the mark. I learnt too that the one-day game could have its sessions, shorter than Tests but still significant. What would be the mood after 10 overs, 20 overs, 30, 40 and then for the last 10?

I was able too to watch the highlights on Channel 4 television. These were execrable. Most viewers know what happened, so they want to know how it happened, but cramming 597 balls into 45 minutes, since I reckoned almost 15 minutes was lost to adverts coming every 5 minutes, gave no sense of the ebb and flow of the game, and in particular of Dhoni and Jadeja trying to get over the line by a tidal wave of batting. Inevitably Jadeja's sword-dance with his bat on reaching 50 got an airing. You would never know that Man of the Match was a bowler, Matt Henry, for bowling 42 dot balls, more than anyone else.

However, it did show the two astounding catches, and the two superlative run outs, the quality of which was proof of how intense the matter was. Jadeja caught Latham with a backward leap in the deep, having in the over before run Taylor out with a perfect throw with his natural left arm. New Zealand were not to be outdone. Karthik went to a diving left-handed catch at backward point by Neesham, and then Guptill ran Dhoni out in the 49th over with a direct hit from backward square at a distance of maybe 40 metres. I had concluded by then that India were most unlikely to make their target but it still did not detract from the magic of the moment.

The Indian run rate at the beginning of the 40th over was 9 an over. In the next 9 overs that run rate slipped away from them: 9 (over 41), 8.85 (42), 10.33 (43), 10.40 (44). So, 52 runs were now required off 30 balls, but the run rate remained obstinately high: 10.50 (45), 12.33 (46, a wizard Henry over), 15.5 (47, a wizard Boult over). And then Dhoni was run out on the third ball of the 48th over coming back for the second run, which he was obliged to do if India were going to retain a chance of winning. Yet if he had made it, or rather Guptill's arrow had missed the stumps, India would have needed 22 off 9 balls. What if Dhoni had then farmed the strike to face the bulk of those 9 balls? What if he had hit two more sixes, and a boundary, leaving 6 to be scored by other means. . . And so on. What is possible is not what is probable, and it is certainly not what is actual. India were 221 all out in the last over, and New Zealand were in the final.

The excitement was palpable. One of the joys of these big tournaments is the context, a contest for a place in the final that transforms excitement, not uncommon in cricket matches, into a unique experience. It may be joy unconfined, it may be anguish inexpressible, but for a moderately impartial observer it was pure pleasure.

9 World Cup Final: Sunday 14 July 2019

How do you describe a game about which so many words have been written already, and so much hyperbole expended? It certainly opened my eyes to what sporting heights white-ball cricket could attain, chiefly because, as it turned out, it proved to be attritional in the best way, a tense contest between bat and ball. Although Stokes was rightly awarded Man of the Match for his heroic innings, in a way it was more a bowler's game than a batsman's. As it happened, Lord's was a wonderful place for the final, not just for its place in cricket history but because it helped to offer a contest between bat and ball. The Lord's slope managed to make it so exciting.

When the dust had settled and the final score cards printed and studied, the following emerged:

- New Zealand won the dot-ball contest: 173 of their 300 balls were not scored from, compared to England's still respectable 160 out of their 300.

- England lost the extras contest: New Zealand benefited from 30 extras, including 17 wides, while England only got 17 extras, including 12 wides, still not respectable for New Zealand but better than England. 5 wides came from Archer.

- Colin de Grandhomme walked off with the economy-rate prize of 25 from 10 overs (2.5 an over), whereas the best of the England bowlers, Chris Woakes, could only manage 37 off nine overs (4.11 an over).

- On the other outsize hand, England won the boundaries contest: New Zealand had 2 sixes against England's 3, all courtesy of Stokes, while they only mustered 14 fours against England's 22, of which 7 came from Bairstow and 6 from Buttler. This bare statistic, as it turned out, would have crucial significance, more brutal than bare.

In the cool hours after the game, there is a risk of a superfluity of analysis that kills rather than enhances the memory of the occasion. Instead a sense of the emotions engendered needs recollecting, and a sense of the tensions involved – probably irrecoverable in hindsight.

In particular how do you describe the opening half of the innings when spectators know even less than the players and the journalists in the Media Centre? However, they do quickly get a sense of how the pitch is behaving, and whether a bowler is bowling superbly, or just well – which may not be good enough. Guptill and Nicholls opened the batting for New Zealand, and Woakes and Archer opened the bowling. Early on Guptill hit Archer for six, producing a wry smile from the bowler, then followed it up with a boundary and 2 singles, making 12 off the over. Was it going to be a high-scoring match? But then Woakes had Guptill lbw for 19 and Williamson came to the crease. Archer then tested him with a near maiden, so was it going to be a low-scoring match? It could not be nerves, surely, as Williamson only does watchfulness. Still, you cannot tell since from behind his beard and his Kiwi impassivity he gives nothing away. At the end of the twelfth over, Williamson had only scored 2 off 21 balls.

When Mark Wood came on to bowl he got his speed up to 150 kph/93 mph. In fact he produced in this game the equal fastest ball (to Archer and the Australian Mitchell Starc) in the tournament at 153 kph/95 mph. Morgan cleverly complemented his pace with Plunkett's guile, and in the twenty-third over it was Plunkett who had Williamson caught behind with a ball showing a deviation of 0.57°. I was unclear as to what to make of this: was it the 'Goldilocks ball', deviating somewhat but not too little, not too much? Nicholls was still there grafting away, looking on as Ross Taylor came to the crease to the strains, equal loudest in the tournament I speculated, of Eric Clapton's 'Layla'. Was this needless or mindless? (Might other candidates be the opening chords of Beethoven's Fifth? Wagner's Ride of the Valkyries? Even Brahms's Tragic Symphony? Something German anyway.) This was not the Lord's of the 'soundless clapping host' in Francis Thompson's poem. A slight dial-down in intensity was signalled by the sight of a spectator with a lion's head and mane, and I felt relieved I had not got a ticket to an England final to find myself sitting behind him. Nicholls had gone in the 27th over for a very respectable 55 off 77 balls, and the fog was beginning to clear: would New Zealand kick on in this middle period? Could England peg them back? New Zealand wanted to get after Rashid, but in the end his 8 overs, wicketless in the event, went for only 39 runs, at a respectable economy rate of 4.88.

At 1.07 pm the television switched from high definition to standard definition (the British Grand Prix taking over the HD slot), which was not quite so good. Be grateful, I told myself.

We were given at this point an aerial shot of Lord's which showed lots of spectators in the nursery behind the media centre and a number of empty seats visible in the stadium. This astounded me, that you would get a ticket, get to Lord's and yet not watch the game live.

At 1.16 pm it was 83 balls since the last boundary. Then in the thirty-fourth over Taylor was lbw to Wood, and although replays showed the ball was missing the stumps New Zealand were out of reviews and so he had to go. This is yet another feature of the modern game that would have amazed a previous generation. Is it a benefit? Probably, and the theatre of DRS is surprisingly admirable, but somehow I do not entirely trust hawkeye, or at least I am inclined to trust the umpire's eye just as much, humans before robots.

The score predictor was now 255 runs for New Zealand and there seemed to be a lull of intensity for spectators if not for the players. Neesham seemed to be aware that he needed to increase the run rate because Morgan forced him into an error and he was caught by Root at mid-on off Plunkett's bowling. This wicket seemed to have been deliberately planned. Clever.

At the end of the thirty-ninth over, New Zealand had got to 5 wickets for 169 and we were given the statistic that Bairstow had saved 24 runs in the match, 19 of them in the outfield. This was impressive.

At the end of the forty-fifth over, the mighty de Grandhomme was yet to hit a boundary, and soon after he was caught by Vince, fielding as a substitute, off Woakes for 16 off 28 balls. New Zealand could only take five runs off Archer's forty-seventh over, and in the next over Latham was another victim of a Vince-Woakes combination, a full toss, undone by the slower ball. There were 9 deliveries left, but when a yorker went wrong and Woakes bowled too high, it gave Mitchell Santner a 'free hit' on the next ball which unfortunately for New Zealand he missed. For the last over, they needed 12 runs to get to 250, a sort of psychological milestone. It was bowled by Archer, and went like this: dot / 1 (near run out) / wide / wicket: Henry bowled / dot / 1 / dot. So 1 wicket and 3 off the final over, and Archer's last 5 overs had produced 1 wicket for only 22 runs. This was also impressive.

At the close of the innings, New Zealand were 8 for 241. Beat that, England. Easy, New Zealand. In fact this game proved conclusive: it was now deemed better to bat first and leave your opponents to chase a total, which clever bowling and captaincy would make hard for them. So it proved on this day at Lord's.

Spectators were still part of the event. Teresa May, days away from stepping down as Prime Minister – in office but not in power, and with time to watch an important game of cricket, *capax imperii nisi imperasset* (see page 25), I regretfully reflected – was to be seen at the game. We were also shown pictures of the 5000 spectators in the fanzone in Trafalgar Square. People were getting engaged, and deriving high enjoyment from the cricket, and if not from the cricket then there was the Men's Final at Wimbledon, which turned out to be an epic also, and the British Grand Prix in which Lewis Hamilton clocked up his sixth win in the event. Amidst all the political discombobulations was this a vision of contentment?

*

When England batted, Roy survived a big appeal on his first ball but was given not out. It was important to try and relax, players, spectators and umpires alike. By the time the sun began to emerge around 4 pm, the game felt very attritional and doubly absorbing: the eleventh over was the third maiden in a row, the run rate being kept to 3.19 an over. Bairstow moved to get into his comfort zone of lusty striking of the ball. He had a four, and then nearly dragged one onto his stumps, the ball happily going to the boundary: good luck or destiny? Roy had gone in the sixth over, so Root was now batting and would surely move the innings along. Except he did not. He had taken 28 balls to get 7 runs, a tribute to the tightness of the New Zealand bowling, especially from De Grandhomme. In the seventeenth over Root swiped at one and missed; the next ball had him reaching to hit it into the off only to edge the ball to the wicket-keeper. Bairstow was the third to go, playing an inside edge onto his stumps. Bad luck or destiny? He was out for 36 runs (to which one should add all those runs he saved in the field) off 55 balls, a measure of the difficulty for batsmen.

Then Morgan was out to a brilliant catch by Ferguson and England were 86-4; gloom began to descend on me and the New Zealand win predictor moved to 51%. Which was more important, overs remaining or batsmen to come? Expressions were grim no doubt up and down England, which the relentless optimism of the advert breaks failed to dispel, and possibly even increased. Boult was brought back on to break the Stokes-Buttler partnership and with 20 overs/120 balls left England needed 127 to win. Mitchell Santner, the New Zealand spinner, came on to bowl and while he only did 3 overs, he only went for 11 runs. There was no question of New Zealand staying well in the game although the win predictor for them had gone down to 38%.

The TV showed a man sporting a Croatian cap. Should I have been surprised? No. This was another symptom of cricket's global ambitions.

"To strive, to seek, to find, and not to yield," came to mind for both sets of fans.

At this point England showed their mettle. A fourth-wicket partnership between Stokes and Buttler began to mean England regaining the momentum lost in the middle overs. With 10 overs to go, they were 170-4: to win 72 runs were required from 60 balls. The run rate was 4.25 an over, and the required run rate (rrr) 7.20 an over, not impossible – at least for Stokes and Buttler. While Matt Henry had been strong with the new ball, the worn ball was harder for him and a psychological advantage was taken by Buttler when he scooped him for a boundary. The required run rate kept creeping up like this:

over 41 (Ferguson) rrr 7.66

42 (Neesham) 8.12

43 (Ferguson) 8.42

44 (Boult) 8.83

45 (Ferguson) 9.20 – and the big wicket of Buttler

46 (Neesham) 9.75

47 (Ferguson) 11.33

This was a crucial moment: Ferguson had kept the forty-seventh over to 5 runs, and had also taken the wicket of Woakes. The order for England was growing taller by the over. Then 10 runs came from the

48th over, bowled by Boult, keeping the rate to 12, or putting it in a more more illuminating way, 24 runs were needed from 12 balls. Neesham took the 49th over and England's arm seemed to be wrestled downwards: both Plunkett's and Archer's wickets fell, although nine runs came from the over, thanks to a six from Stokes. What is more he scored a single to keep the strike for the last over. His partner was Rashid, no slouch with the bat but no Stokes either.

A naked account of the fiftieth over, shorn of its tension, suspense and emotion, went like this:

1) Yorker, Stokes declines single, so does Rashid – 15 to win from 5 balls.

2) Yorker again, a dot ball again, so Stokes wants to hit a six or two – 15 to win from 4 balls.

3) Length ball which Stokes makes into an elegant loft leg side for six, and Williamson gives a wry smile – 9 to win from 3 balls.

4) Stokes swipes full-toss to leg, and in order to keep the strike runs 2. Guptill's full-toss throw hits Stokes's bat as he dives for the crease and ricochets to the boundary, a permissible 6 runs. This time there was no wry smile from Williamson nor from Guptill, but a look of incomprehension. This we could all share. Still there it was – 3 to win from 2 balls. Actually television viewers got a privileged view of this exceptional moment when the camera cut high at 45 degrees to it, a judicious choice from the 38 cameras at the ground by Gary Scovell (let him be named and glorified) for ICC TV production.

5) Stokes hits down the ground, loses his footing but still runs, and then runs a second run, but Rashid is stranded by the throw to the bowler's end and is out. But Stokes is facing the final ball – 2 to win from one ball.

6) Stokes pushes looking cleverly for a gap allowing 2 runs, but Williamson is ready for him since he has placed a longish mid-on in a perfect position to receive it and throw to the bowler's end. The batsmen run 2 but Mark Wood cannot make it. Only one run from the over, making it a tie.

A less prosaic account of the 50th over admires Boult's 2 dot balls, then gasps at the way Stokes slog-swept his third ball for a six, but I still felt – anxiously – that the odds were in New Zealand's favour. This was to reckon without the extraordinary intervention of chance, or rather Chance, shading into fate or Destiny. Among the Homeric Greeks what happened next would be interpreted as the result of divine intervention. Zeus, king of the gods, would have weighed the chances of victory on his scales, England in one pan, New Zealand in the other, and the scales would have showed England's pan being the heavier. New Zealand were going to lose and there was nothing they could do to alter that destiny. This is to rationalise in hindsight the fact that Stokes hit the ball to the deep, wanting two runs. He came back for the second to the keeper's end, and the throw-in from Guptill hit his bat and cannoned to the boundary. 2 runs and a 4 runs made 6: to win England now needed 3 runs from 2 balls, a piece of cake.

Yet so it did not prove. Stokes struck the ball, wanting 2 runs, Rashid obliged but in trying to make his crease for the second run he was run out. This was a noble sacrifice on his part since both batsmen knew England had one more batsman, Mark Wood, to come. Rashid went, Stokes retained the strike, and only needed 2 runs off the last ball to win the match. One run only would tie it, an unhelpful outcome in the circumstances. So two it was that Stokes went for, Wood obliging again, but sharp fielding brought his downfall as it had done Rashid's. England were all out, only one run went in the scorebook, and the two sides had tied on 241 runs each.

How would this be resolved? Just when the commentators first mentioned the 'super over' that would be needed in the event of a tie I cannot recall. But as soon as it happened, they went into overdrive getting the dazed audience up to speed: each side would have one over each, and the side to score the most runs would win. And what would happen if the super over was tied? That was too remote to take seriously, but it seemed that a 'boundary countback' would come into play, i.e. the side that had scored the most boundaries in the substantive part of the match would win. Having scored 22 fours and 3 sixes against New Zealand's 14 fours and 2 sixes, England had this one in the bag. But it would not be necessary surely? These 12 balls must produce a winner.

This was uncharted territory. It was not like a penalty shoot-out pitting one penalty-taker's shooting skill against a goalkeeper's agility.

Anyway, in that case, familiarity has removed the novelty value. The super over was going to be different: novel yes, two batsmen, one bowler, yes, but there was a crucial additional factor since the rest of the team were going to have to be on full alert to take split-second decisions and then to execute them skilfully and correctly. The captain too would have to be super astute in his field placings.

As this whirled around in the national consciousness, at least that part of it engaged with what was happening at Lord's – and by 7 o'clock both the Wimbledon final and the British Grand Prix were over, so newcomers, drunk on sporting spectacle, must have been arriving all the time. A friend of mine who was watching with his son and two grand-daughters told me that just before the start of the super over, the two girls, 'sporty and energetic' by nature, ran upstairs to don their England shirts in order to watch it.

So, 12 balls, except there were 13 since Archer bowled a wide with his first ball. He had bowled 5 wides in the main New Zealand innings, more than anyone else, so in choosing him, Morgan was taking a risk. Would not Woakes have been a better choice? The question is superfluous in view of what happened. In any case, Archer was very cool and skilful; there was no way of knowing that Woakes would have been more so.

The New Zealand over was bowled by Trent Boult. Again his economy rate in the England innings was poorer than the others, giving away 6.70 runs an over, but he was their main strike bowler. Would de Grandhomme, or Ferguson, have been a better choice? Another 'what if' question, another waste of words.

Boundaries would be needed. Two Stokes sixes would do nicely but having scored 84 off 98 balls Stokes was not in mint condition. His partner, Joss Buttler, having hit 59 runs, was fresher, and between them, they could rack up a decent score for the over. And this they did: 3 (Stokes), 1 (Buttler), 4 (Stokes, superbly finding the gap), 1 (Stokes), 2 (Buttler), 4 (Buttler, ditto). Stokes must have worried about that 3 runs – they were energy-consuming, whereas a boundary was energy-saving. Another concern was the sun declining behind Lord's: the pitch was in full sunlight but the outfield on the Grand Stand side was not. When Buttler hit 2 on the fifth ball, the fielder was slow to pick it up in the sunlight, when he might have kept the run to 1. Small things counted.

In the end, England had 15 runs, and I felt a measure of confidence, quite ill-founded, that this would be enough. However, when Archer starts his over with a wide, he drops his shoulders, encouraging others to do the same. His first ball proper goes for two, and his second ball Neesham makes into a mighty six. England hearts take a severe hit: 7 runs to win are needed off 4 balls. New Zealand hearts can be confident. His third ball is hit along the ground to Roy in the deep on the Mound Stand side with the sun in his eyes. A clean piece of fielding and an accurate throw to the wicket-keeper would run Neesham out, but Roy misfields. New Zealand need 5 runs to win off 3 balls. Neesham likes picking out Roy, because the fourth ball goes to him again, but he throws it to the wrong end, sort of. It was remarked that he threw it to the bowler's end when he should have gone for the wicket-keeper's end. But that was a longer throw, and while one directly over the stumps might have done it, the rule seems to be 'one bounce into the keeper's hands' in which case Neesham would surely have got home. As it was, a clean piece of fielding and a clean full-toss throw to Archer right adjacent to the stumps was not a bad choice. But Guptill was still home safely.

New Zealand now need 3 to win off 2 balls. How can Archer handle this? The fifth ball is bowled slightly wider on the crease and Neesham, in trying to swot it for 2 runs or a boundary, mishits it. He takes a single, but it brings Guptill to face the last ball with New Zealand only needing 2 runs to win.

The sixth ball, the yorker, was well squeezed by Guptill towards the mid-wicket boundary. A four would be nice, but in fact not hitting it too hard gave him a good chance to run two. It almost paid off. As it was Buttler cleverly and crucially positioned himself in front of the stumps allowing him to maintain the speed of Roy's throw by the speed of his movements, and furthermore ensure that the stumps would be hit.

This is where the suspense addled my brain. Did it addle the England players at all? It seems not because when New Zealand only got one run they all celebrated extravagantly led by Buttler. And New Zealand behaved in the knowledge they needed the two, so they must have known that the rule of the boundary countback would sink them: they had to have 16 runs off the super over to England's 15.

The one run taken off the fifth ball was crucial since it brought Martin Guptill on strike for the last ball. Guptill is a right-hand bat, so Morgan reset his field and in so doing moved Roy right across it from the sunny side to the shade cast by the Grand Stand. This worked decisively in England's favour. When Archer bowled a yorker Guptill did manage to hit it to the mid-wicket boundary, but Roy saw it perfectly, picked it up perfectly, and threw it perfectly with one bounce into Buttler who moved at warp speed to trash the stumps. We knew it was exciting because the zing bails and zing stumps lit up. But had England won? Did Guptill make his ground? Buttler and the square-leg umpire – and Guptill – were the first to know he had not, and it was by Buttler's reaction that I knew the scales had finally descended in England's favour.

New Zealand had been allowed to nominate which end the bowlers would bowl at, and they chose the Nursery End. This was Williamson's decision but did Boult tell him that was the end he fancied? What it did mean was that a left-hand bat – Stokes or Neesham – in striking the ball to leg would be hitting it to fielders with the sun in their eyes. Was that a consideration at all, or only in hindsight?

*

As an interlude, two random reflections could be made, the first absolutely unimportant, the other absolutely important.

1)   Stuart Broad was invited on Friday by the ECB to attend on Sunday despite the fact that Nottinghamshire's Division One match against Surrey started the previous day, i.e. the Saturday. He was therefore obliged to decline the invitation. Were the ECB administrators ignoring the county championship? God forbid.

2)   At the beginning of the day the ECB had been talking cautiously about an audience of 4 to 5 million being a decent figure for the day. (By comparison in the Ashes 2005 summer, the audience on television had peaked at over 9 million.) In fact nearly 8 million tuned in to watch the climax. There were also 8 fanzones across the country, in-

cluding in Trafalgar Square where there were 5000 fans. The #CWC19Final hashtag hit some 40 million page views, while there were 3.9 million unique browsers on the @BBCSport live page. It had been hoped that the World Cup would reconnect the English sporting public with cricket – and so it seemed to prove.

*

When a friend said to me that the result in the World Cup was no cause for triumphalism, my initial reaction was to agree. Yet on reflection it did not feel quite enough: if I, or any other English person (not to mention the Irish, in view of Morgan's contribution) wanted to take pride in what had happened, why should we be denied? But then I scratched my head: what did triumphalism look like? To get a feel for this I turned to how The Sun newspaper had covered the final. This is not my regular reading, but since its circulation is reckoned to be over 1.3 million it was tuned into a much larger audience than, say, for The Times which had a circulation of a little over 400,000.

The Sun's headline read: "Wowzat! England cricket fans go WILD after knife-edge World Cup win sees team lift trophy for the first time following 'greatest match ever'." There was nothing erroneous in that, but nationalism crept in with photos of Union Jacks and England flags being waved by the fanzone crowds in Trafalgar Square. Yet I could not feel even a spark of disapproval: it is a merit of sport that it provides a lightning-rod for nationalism. I learnt too that the anthem 'Cricket's Coming Home' was "reverberating around the bouncing Home of Cricket". That sounds as if it might be triumphalism Lord's style, and yet the paper carefully reported that the Queen's message included both congratulations to England and commiserations to New Zealand, "who competed so admirably in today's contest and throughout the tournament".

The Daily Mirror, which has half The Sun's circulation, was admirably factual, "England beat New Zealand as epic cricket World Cup 2019 final goes to Super Over," and gave a sobering account of the game with the fall of wickets etc.

Quite as intriguing was another Sun headline on 15 July: "Huge respect" about "Muslim duo Ali and Rashid" who "run for cover from champagne spray during England's celebrations and cricket fans love it." Somewhere in the ether, Saad tweeted the 'huge respect' idea and praised Ali and Rashid for "celebrating within limits". This appealed to me: nothing succeeds like success, nothing fails like excess.

Two weeks later there was a footnote: on 2 August The Sun reported that on the opening day of the first Ashes Test at Edgbaston, a plane flew over with a 'cheeky' banner, calling for Ben Stokes to be knighted "as cricket fans get into the spirit". The photo showed a plane pulling a banner, "Arise Sir Ben Stokes – Barmy Army." Apparently the BA had paid for the flyover, but "alas, Stokes was not in sight to witness it."

So that was triumphalist too, but of the kind that cheers, and does not depress.

It remained the case that Kane Williamson's composure was admirable. He scored 578 runs in the tournament and was awarded the Man of the Tournament prize, as much for his captaincy as for his batting. It is hard to discern at all what he is thinking as he strokes his beard but he comes closer than any other captain to treating triumph and disaster just the same. At the press conference afterwards he said in a deadpan tone, "Was it boundaries or something?" On the little matter of the ball hitting Stokes's bat and going for four overthrows, he commented, "You can't look at that and think that perhaps decided the match, there were so many other bits and pieces. It was so many small parts in a match that could have gone either way." In the post-match interviews, first in line was Bairstow and his first comment was to offer commiserations to New Zealand. This too was correct behaviour.

After 48 matches, 22,401 runs and 662 wickets the World Cup came down to the super over. Archer said that before he bowled it, Stokes came over and told him that, win or lose, today would not define him as a player. These were insightful words and a wise message at a good time. It will be extraordinary for Archer to have played in a match that would count as a pinnacle of his career just as he is setting out on playing international cricket. Nothing will ever be quite the same, will it?

In the New Year honours, Morgan became CBE, Stokes OBE, the coach Trevor Bayliss OBE, and Root and Buttler MBE (was that for the way he trashed the stumps at the climax?). For Captain Morgan there was a fairy-tale quality to his journey from a Dublin housing estate to this point. After the game he let slip that Rashid had felt that Allah was on England's side while Morgan felt that England had had the 'rub of the green'. This phrase derives from golf, but Morgan was using it as an equivalent to the 'luck of the Irish'. As a boy in Dublin Morgan proved to be so good at cricket, and so self-confident that he was ambitious to play for England. Opportunities to play international cricket for Ireland were fewer then than they are now, so he started playing first-class cricket for Middlesex in 2006 and soon after started playing for England. The point has been made that, not being brought up according to ECB rules, and having been grounded in Gaelic Games where he developed the necessary wrist play, he had the cheek to invent his own repertory of shots. His Middlesex colleague, Steven Finn, reported seeing him hit a six with a scoop shot at Chelmsford when playing against Essex. "No one had ever seen anyone do that before." It was in Ireland too that he learnt that a good strike rate was more important than the traditional average. Thus it was that he developed a winning cavalier style that took England to victory in July and him to the award of a CBE in the New Year Honours.

*

How could the rest of the season measure up to this extraordinary game? Nothing was so remarkable in 2019 than the fact that it did measure up, by virtue of an epic Ashes battle, a scintillating Blast Finals Day, and a final arm-wrestle in the county championship.

I learnt too that Britain was set to bask in a 'continental heat dome' with above-average temperatures over the next 3 months. High temperatures were given a higher probability than cooler ones in the south of England by the end of August, and well into September. This would help the Test series against Australia, but also the rounds of championship games scheduled for 10, 16 and 23 September. This was an encouraging prospect when one could be forgiven for thinking at the beginning of the season that it had been extended too far and some crucial games might be affected by weather.

*

By the end of the year the World Cup win was being mythologized: the Royal Mail produced a set of commemorative stamps -

Part 3 FURNACE

10 Interlude: England v Ireland Test, 24 to 26 July, Lord's

Every narrative benefits from twists and turns. A promising framework for the season was set up by having two monumental cricket events in the World Cup (finished 14 July) and an Ashes series (starting 1 August). Not all those involved in the former would be playing in the latter, but the impression was given of a certain seamlessness between the two events. Still, I needed a rest, let alone the England players.

Inserted in the schedule between the two was the small matter of a first ever Test match between England and Ireland, a slim Greek goddess between two Norse giants. It was 'small' because it would be an entertaining *entr'acte*, scheduled for four days rather than five. I had no qualms about it happening since in the shifting politics of Anglo-Irish relations, an *entente cordiale* between England and Ireland might not come amiss. Might Ireland bring off a creditable draw?

Political relations were about to enter a new phase with the election of Boris Johnson as leader of the Conservative Party, and thus Prime Minister. To signal the event, on the steps of number 10 Downing Street on his first day as PM (24 July) he gave the Sheldon Cottrell Sa-

lute. I recognised it immediately, and concluded that cricket had made one of its rare break-outs onto the wider national stage, a sign that it was regaining the nation's affections. Johnson had popularised cricket in a way that a dozen cunning ECB plans could never do. I then learnt that this flaunting gesture in the modern manner, jocular in the Johnsonian manner, superficial if you prefer, certainly vulgar, was lost on the population. A friend of mine had never seen or heard of the Cottrell Salute (which for the hard of understanding was what the West Indies fast bowler makes to his team on taking a wicket). Fancy not knowing that, but then there are more things in heaven and earth than are dreamt of in my cricketing philosophy.

I was busy on Wednesday 24 July at the beach with the grandchildren so I did not follow the first day of the Test match at Lord's. When I discovered that England had been bowled out for 85, I was not so much aghast as astonished. Hubris is a necessary component in the drama of life, so I could only interpret this low score as come-uppance for the triumph of the World Cup. Yet this was a complete misinterpretation. For those players who had been in the World Cup (Root, Roy, Bairstow, Woakes, Ali) what they needed was not a Test match but a rest, or low-key cricketing practice: how about some county cricket for example? For the non-World Cup players (Burns, Denly, Curran, Broad, Stone and Leach) there was less excuse, and indeed the Test offered them a useful bridge from county cricket to the series with Australia. Then there was the Tim Murtagh factor. He had bowled for Middlesex since 2007 and could be said to know Lord's quite well. Now he was playing for Ireland. But was he a mere cricketing journeyman? Not on this day. The England innings lasted all of 23.4 overs of which Murtagh had bowled 9 and taken 5 wickets for 13 runs, at an economy rate of 1.44. His victims were Burns, Roy, Bairstow, Ali and Woakes, a roster of heroes whom he had made into zeros – literally in the case of Bairstow, Ali and Woakes, who were all sent back to the pavilion for nought. It was enough to make an Englishman apoplectic, except all I could feel was a mild disappointment and a warm cheer for Ireland as the score would give them great encouragement. I had a radical thought that an Irish win would be more inspiriting than an English defeat would be dispiriting. My son, over from America on business, found himself in Dublin on Day Two of the Test, which allowed the taxi driver to say to him, "You won the World Cup thanks to the Irish; and now we're beating you in the Test." If you weren't English, this was one of the cricketing jokes of the year, and if you were English you would want a chance to talk to the taxi driver after Day Three.

In fact, the England-Ireland game, having begun with agony for England and ecstasy for Ireland began to enter a grinding Act Two. On Day One, in reply to England's feeble 85, Ireland had got to 207 all out, a modest but threatening total. Andrew Balbirnie had top scored with 55 and when he was bowled by Ollie Stone, Ireland were 138-4, 53 runs ahead and ready to make an imposing score. That they did not succeed in doing so was down to their last six wickets falling for 69 runs, which was to the credit of the England bowlers: Stuart Broad bowled 19 overs and took 3 wickets for 60 runs, while Stone and Curran took 3 wickets each. Where was Woakes however, bowling on one of his favourite grounds? 10-0-34-0 is the answer, perhaps a case of WorldCup-itis. This will have got under his skin: how much could he salvage?

England had to face one over at the end of Day One, and for Burns as opener his partner was the number eleven, Jack Leach, in the team to provide a spin option to Ali, but here opening the England innings. He had been given 3 overs in the Ireland first innings, and been hit for 26 runs, a lack-of-economy rate of over 8 an over, which is not even acceptable in white-ball cricket. He was yet another player with some convincing to do. His opponent was Murtagh, who was no doubt eyeing up a second five-for, but Leach survived to fight the next day.

And he did fight on Day Two, the drama turning into fairytale. Finding a moment on the Thursday to catch up with progress and not expecting any, I learnt that the tanker had been pulled around, and what had done the pulling was Leach's tiny pilot ship. Leach knows he is a number eleven batsman but has had the nous to hone a defensive technique which would allow him to partner a stroke-maker: this would prove potent in the Ashes, and here at Lord's he had a partnership with Jason Roy of 145 runs. However, it did not necessarily appear that he played fifth fiddle to Roy's first violin, but instead unleashed his inner cover drive, hitting 16 boundaries in scoring 92 at a strike rate of 56.79, perhaps succumbing in the end to fatigue. *Cunctando restituit rem* – 'he rescued the situation by being bloody-minded' (as was said of Quintus Fabius Maximus in the third century BC), not just by his patience over

162 balls, but by the need to prevent his glasses steaming up: a ritual developed of him removing gloves and helmet to wipe them, and then replacing helmet and gloves, and picking up his bat again. This was unexpected theatre, like an attendant lord stealing the scene from Hamlet. He had his luck, being dropped on 72, but then luck is the privilege of batsmen: where would they be without it? What finally did for him was cramp in forearm and quad. In the nervous 90s, he eyed his century, and got caught off the bowling of Murtagh. Famously David Steele, in defying the firepower of Lillee and Thomson in 1975, helmetless naturally, was labelled 'the bank clerk who went to war'. Leach's achievement was more prosaic, so more apt for him would be: 'the librarian who went to work'. This was all watched by Teresa May, now ex-Prime Minister , pleased (I hoped) at being present at this carefree moment.

At close of play on Day Two, the folktale was poised between a happy and an unhappy ending, depending on your point of view. England had got to 303-9, 181 runs ahead. One feature of the day had been the heat dome, since the temperature climbed to 37°C, another factor to excuse Leach not getting his century. At number ten Broad had thumped his way to 21 off 25 balls including a six, when thunder and lightning took them off before the downpour came. The commentators quickly passed judgement, by inclination and habit unfavourable, while the spectators joined in this censorious fit by booing the umpires, and despite having had 76 intriguing overs during the day. Taking an Irish point of view, I felt sure that they were glad of some respite from the ferocious heat. Which had been worse, batting or bowling? Fast bowling requires so much energy, but then batting in all that padding requires an energy of a different kind. The players were surely happy to call it a day, especially Gary Wilson, the Ireland wicket-keeper, who in his padded state had to move on every ball.

Day Three dawned. Could Broad and Stone get the England lead to 200? This hope had to be abandoned pronto when Stone was bowled by Stuart Thompson on the first ball of the morning. Ireland only needed 182 to win, England only needed 10 wickets. Put your money on Ireland, since 182 is a perfectly manageable fourth-innings run chase. To win England needed to bowl as a quartet: Broad, right arm, quick, accurate with a high action and years of experience; Woakes ditto, albeit with slightly fewer years; Stone, right arm, very quick; Curran, left arm, pacey, skiddy. On this pitch the spinners would not be needed, although if Leach were to come on and take wickets this would surely make him Man of the Match. Ireland could be 60-0 and England still win, Ireland 100-1 and England still in it, albeit by a narrowing margin. In the dressing room they would want to get Ireland on something like 50-3 in order to seize victory. Technically, one wicket was needed every 18 runs. For both sides Tennyson's 'not yielding' would be their mantra.

So, from horror show, to folktale, to wrestling match. What would the final act bring? *Peripateia*, as it turned out, 'reversal of fortune', agony for Ireland, ecstasy for England. Broad added 4 wickets to his 3 in the first innings, while Woakes, maybe stung awake by his personal performance so far, had figures of 17.4-2-17-6. The Ireland bubble was punctured even more comprehensively than England's had been in their first innings as they finished 38 all out in 15.4 overs, James McCollum top scoring with 11. Was this ecstasy for England? It should not have been, merely the overdue restoration of the *status quo ante*.

After the game, Root criticised the Lord's pitch as 'substandard', which prompted indelicate comment in the press about it being the first Test pitch the new groundsman, Karl McDermott, had prepared at Lord's – and he happened to be an Irishman. That was gossip. More searching was the question of whether Root should have played. It was admirable that he did, as he wants to be a leader not a shirker. However, he had played two rounds in the county championship in April, an ODI against Ireland, a T20I and five ODIs against Pakistan in May and 13 World Cup matches. He did skip the World Cup warm-up match against Australia in May, but he was entitled to feel physically and mentally stretched. In the Ireland match he had won the toss, decided to bat, and his team had collapsed to 85 runs. For this decision heads needed to roll, i.e. Root's. Then he had been out for 2, providing more grounds for complaint. He had managed 31 in the second innings off 64 balls which was a captain's contribution in its way. He did not try to excuse himself but he was quoted as saying, "It's been ten weeks of hard cricket and of high emotion and of ups and downs. It does take a lot out of you. . . But we've dealt with it pretty well." This is an admirable statement of the principle of not yielding. Yet all these words cannot quite capture an image of him by the photographer Philip Brown: the attractive boyish look of his springtime as a cricketer has been replaced by the weathered look of a hard summer of rain and sun, so that the eyes have narrowed and he is gazing into the distance towards a future that is not easy to decipher. Sport tests character, and long, slow cricket does it more than any other, which offers yet another reason for preserving and sustaining it.

That Friday 26 July I was due to see the hospital consultant in the afternoon who confirmed I had an aortic aneurysm and that it needed repair straight off. This was sobering but I was buoyed that day by Jack Leach being made Man of the Match, despite only bowling three indifferent overs. I felt I had a personal interest in him having first encountered him in 2016 at Taunton when Somerset rolled over Durham, especially in the second innings when Leach shared the bowling honours with Roelof Van der Merwe. I was so impressed that when I had the opportunity to do so after the game was over, I congratulated him, and had my picture taken with him.

Ever since I had watched him stumbling towards a place in the England team. He had been one of three spinners in the three Tests played against Sri Lanka at the end of 2018, and, as a result of Moeen Ali's jaded performances that summer, looked ready for a place in the England Ashes team: in the event he played four Test matches. I saw somewhere that he was described as 'honest Jack Leach' but that sounded patronising – unless it contained the notion of him doing an honest day's work, an idea which rang true enough. Later in the season he would be considered a candidate for the Sports Personality of the Year, which was hyperbolic and did not square with my picture of the journeyman cricketer going to work. I was content to think of him as plain Mr Leach, a cricketer of my time.

11   Interlude: 15 to 31 July

As the World Cup was reaching its showdown, in the county championship the show had to go on without such distractions. Another 8 games in Divisions One (**tenth CC round**) and Two had begun on Saturday 13 July (see page 68). All the players at least, and probably a lot of the supporters, would have taken them seriously, particularly those at Somerset and Essex. There was the prospect of a juicy game at Chelmsford, where Essex were taking on Warwickshire. Would the Essex bulldozer continue on its way, or could Warwickshire throw itself in front and hold up its progress? There was an even juicier prospect at Headingley where Yorkshire were hosting Somerset, the latter keen not to allow their season to falter, Yorkshire keen to prove its quality at the highest level. Leeds was the first choice to attend, but Chelmsford was a lot nearer, so Chelmsford it was.

As it turned out, on the morning of Monday 15 July, the morning after the momentous day before, Somerset were in a decidedly delicate position like a bus on the edge of a sinkhole. Yorkshire had batted first and piled up 520 runs (Ballance cashing in again with 111 runs), while at the close of play on the second day, Somerset were 4 wickets for 76. They had to shift the weight of the bus back onto level ground by avoiding the follow-on to have any chance of a draw, let alone a victory.

Essex for their part had batted first but only scored 245 runs, of which a third had come from Alastair Cook with 84 runs. But Warwickshire had not fared well in reply. Peter Siddle, continuing to get in practice for the Ashes, had taken 5 wickets for 33 runs, but Matt Quinn and Aaron Beard had contributed, while Harmer had wheeled away for 27 overs and taken 2 wickets. At the close of play on the Sunday, Essex were one wicket for 73, with Cook in his second innings still at the crease. By going to Chelmsford I would have another chance to see him in action, having missed out in May. Essex were 157 runs ahead, so another 200 would leave Warwickshire chasing some 350 runs at the fortress. It was an enticing prospect. When I arrived at the ground, I learnt from someone that he had booked a taxi at 6:20 pm, only to be told by the taxi firm that Essex would have won it well before then. While it is sometimes claimed that taxi drivers have a special insight into the world, on this particular occasion such insight had escaped them. By the start of the third day Essex had got to 73 runs at 2.5 runs an over, with Cook on 34 not out, remarkably similar to their rate of 2.6 an over in their first innings and Warwickshire's 2.4 an over in their first innings. Assuming a rate of 2.5 runs an over, with some 90 overs in the day, Essex would only have added 225 runs to their present lead of 157, that is to say 350 to 400 runs ahead, leaving them Day Four to knock over Warwickshire a second time. The game was therefore unlikely to finish on Day Three let alone finish early. I was in for some slow cricket in pleasant contrast to the frenetic excitements of the day before, except that one of the pleasures of the season was the way the brain could encompass both these things, and it did not have to be the case that one excluded the other.

Unlike in May, this time I was in my seat for the opening over which started with Cook leaving the ball outside off stump, an essential ritual of slow cricket. The bowler was Ollie Stone, Norwich's fin-

Stone's long stride

est, since from 2011, at the age of 18, to 2017 he had played for Norfolk County Cricket. At the other end was Jeetan Patel, who was proving a handful. The loudest voices were from the players on the field: "Come on Stoner" (variation Stony) and at the other end "Come on Jeety" (variation Cheetah). At 11.30 Cook moved to 51 with a lovely off drive off Henry Brookes ("Brooker"). At the other end Quinn, who had been on nought not out overnight, had managed to score only one run in the first half hour, but then he had come in as the nightwatchman, and doubtless was under instruction to stick around and 'break

Warwickshire's will'. This was the first time in the season I had seen a number eleven batsmen with a good enough defensive technique to stick around while stroke play at the other end moved the score along, but it was not to be the last.

At noon Will Rhodes came on with his medium-fast bowling, who had taken 5 wickets for 17 runs in the first innings. The cries rang out: "Here we go, golden arm!" or "Here we go, Rhodie" affirmed with a "Yeah, Rhodie". Cook was on 73, but twenty minutes later, after he had scored 10 more runs, he was lbw to Rhodes for 83 off 168 balls. Once again he had anchored the innings leaving the other Essex batsmen to build an impregnable lead. Rhodes's next wicket was Tom Westley, out for 4 runs off 5 balls. There was a disgruntlement amongst the spectators near me at his flashing at a ball that should have been left. "He's done that before." Around 12.40 the cricket seemed to take a step up in urgency. Quinn finally departed for 9 runs off 69 balls, and Warwickshire needed to press further. At lunch Essex were over 300 runs ahead with 6 wickets in hand. Jeetan Patel had bowled right through the morning from the river end.

Essex must have come out after lunch with the intention of pushing on. Perhaps as a result, Rishi Patel was caught at second slip off Brookes. Warwickshire saw a chance to push back by taking wickets. The new batsman was the Essex captain, Ryan ten Doeschate, and his arrival was greeted with a shout to the bowler: "Two in the over, Brooker" and sure enough, Brookes obliged: wicket (Patel) 2 3 2 1 wicket (ten Doeschate), with Brookes knocking his stump out of the ground. Essex 6 wickets for 177. Shortly after, I heard a comment, "Who is this Brookes?" This was quite a compliment, really.

Dan Lawrence had come in for the fifth wicket and in his unobtrusive way began to take over the Cook role of anchoring one end at the same time as scoring runs. Stone came on at the Hayes End, but the score moved on. Essex reached 200 with an imperious drive from Lawrence, and Adam Wheater, who had come in at number eight, was now 16 off 17 balls. Patel's first over back on after the break went for 7 runs, but in trying to reverse sweep him Wheater was very well caught at short leg by Rhodes. Next up was Simon Harmer, a very good batsman at pushing the score on. He walks like a teddy bear, stocky despite his height, and with his feet slightly splayed, yet he is not to be underestimated as a lower-order batsmen. A Harmer boundary took the lead to 303 runs, with the batsmen eyeing as their next stop a lead of 350. At 2.54 pm the new ball was shared by Stone and Brookes, but in the 85th over Lawrence took Essex to their next milestone by thumping the ball to the boundary for his 50. Next ball he hit down the ground, and the next ball likewise. The bowler then got a dot ball by putting the ball down the leg, and then bowled 2 bouncers which Lawrence ignored by ducking under them. Dot balls but no upper hand. So 12 off the over. Lawrence was beginning to up the scoring rate, but it felt without risk. His strokes were smooth, Harmer's lusty. Just before tea Harmer hit Rhodes for a straight six. This being red-ball cricket, and my eyes needing a cataract operation, I did not see it but I knew by reactions it had gone a long way. Tea loomed when Essex might declare, giving Harmer, on 38, 6 minutes to get to his 50. Would this be a moment to go after Patel? I waited in anticipation of a blast but more compellingly Patel's 91st over only went for one run. Harmer was now facing Rhodes, and three was taken from the over, two from the next off Patel. When the players went off for tea, I thought a declaration would be made, but after tea Essex resumed. Did Lawrence want his ton, with very little time to get to it? This might explain the mighty swipe to Rhodes bringing his downfall in the 94th over, while one over later Harmer chasing his 50 holed out to long on for 43 off 67 balls. The tail-enders were giving Warwickshire fielding practice, but when at 4.22 the lead was finally 400, Essex declared on nine wickets for 316. A run rate of 3.26 was not princely but on this pitch Essex were forcing the pace. They now had some 25 overs to bowl at Warwickshire in the last session. This was an enticing prospect, and I had been able to move to the upper tier of the stand at the River End, giving me a good view over mid-on to the right-hand batsman at the other end. The declining sun was making shadows and moving the game into the golden hour.

At 4.45 pm, in order to encourage the faithful, someone shouted "10 for 1, 20 for 2". Siddle (Australia) and Quinn (New Zealand, but with a British passport) opened the bowling without getting an immediate wicket. Ten Doeschate turned to Harmer (South Africa) after seven overs, so I had the pleasure of watching him from the higher level, which was just what I wanted.

When Banks drove Harmer for 4 runs, and Rhodes then hit Quinn for 4, there were cries of encouragement from the Warwickshire balcony. In the thirteenth over Warwickshire had scored 50 runs off 74 balls, so they were not retreating into their shell. While the Essex players gave a lot of encouragement to Quinn, Cook in the slips was quiet, "refined out of all existence, indifferent . . .". Two maidens ensued, with Warwickshire keen to play out their innings to the close without losing a wicket. Aaron Beard (Chelmsford) came on, right-arm fast-medium, 21 years old, and another product of the Essex stable of county cricketers. A Beard too young to be revered, but certainly to be cheered and if possible feared. For Warwickshire to be jeered. In the nineteenth over, with about 7 overs left, Beard had Rhodes lbw for 25. He was replaced by the 20-year-old Rob Yates, youth against youth. Essex were now pressing for a second wicket before the close, Warwickshire just to survive. 10 minutes later, Yates was yet to score. To Harmer he was surrounded by a silly mid-off and a silly mid-on, with 2 slips. For the last ball of the over a second silly mid-off was brought in. This was the fortress in action, although it is an odd meta-

phor because it is Essex who do the besieging while their opponents
play the role of the besieged – or perhaps prisoner.

Yates retained his composure unafraid to take a single off the last
ball to keep the strike, first from a Harmer over, second from a Beard
over, the last of the day. This was pressure but it was not disconcerting
him, and in facing Harmer he was facing a world-class bowler. This
was another moment that the county championship did not feel like
such a poor relation to Test cricket.

While Essex had spent the day tightening their grip on the game,
at Headingley Somerset had had a sobering day. In reply to Yorkshire's
520 they had been bowled out for 196, the destroyer being Keshav Maharaj, the South African slow left-armer, whose figures were 26.3-9-52-
7. 135 of the 159 balls he bowled were dot balls. Somerset then had to
follow on and by close of play were 159-4. Banton had battled to 58 not
out, which showed a necessary propensity to take care. For such a free
hitter of the ball, his challenge will be to develop the patient side of his
game; this innings suggested that he might be *capax* surely? His captain,
Tom Abell, had played a part in an opening partnership of 89 with
Azhar Ali. But then number three, James Hildreth, had succumbed to
Maharaj, weaving his magic, for one run. It is at moments like these
that the difficulty of victory turns to the inevitability of defeat. The next
day, 16 July, confirmed this prognosis: they were all out for 251. Maharaj took 3 wickets for 75 runs off 34 overs, even more than in the first
innings, and bowled a similar proportion of dot balls (170 out of 204
balls), but the chief wicket taker was the seasoned Yorkshire campaigner, Steve Patterson, taking 4 wickets for 54 runs. These two must have

been hunting as a pair. Banton had lasted only 10 overs in the morning to move his score from 58 to 63 before being bowled by Patterson. Among those who followed him to the crease was Dom Bess, who had been loaned to Yorkshire earlier in the season to give them some spin scalpel, but his return to Somerset had led to his replacement by Maharaj who provided some spin butchery. Left at the end was Jack Brooks on 2 not out, Yorkshire's former fast bowler who had moved to Somerset with only modest success. This was a very satisfying result for Yorkshire.

How unsatisfying the result was for Somerset was shown by Essex moving above them in the Division One points table by 4 points. Yorkshire were well down at third place, 34 points behind Somerset. This would give Essex a strong platform for the final rounds beginning on Sunday 18 August. Until then the county championship was in lockdown to be replaced by the Ashes series and the T20 Blast competition.

In Division Two Lancashire, having achieved 5 victories in 10 games, were surging ahead, 38 points ahead of Glamorgan in second place. Other contenders for promotion seemed to be Northamptonshire, Durham and Middlesex. Gloucestershire had completed their game against Leicestershire on 18 July and had only 106 points to Lancashire's 157. However, they did have a game in hand, to be played against Worcestershire beginning on Sunday 21 July as part of the Cheltenham Cricket Festival, one of those long-established events in county cricket that was clinging on in the gales being caused by the changes to the game, as was the Cricket Festival at Canterbury.

Gloucestershire's defeat of Leicestershire had sounded particularly exciting. With 48 to win off 8 overs they got there with 3 balls left. It came down to 15 runs needed off 7 balls. Ryan Higgins, their number three batsman, drove Mohammed Abbas for a six before going into the last over, bowled by Chris Wright. 9 runs were needed off 6 balls, easy in white-ball cricket maybe not so easy in red-ball cricket, so Wright needed to bowl a deathly death over. However, the first two balls allowed three runs, leaving three runs needed off 4 balls. Matters were settled by Gareth Roderick hitting the next ball for six. Game over, and perhaps a harbinger of Gloucestershire's intent. At least they thought that staying in Division Two was not inevitable.

Test players were on show in Division Two. Although we did not know it at the time, there was particular significance in the fact that Marnus Labuschagne, playing for Glamorgan, had achieved an average of 65.52 in 18 innings. Dawid Malan, another player to have come and gone from the England Test team in the past few years (15 matches played) now had an average of 63.21 in 15 innings for Middlesex. Middlesex had just trounced second-placed Glamorgan and, what with its name and its history, might be thought to be a prime candidate for promotion to Division One. Toby Roland-Jones, who like Malan had had his moments with the England team before suffering a terrible back injury, had 9 wickets in the match. That would have been a good game to watch, if only there were not other distractions in my head. Sometimes it felt as much as I could do to keep up with Essex and Somerset.

Division Two continued to attract attention when Gloucestershire's Cheltenham game against Worcestershire was won by 13 runs, a thriller that had gone to the fourth day, and another signal of Gloucestershire's intent to put themselves forward for promotion. After the 10 matches, like Glamorgan they now had 129 points, and a group of six counties, Glamorgan, Gloucestershire, Northamptonshire, Durham, Middlesex and Derbyshire were all covered by 20 points, and all were in contention for the two out of three promotion places to Division One. *

In this addictive state on the night of 15 July I had a cricket dream which turned into one of anxiety. I was in a municipal park which for some reason not revealed to me seemed to be a Notts outground. While it was Nottinghamshire playing, there were only a few spectators on the scattered benches, and on the pitch adjacent to it a club game was going on. There were other cricket pitches as well but they were free of cricket, so the scene had the air of parkland, leafy, summery, low-key. Nor was I merely an observer. I think I was meant to be playing in the Notts game, but that is where the anxiety crept in. Where was I meant to go? And which team was I playing for? Anyway they were already playing so I was superfluous, and had probably let someone down. In this disconcerted state I emerged slowly to consciousness.

This obsession with cricket I was linking to a stimulating encounter with English history in the 1000-page book by Robert Tombs, 'The English and Their History', published in 2015. In it he remarked that in the nineteenth century both county and Test cricket retained leisurely pre-industrial timetables, making the game deliberately unsuitable as a mass spectator sport (something the ECB is currently still thinking to put right). Despite this, it was held in esteem on the grounds that it fostered virtues "claimed to be quintessentially English, such as team spirit, fair play and coolness under pressure". Equally striking was the notion that "gentlemanly amateurs . . . deplored commercialisation, were shocked by rowdy and partisan crowd behaviour, and accused professional players of cheating and violence." This felt like a suitable lead-in to the fact that the T20 Blast was due to begin on Saturday 20 July and would continue until Finals Day on Saturday 21 September, all alongside England's Test Matches against Australia.

*

When the Blast started, I obliged myself to take an interest in it this year. I was struck by how it is marketed: first the synthetic names of the teams involved – Sharks, Eagles and so on – and then the focus on stars: 'Come and see De Villiers smash 88 not out to help Middlesex beat Essex' (18 July). Alternatively see Ten Doeschate trying to rescue the Essex innings with 74 not out. Cricket success is built from team effort: here the impression is given it is down to individuals, batsmen mainly. You would not market a game as 'Come and watch Rashid Khan bamboozle the batsmen!' even if Sussex had signed him for the purpose. It feels more nakedly mercenary, too. And is the list of top run-makers more interesting than the top wicket-takers? But it seems to be still a game of character: against Middlesex Harmer went for 38 runs without a wicket at an economy rate of 12.66 an over! Was it De Villiers punishing a fellow South African for fun? Is white-ball cricket not Harmer's thing? In fact T20 is emphatically Harmer's thing, as I was to discover. There is something about the game that is very easy to mock, and maybe that is even part of its allure. This game at Lord's was watched by a 28,000 sell-out crowd, which is a bit different from Chelmsford. I can see how much the players would enjoy that.

The next day, 19 July, Essex salvaged their reputation by beating

Surrey. However this does not feel a quite accurate description of what happened, since more precisely Cameron Delport (a name new to me but I have to keep up), as much as Essex, beat Surrey. In scoring 226-4, Delport scored 129 off 49 balls in a game reduced to 15 overs a side. That is 180 balls in the whole match, not far off the 200 balls that The Hundred is proposing. Is this game a harbinger of the future? Delport certainly stole headlines. Here's how: dot dot 1 1 1 4 dot 1 4 6 4 dot dot 4 6 6 6 4 2 1 1 1 6 dot 1 6 dot 6 1 6 6 6 1 1 dot 4 dot 6 4 dot 1 dot 6 dot 6 1 6 2 out! He sounds like the archetypal new cricket mercenary, having played in his career for some two dozen teams (so far), including Boost Defenders, Chittagong Vikings, Dhaka Dynamites, Essex Eagles, Guyana Amazon Warriors, Islamabad United, Kolkata Knight Riders, KwaZulu-Natal and KwaZulu-Natal Under-19s, Lahore Qalandars, Lantau Galaxy Riders, Leicestershire, Paarl Rocks, Pakhtoon XI, Paktia Panthers, Royal Bengal Tigers, St Lucia Zouks, Sydney Thunder and Trinidad & Tobago Red Steel, plus South Africa A. It makes my head spin. However, it was not as head-spinning as the Batting Impact Index devised by Elgan Alderman in The Times: runs per innings x runs per over divided by 100; the Bowling Impact Index is strike rate x economy; and the All-round Impact Index is the Batting Index divided by Bowling Index x 100. It's so simple a child of ten could understand it. The trouble is I am 71.

In terms of crowds, the two games in the London derby between Middlesex and Surrey had capacity numbers. Middlesex, despite only a moderate season so far in four-day cricket, beat Surrey twice. On 23 July Malan hit 117 off 57 balls in getting Middlesex to 209, to which Surrey could only manage 172, although I noticed the return of Ollie Pope (47 runs off 31 balls) to action after recovery from a bad shoulder injury. This boded well for red-ball cricket, as he is a remarkable prospect. And then on Thursday 8 August at Lord's, Middlesex went one better, scoring 210 thanks to 64 from De Villiers and 70 from the heroic Irishman, Eoin Morgan. Steven Finn, a man with a brilliant future behind him in Test cricket, helped to rattle Surrey to 146 all out with 5 wickets for 16 runs. Perhaps bowlers can make more of an impact than I am crediting them with. These crowds were reflecting a healthy demand for tickets in advance of the T20 campaign, and I could not help feeling that these numbers were being partly driven by marketing for The Hundred, in obedience to a law of unintended consequences. At Old Trafford a 300% increase in sales since the World Cup Final were being put down to that event rather than anything to do with The Hundred.

Surrey made a much better fist of it on 25 July. Glamorgan, having won the toss, decided to put Surrey into bat, a decision that seem to have paid off when they could only manage a modest 141. Towards the latter part of their innings, a fox ran onto the outfield and would not move, thus holding up play. Not even the marketing department could come up with such a brilliant piece of theatre. But then it all went wrong for Glamorgan when they were all out for 44 with Tom Curran taking 3 wickets for 3 runs, Gareth Batty 3 wickets for 7 runs, and Imran Tahir, leg-spinner for South Africa, 3 wickets for 8 runs. No animals were hurt in the playing of this game, but possibly some egos got bruised.

Also on 25 July, Lancashire won a thriller against Yorkshire at Headingley. In front of a crowd of 18,500, they made 170-6, and Yorkshire were 9 runs short at the end. What is more the man of the match was a bowler, Saqib Mahmood who had taken 3-33. I wish I had been there. 88 out of the 240 bowled were dot balls, and the suspense of whether Yorkshire would make it was what made T20 especially worthwhile.

It was commented that the ECB appeared reluctant to promote the Blast competition this year, but with strong ticket sales, why should they have to? Surrey and Lancashire, who seem particularly attached to the competition, issued a press release revealing record ticket sales. Several counties are supposedly convinced that the ECB does not want the 2020 Blast competition to threaten The Hundred. It turns out that they have a huge marketing budget for the new competition, with each of the 8 franchises getting £800,000 for promotion, approximately £200,000 for each of their home matches. In addition, a combined total of £6 million is available for 'event production', one of those mysterious phrases that crops up in modern management.

There is a sense that an audience is being coerced into loving the new competition. While I can express disagreement, and even rant and rail against it, there is an extra frustration added from the sense of battling a great machine.

The development of T20 Leagues around the globe represent cricket's strongest bid so far to be a global game, free from the colonial history embedded in Test cricket and more in tune than the one-day game with the big money power games of the global economy. To resist it feels foolish, like trying to get the whiff of cordite back in the cannon.

*

A more attractive aspect in the development of the global game is the growth of women's cricket, fighting for attention in the pond of big male fish. Since it is as much a game of brain, agility, and hand-eye coordination, as of sheer brawn, cricket feels a very suitable sport for women. Like tennis, can one envisage the female version coexisting with some equality with the male version? With that in mind, the series between England and Australia Women had been scheduled for this August (see page 64). This was well-intentioned, even if it was bold, and while I do not have figures for audiences at the various games, it felt swamped by other cricket events. What is more the utter dominance of the Australia women over England further helped to deflate the whole event in this country. I daresay they felt differently about it in Australia.

*

Amidst all the cricketing noise in my head, I noticed too that on 5 to 13 August, a cricket World Series for Disability Teams was played in Worcestershire. This was further evidence of cricket's strenuous efforts to reach out, fuelled I imagined by the efforts of players and organisers rather than of money.

12 FIRST ASHES TEST:
1 to 5 August, Edgbaston

The results of the 2019 Ashes Tests are public knowledge so they are listed here at the beginning of the story. To publish them is not to spoil that story since the suspense is not in the what but in the how.

*

First Test, Edgbaston: Aus. 284 & 487-7d; Eng. 374 &146. Aus. won toss and chose to bat. Australia win. Australia 1, England 0.

*

Second Test, Lord's: Eng. 258 & 258-5d; Aus. 250 & 154-6. Aus. won toss and chose to field. Draw. Australia 1, England 0.

*

Third Test, Headingley: Aus. 179 & 246; Eng. 67 & 362-9. Eng. won toss and chose to field. England win. Australia 1, England 1.

*

Fourth Test, Old Trafford: Aus. 497-8d & 186-6d; Eng. 301 & 197. Aus. won toss and chose to bat. Australia win. Australia 2, England 1.

*

Fifth Test, The Oval: Eng. 294 & 329; Aus. 225 & 263. Aus. won toss and chose to field. England win. Australia 2, England 2.

Series drawn; Australia retain Ashes.

*

For the First Test against Australia, Edgbaston was expected to make over £5 million through food, drink, tickets, hospitality and merchandise sales. The ground was likely to be at its full capacity of 25,000 for the first 3 days, and 90% of Day Four tickets had been sold. So, 95,000 spectators were expected to attend the First Test, including 3500 hospitality tickets and about 1700 complimentary tickets. There was an appetite for cricket. In the week before the First Test began more than 52,000 additional tickets were sold for Blast matches, and advance ticket sales were up 8% on last year.

*

"You cannot win an Ashes Test with only 10 players."

I was in Cornwall on holiday on Thursday 1 August, when the Test started. Only casual checking of the score was possible, when I learnt that Australia had won the toss and chosen to bat, very sensible until they were 99-4, then 112-6, then 122-8. Such casual engagement on my part disguised the progress of Steve Smith, and I had missed the fact that Anderson could only bowl 4 overs before having to withdraw from the game crooked in the body, and then pained in the mind. Peter Siddle, Essex finest, came to the crease, a seasoned campaigner even with the bat, no doubt with an instruction to hold up the other end while Smith went on. Somehow, conditions seem to have eased, and Australia were wrestling some sort of psychological advantage back. Siddle was no violet to Smith's sunflower, striking 44 off 85 balls. When he was out with the score at 210, Nathan Lyon came in, and what with Smith farming the strike, managed 12 runs off 26 balls. The Australian innings finally ended on 284 when Broad bowled Smith with 144 to his name. When Smith was interviewed by Mark Nicholas on the highlights that day, you had to warm to him. He had been booed at all points, apparently, including on reaching his century. When he was finally out, he rushed from the field so that Australia could have a bowl at England. Only when the Aussie fielders left at the close of play was he pushed to the front to take the applause. My first thought was to regard it, rather glibly, as a redemptive innings. However, if this was redemption, it turned out that there was a lot more redemption to come.

Naturally, the 'what if?' question for supporters was whether, if Anderson had been fit to bowl, he could have taken Smith's wicket. We shall never know, but instead learnt that the other England bowlers found it extremely difficult. It boiled down to the headline in the Sunday Times on 4 August: "Stop Smith!"

Smith was not the only person to be booed. David Warner and Cameron Bancroft copped it as well. Warner spent some of the time fielding on the boundary where he was the subject of constant mockery. He seemed to be taking it good-naturedly, but in view of what was to happen in the series, it may have had a mental effect. As for

Bancroft, I felt I should keep a weather eye on him, since he had made a very good job of both captaining Durham and regularly scoring runs for it. He had no doubt been sent there to keep his hopes of Ashes selection alive by learning more about English conditions. Alas, putting the booing on one side (which was possibly only quarter hearted in his case, the real villains being Smith and Warner), he could only manage 8 in the first innings and 7 in the second. This was not what the Aussie selectors wanted. On the other hand, it was more runs than Warner managed (scores of 2 and 8). But there was also the dignified sight of Warner walking without hesitation on being given out. On the eve of the Test, Tim Paine, the Australian captain, had laid out his team's strategy in a newspaper column, in which humility, discipline and patience were key words. Certainly they were on display at Edgbaston and indeed won Australia the Test.

For England supporters who valued the link between county and Test cricket, the Rory Burns story was more uplifting. At the end of Day Two he was 125 not out, having spent 37 minutes on 92, and faced 10 balls while on 99. The assumption was that this reflected nerves, but it also reflected grit: he said afterwards that while on 99 he talked himself out of sweeping against Lyon. Having watched him a little in 2018, in particular Surrey's game against Yorkshire at Scarborough, I had reached the tentative conclusion that he was of Test quality. There was technical ability, and the sense that pressure could bring out the best side of him. By the time he came to the Ashes, he had played Tests against India, Sri Lanka and West Indies – and against Ireland in July. He had done well in the county batting averages in 2018, and, as Jonathan Agnew shrewdly pointed out on TMS, his run of poor scores was on difficult pitches. This did not account for his poor form in county cricket in 2019 where he was one of the players grafting away while the World Cup was going on. The game at Lord's against Ireland, when he scored 6 and 6, was on a particularly difficult pitch but the selectors had retained faith. All the noise was coming from the critics, since commentary in all kinds of media is established on an adversarial system. For their part, the selectors just have to wait for their selections to perform. Getting a century in this Test raised the intriguing question for him. Assuming selection for the rest of the series, he had 9 more innings. Would he target a century off two of them, perhaps a 50 off another two, and getting an average of 40 for the series? What should the ordinary England supporter expect of him?

There was also pleasure in Root making 57, and indeed in taking 57 balls to make 11 runs. For such a deft manipulator of singles and of rotating the strike, this was out of character, although it must have reflected the quality of the Australian bowling and Root working hard to adjust from one-day mode to 5-day mode.

The other county cricketer on the field was Peter Siddle who had played several games for Essex in preparation for the Ashes. In England's first innings he had bowled 27 overs, taken 2 wickets, and gone for 52 runs at an economy rate of just under 2 an over. This was impressive and vindicated his work in county cricket. As indeed it had for Stuart Broad, labouring during the World Cup in the Notts vineyard, of very indifferent quality, but he had kept going (compare Siddle being part of a strong Essex team, much more inspiriting) and at the age of 33 taking the opportunity to learn more about how to bowl, even with well over 400 wickets to his name. County cricket had had a particular role this summer.

At the start of Day Three, questions arose: could Burns go on to an even bigger score? Answer no: he was out for 133. Could Stokes's solid 38 not out on the previous day prove a platform to something much larger? Answer not really: he was out for 50. Could Bairstow, Ali and Woakes really start to take the game away from Australia? Answer not really. While Woakes was not out 37 at the end, Bairstow and Ali had gone very cheaply, although there was the pleasurable sight of Broad rediscovering a tailender's batting touch in scoring 29 runs. For the Australians, the question was whether their bowlers could get 2 or 3 wickets cheaply and shift things back in their favour. I had a notion that, judging by past performances, they were due to win a session. The day before England were 4 wickets for 267 runs. By lunchtime this promising position was only modestly moved to 8 wickets for 328 runs. This was another marker for the series. The Australian bowlers were in their way superb in keeping the England batsmen tied down. The innings ended with England 374 all out.

By close of play Australia were 3 wickets for 124 runs, only 34 runs ahead, with Smith on 46 not out. "Stop Smith!" indeed. England's challenge was to win the first session by getting him early; Australia's was to win the session by having him still there at lunchtime. For an England supporter it was important to keep the Australia lead to under 200. In fact Australia got 240 runs ahead with 6 wickets in hand at the end of the first session, and at the end of the second session were 5 wickets for 356 runs. By that point the game had changed completely.

England started their innings at the end of the day and survived 7 testing overs. Day Five brought the hardest trial of all: no one would give them a chance to score the necessary runs to win, so they had to bat out the day against the Australian quicks, and now, coming into the frame, the skill of their spinner Nathan Lyon. In particular could Root produce an outstanding innings to anchor England and secure a draw? If cricket is fought solely in the mind, each batsman down to number eleven had to prepare themselves to preserve their wicket. If cricket is fought solely with technique, then that has to be in very good shape against such a high-quality spinner. Rain would help, but they had to bat as if it was unlikely to happen. It was a question of somehow break- ing the Australian will. None of these hopes materialised for England, and indeed they broke the England will. I calculated that to get the draw England were only allowed to lose one wicket per hour. At 11.17, Burns was out; around 12.20 Roy charged Lyon with his bat over 2 feet away from his front pad so that he was bowled as the ball turned past the inside edge, the cavalier who threw in the towel. Pity. He had sur- vived 1.25 hours against the quicks. This was Lyon's third over and the mantra of 'being positive' is double-edged: success makes you feel like superman; failure superflawed. From hero in World Cup to zero here. Denly then was out at 12.37, and, alas, Root as well at 12.50, having sur- vived 57 balls. By 3.15 England were 146 all out, and Australia had won by 251 runs at Edgbaston, their bugbear ground.

There were suggestions that the emotional intensity of the World Cup had weakened some of the England players. The names of Ali, Bairstow and Buttler were mentioned. Moeen Ali, with scores of 0 and 4, and 3 wickets for 172 runs, even I could see needed a rest. Bairstow, on the other hand, was given out in the second innings on a technicality, still out, but the ball only just touched his glove, which seemed to go further up his arm than was necessary. The ball before he had dropped his hands and taken it on the chest – he should be given credit for that, a sort of Brian Close moment. As for Buttler, involved in red-ball cricket for the first time since March, he was bowled by an exceptional ball from Cummins, who in this series was an exceptional bowler. For his supporters, Buttler was unlucky; for his critics he made his own bad luck.

The result was undoubtedly depressing if you supported England, and inversely uplifting if you supported Australia. For the detached observer, it was all fascinating: after all, the Test had gone the full 5 days. There was a reversal of fortune of a dramatic kind, such as cricket is very good at: Australia had gone from 122-8 to a 251-run victory. Steve Smith's 286 runs had won the match for them. For England it was a train crash: the train had been shuttling along merrily but then found the rails removed, so that it ploughed on only to tip slowly and plunge down the embankment. Terrific spectacle really.

There was a hubristic touch to the creation of #fortressEdgbaston on Twitter. The lowlights on tv began with Mark Nicholas in the Hollies stand, hobnobbing with supporters. Somehow, knowing the result, I found this jarring.

Christian Prudhomme, director of the Tour the France, was reported as describing the Tour as "life, condensed . . . All the wonderful, exceptional, disconcerting, unfortunate things that can happen: it is life." Although he was not thinking of cricket, it was a pleasure to read a Frenchman describing it with such articulacy.

The Test was marked by 3 'not cricket' incidents. The first was when Joe Root was batting and the ball grazed the stumps without removing the bails, arousing justifiable amazement among the Australians. How did that happen? A stroke of bad luck? The Australians were determined to get compensation, which they did by pressing for the ball to be changed. This we were told by TMS was within the rules, but it was also commented that the replacement ball which they finally got had more red on it, and could well have had a slightly prouder seam as a result. The ball then began to behave as the bowlers wanted, and Denly was lbw for 18, and five runs later, Buttler was caught off Cummins for 5. This was good luck for the Australians but not good for cricket. Naturally the England team have not been slow in pursuing this tactic as well. A remarkable photograph was published afterwards of Root offering the ball to the nose of umpire Joel Wilson after James Pattinson had struck a six and the ball landed in a glass of beer. The ball was changed (on what grounds?) but it felt rather academic as by this time Australia were romping away in their second innings.

Secondly, perhaps DRS, the television umpire, has never been more important. Over the five days, eight of Wilson's decisions had been overturned on review. It could be argued that the system worked, but to work properly, oddly enough, it does need the umpires making the correct or near-to-correct call.

The third unsettling element was the booing, except that the booing of Smith, by mere dint of repetition, had become a mark of respect. I did not relish the prospect of 20 more days of this.

In the end, this was mere ornament. The substance of the matter was that England were left with two headaches: how to get Steve Smith out; and how to find a spinner as effective as Lyon.

13 SECOND ASHES TEST: 14 to 18 August, Lord's

On Tuesday 13 August I swung from the low and slow to the quick and loud by going to watch a Blast game at Bristol (see chapter 14). That had taken place on Tuesday evening, and on Wednesday I returned to Norwich by train, conscious that Day One of the Test was due to start that day at Lord's, so as a rail traveller I wouldn't be fully involved. But by a stroke of luck rain prevented any play that day, so I missed nothing. Lucky for me, but as it turned out not for England who could have done with that fifth day.

*

"You cannot win an Ashes Test if you lose 5 sessions to rain."

So it started on the Wednesday with some anticipation. In view of Smith's ascendancy in the first Test, something special would be needed to deal with him. To win it is no good only taking 18 wickets. Jofra Archer had performed very well in the World Cup but there had been a feeling that he needed a rest. But the first Test raised an alarm: Archer, your country needs you! However, he needed some red-ball practice which led to the curious sight of him playing for the Sussex Second XI against Gloucestershire at the Blackstone Academy Ground in West Sussex. There he got his eye in by taking 6 wickets and scoring 108 runs off 99 balls. He bowled 12.1 overs in the Gloucestershire first innings and they were bowled out for 79. The first spell was of 8 overs which prompted the thought that if he hadn't run through the wickets so quickly he would have had more practice. Hats off – and helmets on – to the Gloucestershire batsmen, especially the youthful ones obliged to face one of the fastest bowlers in the world. Another gold star to county cricket, I felt, in laying this on. Matt Brewer, 18 years of age, played for Gloucs, and commented afterwards: "I don't think I was frightened, but my adrenaline was through the roof." Archer's figures were 12.1-4-27-6, at an economy rate of 2.22. Step aside, Gloucs seconds; step forward Mr Smith.

There was the ticklish matter too of finding a spinner. Moeen Ali was finally rested, and since he seems a wise person, perhaps a part of him did not mind having a rest. Nor was he going to be out of mind, since he came back into full sight in the Blast. So, Jack Leach finally got his chance in a home series, after a stuttering run-up to international cricket. They also serve who only stand and wait – but better still to play a major role.

Thus we arrived at an Ashes Test at Lord's. For reasons I find difficult to fathom, opposition teams in recent decades have tended to do well here. Is it extra motivation at the prospect of beating England at the Mecca of cricket? This sounds fantastical. What is more, you would think that England bowlers would have an advantage since they know the Lord's slope intimately. At least, that is one reason why Murtagh ran through England in July; years of playing at Lord's gave him a special familiarity. On this occasion, England needed a win to pull the series back and keep it live.

Australia won the toss and elected to field. Was there a game plan to get England out quickly, make a big score, and then bowl England out again with their quick bowlers operating as the battering ram and Lyon as the spear point? To justify this decision, Australia needed to rattle through England. At lunch England were only 2 wickets down but they had only scored 76 runs off 27 overs. At tea they were six wickets for 201 off 61 overs, and after tea were 258 all out. Cummins, Hazelwood and Lyon each took 3 wickets, so Australia must have felt happy with Tim Paine's election to field.

When England batted, after Cummins had opened the bowling with a maiden to Burns, Hazelwood bowled to Roy, and on the third ball had him caught at the wicket. Definitely one up to Australia, and one down to England, with a strong dose of one down to Roy. This brought Root to the crease a lot earlier than he would have wished. His preferred position is number four, while batting at number three. A very early wicket turns him into an opener. So, in addition to his responsibilities as captain, he has to wrestle with mastering the bowling in an unfavoured position. He duly battled for 37 minutes to score 14 runs. As the day proceeded only Burns (53 runs) and Bairstow (52 runs) made the England score look like anything. Buttler could only score 12 off 23 balls, causing the vultures to circle. Yet if it really did seem the case that the pitch was a difficult one to bat on, more credit needed to be given to those who scored runs – even Denly's 30 – than to those who did not.

Australian experience will have known that a proper judgement on the decision to field needed to await the Australian innings. In the last session England managed 13 overs and got one wicket, that of David Warner to Broad. The media were really looking forward to the Archer-Smith battle, but in keeping Australia to 250, Broad and Woakes were crucial contributors, Broad with 4 wickets for 65 runs, Woakes 3 wickets for 61. The morning of Day Three (in effect Day Two) was definitely England's. Australia went from 30-1 to 80-4, but then it rained. Apparently England had not bowled well initially, but then found an outstanding groove, enabling them to make psychological inroads and remind Australia that they were not going to have it all their own way. Still, Smith was there on 13, and the gladiatorial battle between Archer and him was postponed to Day 4 on 17 August. This was serendipitous: that day was a Saturday, and so the battle could take place before a Saturday Lord's house, a highlight of the season. The anticipation was immense, and quite eclipsed the rueful thought that there might not be enough time for England to force a result.

The tone was set by an announcement at St John's tube station over the public address (as reported by Mike Atherton in The Times): "If anyone knows how to dismiss Smith, please make your way to the England dressing room." The first wicket of the day fell to Broad, and I felt compelled to subscribe to Now TV in order to watch rather than listen on the radio. Almost immediately the camera gave a panning shot across a packed house at Lord's. Anticipation and concentration in equal measure: what could possibly be wrong with the world? The suspense was powerful and brought to mind Oscar Wilde's witty idea: "I hope it will last." In the 52nd over, Archer bowled a maiden to Smith with six different balls. I was wondering if Leach would get a spell before lunch, especially as he was fielding from long leg to long leg, a version of the loneliness of the long-distance fielder. It also appeared to be the case that Archer was not bowling flat out, perhaps on instruction. The commentariat wanted to see Archer in action, but at the same time kept warning about overusing him. At 12.33 Leach came on, bowling without glasses. He started with a maiden, but did not really trouble Paine. At 12.50 Smith hit a boundary to go to 52 – 107 balls, 6 fours, 184 minutes. The session had produced 75 runs for 1 wicket, so it could be said that Australia had just shaded it. Their tactics would be to keep grinding on, and even go beyond the England total in order to put them under pressure. For England's part, they would be working to keep Australia within the 258 first innings total, and then score enough to set a target on the last day.

After lunch, Paine was the next to go, in the 67th over. And then it happened. At 2.11 Archer hit Smith on the unprotected arm, producing an egg-size bulge. He popped some painkillers and carried on. At the other end from Archer Leach was bowling tightly, leaking only 8 runs off 6 overs. Archer found extra pace to bowl at 154.5 kph / 96 mph to Smith, a pace which was taking the pitch out of the equation (as Alastair Cook remarked on TMS). The ball hit his gloves, but being Smith he kept it down, otherwise it would have gone to Buttler at forward short leg. To relieve the tension, a comic moment ensued when a boundary by Cummins off Archer had Leach running for it like a speeded-up Groucho Marx. And then it happened again. At 2.37 Smith turning his head away and thus taking his eye off the ball, and having eschewed a helmet with stem guards, was hit behind the ear, and horizontalized. The England fielders stood in a knot nearby; medical attention was provided from both teams. Smith stood up to a round of applause (very welcome) and an earnest conversation followed between him and the team doctor and team physio. At 2.40 he came off under the new 'concussion protocols', up to this moment a complete blank in my brain, which this incident made all clear. As he came off, there was a lot of clapping, I hope also from England fans. There was some sporadic booing but why keep condemning him for his worst 15 minutes when you could praise him for his best 15?

From an England point of view, at least they were into the tail proper, if such a concept still holds in Test cricket. Archer's stamina showed no sign of diminishing and he and Leach bowling in tandem made a powerful pair. In the first four balls of the 76th over, Archer's speeds were 91 mph, 92, 92, 95. It emerged afterwards that Archer's

25th over in this innings was "the fastest by an English Test bowler since records began". The average speed was 92.79 mph; the six balls registered as 90.9 mph (a bouncer), 93.7 (fuller and driven for four, the ball departing like a rifle shot), 92.7 (beat outside edge), 93.9 (fended down to short leg), 92.4 (beat bat on off), 92.2 (beat outside edge again). The recipient of this largesse was Pat Cummins, who deserves some recognition for playing through this over with his wicket intact.

The Australian manager, Justin Langer, had opted for a bit of Aussie needle in the press – or should that be called a manager's sledge? a breach of discussion protocols? – to suggest that Archer's stamina was untested, and therefore open to question. Australian tactics would therefore be to get him back into his second or third or fourth spells. In fact he bowled 8 overs in the morning, and then 8 in the afternoon, the average speed of his twelfth over being 92.8 mph. He managed to bowl 16 balls in succession in excess of 90 mph. This was a different type of bowler to what England was used to, and he had brought England back into the frame with a riposte of a kind to Langer. A graphic in the Sunday Times on 18 August (courtesy of Simon Hughes, naturally) showed that Archer had bowled ever so slightly within himself on Days One, Two and Three, and it was the afternoon session at Smith that had produced his fastest spell. That showed tactical nous from England, and impressive control from Archer.

Now facing Archer was Peter Siddle, and the gap between Test and county cricket suddenly seemed to have widened. When his wicket fell Smith came back out to bat to a rousing reception from the Australian supporters, plus some booing by spectators. The Times had a story headlined "MCC member ejected for 'abusing Smith in pavilion'." This individual was understood to have booed Smith and made disparaging remarks as he made his way to the dressing room. The answer came to me suddenly, "Send the lot to Botany Bay."

Smith has an extraordinary will to make runs, and probably had his eye on the prospect of getting four successive centuries in Ashes Tests, in order to metamorphose a great achievement (three centuries) into a truly superlative one (four centuries). At 3.24 he smeared Woakes for four, and then had a second boundary, as good an example as you could wish of "striving, seeking, finding, and not yielding". In a characteristic bit of Aussie boosterism, Shane Warne commented that Australia was the only team that could win this match. At 3.34, another boundary took him to 92. The next ball from Woakes produced an appeal but it was given not out as it was running down the hill. At 3.35 England appealed again for lbw and this time it was given. Smith departed while at the same time asking the umpire to review it, yet knowing it was out since he has such an acute awareness of exactly where his stumps are, a knowledge which informs how he plays.

The review was unsuccessful. By dint of a slight change of the seam position, Chris Woakes had produced the magic inswinger and the magic wicket. Thus it was that when Leach had Lyon lbw, and at 4.10 Cummins fell to Broad, Australia were all out on 250, 8 runs behind on the first innings. The session had produced 95 runs, 5 wickets, and 29.3 overs. Evens I felt.

The last session of the day was England's chance to assert its position of strength. The difficulties with which the innings opened only underlined the bowlers' dominance in this match. In the 15th over, bowled by Cummins to Roy, who at this point had only scored 2 runs off 13 balls and was perhaps feeling frustrated with red-ball cricket, in trying to hit the ball round to the leg side he got a leading-edge and was caught and bowled. Root was again much earlier to the crease than he would have wished, which had consequences since he was out first ball to a very fine delivery. This was his first golden duck in 153 Test innings, a record waiting to be broken. Free will rules okay. Joe Denly survived the hat-trick ball and he and Burns battled for 16 overs until the former went for 26 off 51 balls, and the latter for 29 off 52 balls. The run rate was around 3.5 an over so the England batsmen had not frozen, but at 71-4 someone was needed to construct a total that would ward off, and possibly defeat Australia. This was Ben Stokes's year so there was no more reassuring sight than to see him at the crease. He was soon joined shortly afterwards by Jos Buttler, in a partnership on which England's hopes rested. It was natural to think of their performance together in the World Cup final, but that was then and this was now, and that was white ball, this was red ball. For Buttler in particular it was a test of his skill and of his mind. He was not found wanting. In criticising the England batting, it was important to acknowledge the quality of the Australian quartet of bowlers: Cummins, Hazelwood, Siddle, Lyon. They would have been striving to put themselves in the frame for victory, but Stokes and Buttler held on to be 16 and 10 not out at close of play. England were 104 runs ahead, but 4 wickets down. Honours in the last session seemed shared, although in hindsight England shaded it.

*

So what was going to happen on the fifth day? I thought we would get a result, which was a long way from what was expected at the beginning of Day Four when the match, after a lot of rain, seemed to be heading for a draw. The England scenario is another hundred-plus runs: 25 each more from Stokes and Buttler, and 25 each – why not? – from Bairstow and Woakes. A total of 200 or so would pose a challenge for Australia to win on this pitch, and in opting to go for a draw they might open the door for the English bowlers. Yesterday the WinViz 'statistics' were flashed up: 48% draw, 11% England win, 41% Australia win. These are not objective numbers but a subjective assessment of probabilities, a big push by Determinism to finally put paid to Free Will. It won't do: the players go on the field with the will, skills and a plan to win. The unlikely can become the probable, the likely the improbable.

In the last half hour on the Saturday, Stokes and Buttler, having swapped positions in the batting order, were under the cosh of the Australian bowlers, especially the left-handed Stokes facing Lyon. He had survived if not prettily, yet despite one or two (very difficult) chances going down, intelligently and, most notably since this is Stokes 2.0, restrainedly. It had the epic ball-against-bat quality. It was epic in the sense that the contest is not completed in a few overs; one hopes it will continue on the next day, and is rhymed with the gladiatorial struggle of the afternoon session between Archer and Smith – the blacksmith standing firm against Sagittarius darting his arrows. This was a ball-by-ball contest. I wanted Archer to get him out, but I also did not want it to end, and thus found myself in curious harmony with the Aussie fans who will have wanted Smith to resist to the last. At the other end Leach had strangled the batsmen, something which added significantly to the tension of Archer versus Smith.

Play was delayed on the last day, restarting around 12.10 and at around one o'clock only 11 overs had been bowled and 27 runs scored. The 50 partnership between Stokes and Buttler came in 143 balls, and it was only just after 1 pm that Buttler struck his first boundary – in 74 balls! At lunch England were 157-4 so it was probably England's session, but now only a minimum of 67 overs remained in the game. On the other hand, the pace was beginning to pick up. Lyon's figures so far were 20-2-65-0 at an economy rate of 3.25 runs an over. I wondered whether the damp had caused something to go out of the pitch. Why that should be I could not work out, but if it was true, it would not be helpful to England's cause in trying to bowl Australia out for a low total. Rain had not just removed time from the game, but seemed to have affected the pitch.

Shortly after lunch, Buttler was out, but Bairstow then helpfully partnered Stokes to a very fine century. England declared on 258-5, Stokes not out with 115 off 165 balls. They were 266 runs ahead: was this more than was needed? Or nicely judged? Only in hindsight might one conclude that they could have declared earlier. England showed strong intent: when Australia batted they lost 2 quick wickets to Archer, and we next had the novel sight of Labuschagne walking out in place of Smith. His name was not completely strange since he had featured so prominently in Glamorgan's cricket season so far, but here he was as the concussion substitute for Smith. Another strange link between Test and county cricket. Cometh the hour, cometh another Smith? That could not possibly be the case, yet Smith's concussion was Labuschagne's opportunity. He took it. At 5.20 p.m., the sun was out after all the rain, and there were 30 overs to go. One hoped the stage was set for a tremendous climax but seven Australian wickets had to fall, Archer was now in his ninth over and Leach's bowling – he bowled 16 overs in the innings – was slightly losing its tidiness.

Curiously, it was listening on the radio that I found the life was being sucked out of the game. When England were batting there was too much fruitless discussion on when Root should declare, a neat runs versus overs equation. However it was noted that, since it was the captain's decision, he was likely to err on the side of caution, since there is such opprobrium directed at him if he gets it wrong. This should have settled the matter but it did not quell speculation particularly – somehow that seemed more interesting than what was happening on the field. In the end Root called the declaration reasonably well – not that anyone could be heard in the commentary box acknowledging this.

Much more egregiously, later in the day they concluded that the match in the late afternoon was moving to a draw so the speculation was now as to when the captains should call it a draw. As it turned out, Root and England were far from doing so since they played to the very end: Leach bowled the final over at 7.22 pm. It would probably be unfair to suggest that the TMS commentators just wanted to get back to their hotel or get back home, but I sensed a distinct shortage of stamina. I felt that Root's striving and not yielding was much the better approach. However, it must be admitted that when Head was dropped in the slips by Roy off Stokes just after 6 pm, maybe Roy's stamina was fading too. It was the end of a long day, the end of a long match, and maintaining the concentration levels to match hand and eye to hold a ball rocketing at you cannot be easy. A moment of yield when not to yield was essential: it felt like a milestone on the way to a draw instead of one to victory.

Australia's hero was Labuschagne, who refused to let England pass: early in his innings he was floored by an Archer bouncer – and then got up to carry on. This was impressive, and he went to 59 runs in 100 balls. So much toiling in the vineyard, not least that of Glamorgan, had paid off.

Both sides had batting fragilities, and the side that would win the series would be the one with fewer. The next test, at Headingley, was only 4 days away, but despite this I thought Smith would insist on playing. In view of Archer's performance, it was commented that Mitchell Starc would surely play in order to razz up the England batsmen similarly.

*

Watching the Archer-Smith contest on the Saturday, I had had no qualms during it. Yet when a friend mentioned to me later that it had made him uncomfortable, I began to have doubts. If we describe it as 'compelling', which was the word commonly used in the press, what does that say about us? That gladiatorial contests are to our taste? In the arena at ancient Rome, men were killed publicly in front of excited crowds; with our 21st-century mindset we either find this distasteful, or deplore the Romans for it. On the other hand, the Roman orator and politician, Cicero, could see the behaviour of gladiators as virtuous in a way that reminded me of Smith: "What blows gladiators endure! How the ones who are well trained prefer to take the blow rather than disgracefully avoid it! How often it looks as if they prefer nothing to giving satisfaction to the crowd! What gladiator, even a mediocre one, ever groans, what gladiator ever bats an eyelid?"

Can we attune our current mindset away from the point of view that, provided there are stemguards on the helmet – and it is odd that Smith did not have these – and provided the concussion protocols work satisfactorily so that they are embraced by player and spectator alike, then we carry on, and we carry on taking pleasure from it? I wonder whether someone with, say, a 23rd-century mindset might not think that bowling a hard ball very fast into unprotected parts of the body was not right, and to enjoy it was even more odd.

14 August counterpoint: Blast and County Cricket

The Ashes war of attrition had begun but August was not just Ashes cricket, even though the Headngley Test starting on 22 August was so magnificent that it obliterated other cricket facts from my mind. Blast grenades were exploding in the background. On 7 August Colin Acker-mann, a stranger name to me then Marnus Labuschagne, took 7 wickets for 18 runs on behalf of Leicestershire against Warwickshire, a.k.a. Bir-mingham Bears, thus becoming the first person to take 7 wickets in a T20 match – and did so in 4 overs. He commented engagingly: "It's the first time it's turned here at Grace Road [in Leicester] in 20 years, which is fantastic for the spinners." What on earth took Leicestershire so long?

At Chelmsford, on Wednesday 7 August, championship contend-ers Somerset (225-6) beat Essex (111 off 12.5 overs). Harmer's figures were 3-0-45-0, economy rate 15 runs per over. Fortress Chelmsford?!?

On Thursday 8 August, Middlesex played Surrey at Lord's in the second London Derby (see page 104). The significant statistic was that the crowd of 27,773 was the highest attendance for a domestic T20 match in England. If The Hundred is intended to replace the Blast, it will be no pushover or pushaside.

*

Forget the Ashes, ignore the Blast. It may not be the loftiest level of cricket, but at least it is on my doorstep: as a complement to the high-intensity shenanigans going on (not just in the government), I went to spend a day watching a shadowy long-form game, a match between Norfolk and Northumberland in the Minor Counties Championship. I was due to break the habit of a lifetime and go to a Blast game on Tues-day 13 August, and the Second Ashes Test was due to start the day af-ter that, so I felt a day at the Norfolk Cricket Festival played at the Man-or Ground at Horsford north of Norwich was called for. It could be deemed a visit to a cricket outground. This was a low-key event but not without its pleasures: it felt long-form enough, with 193.3 overs being bowled, 33 wickets falling, and 857 runs scored in the match. A further reason to go was that Norfolk were second in the Unicorns Championship Eastern Division playing Northumberland who were bottom.

I was able to purchase the traditional scorecard which was reassuring, but the names of the players were quite new to me, and because the scoreboard was slow to react, it was not easy to work out who was who. Doing so would keep me engaged. A comfortable bench was found; the atmosphere had its own festive quality, with little tents round a section of the boundary as if at some mediaeval tournament.

There were spectators round the boundary too, a number finding it a pleasant place to read the paper. This was cricket for Old Believers, and I overheard one delightful comment: "I am going to do a walk round to see if everyone I know is still alive."

Norfolk, batting second, were in pursuit of Northumberland's total of 332 in the first innings. The batting was proper slow cricket, since after 37 minutes only 18 runs had been scored. Ten minutes later the ball was pulled and went racing between two little tents. A fielder disappeared, then after a gap re-emerged with the ball. Two minutes later the same thing happened again. No one seemed to mind the delay, nor was there a rush of spectators to help find the ball.

The Northumberland quicks were the willowy Finn McCreath and the blacksmith-like Adam Hickey. Excitement was only really injected when Northumberland's Ollie McGee came on just before noon to twirl with his left arm, aided briefly by a substitute fielder in black T shirt and shorts. Andy Hanby played forward and was bowled; the cricket was about to get interesting. While Hickey held down the other end, McGee worked away, the batsmen finding him tricky enough that the boundaries dried up. Tom New was trying to anchor the innings and keep the score going: a classic slow-cricket challenge, at one point taking 40 minutes to score 7 runs. Just before lunch Norfolk went past 200, without any applause ringing out. When a drive from the batsman went through a fielder for a four there was a ripple of shock. Maggie commented to me, "He needs his lunch." And then it happened again with another mild ripple of shock expressed alongside a subdued but satirical clap. Matt Williamson, right arm, was now on with McGee's left arm, but slightly quicker. Norfolk started pressing: Marillier took two sixes off him but then pressed too hard so that he was run out on 37, scored off 50 balls in a welcome touch of the Blast game. When he went, the score was 240, under 100 runs behind with five wickets in hand.

Play resumed after lunch at 2 pm, with Norfolk seeking to go on the front foot. While New carried on sedately, Rogers at number seven hit Williamson for six, then was skipping down the ground to hit the ball over extra cover then executing a ramp shot over the wicket-keeper. Even Minor Counties cricket was not immune to revolution. McGee then had him stumped (see over) but the horse was bolting. (At the side of the ground opposite was a row of trees. A buzzard rose heavily, flapped and glided off. Had it seen enough?) Norfolk were now 280 runs for 6 wickets. At 2.40 New finally went for 73, and very soon Norfolk were all out for 314. Their cavalier batting, far from being reckless, displayed a confidence that they could skittle Northumberland out easily.

So it proved. The Northumberland second innings commenced at 3 pm, and they lost a wicket on the second ball. Wickets then fell at 25 runs, 32, 39. After an hour the Norfolk captain Ashley Watson came on to bowl left arm. He had taken 5 wickets in the first innings, and I overheard that he had got 7 in the week before. His first 2 balls provoked 'oohs and arghs', his next 2 were thumped for four, and the last 2 carefully defended. The prize wicket was Tom Hewison, but Watson bowled him just before tea for 38. We left at that point but checking the scores later I found Norfolk had bowled Northumberland all out for 96, Watson securing another 5 wickets. So Norfolk's target in their second

Rogers stumped
off McGee

innings was 115. Could they get them inside this second day? The game was still going at 6.55, Norfolk scoring at 5 an over which took them to a win by 6 wickets. It would have been a long day to stay to the end, but worth it. I felt for Northumberland. Did the team trek back up north that evening? Not a great feeling.

The first day of the match had produced 12 wickets for 560 runs in 125 overs, while the second day, which we had attended, produced 21 wickets and 507 runs in 106 overs. This was not one-day cricket but certainly a different time-frame to four-day cricket. Without the television, or replays, or a commentary, sometimes what was happening was baffling to the spectators. When the sides went off for tea, I wondered whether I had missed a wicket such as a run out or a catch. No, it was a declaration and I could now see that the Norfolk captain had told his team that he would declare at tea. This explained Rogers' madcap innings, and Watson being insouciant before being bowled. Hence maybe Marillier's unwise run out. Runs were more important than wickets. Yet why? There was a day and a session to go. Did they predict Northumberland would fold for 90 runs? And do so leaving enough time for them to knock off 115 to win before close of play?

The win moved Norfolk 12 points clear at the top of the MCC East Division. It was one of those games where you felt that Northumberland rated their chances of winning as low and were anxious to get back home. Two photos in the Eastern Daily Press next day showed Max Richardson and McGee being bowled by Watson with the bat finishing in a mighty slog position, suggesting they were not playing with due care and attention.

*

And then it happened. The day after watching Norfolk play Northumberland at Horsford, as low-key and traditional as you could wish, I went to Bristol to meet up with my three grandsons to watch a Blast game, as razzmatazz and novel as you could wish. I did so because at the new year in New Zealand I had promised to take them to a cricket match. That it was Bristol was a compromise between my home in Norwich and their home in South Devon, so we started from opposite ends of the country, but by virtue of good transport links and an exercise of

the will it was all made possible. I am sure the ECB would have approved.

Was it overwhelming? Was it underwhelming? Well, the latter. I did not know the Gloucestershire team at all but Hampshire had several recognisable players and in any case I had seen a number of them at the One-Day Cup Final at the end of May. A question for a novice like myself: if you win the toss, do you elect to bat and set an imposing target? Or do you field in the confidence you can chase down however many runs the other lot score? Do you bowl and field first when the crowd is quieter and you can concentrate better? Or do you bat second in the belief that the racket from the crowd can help you ramp up the scoring rate? I realised that I had absolutely no idea.

Anyway, Hampshire won the toss and elected to bat. A bar chart of the innings would show that the run rate per over was a healthy 9 in the first 6 overs, and then it stalled, so that when the innings closed on 139-6 off 20 overs, the overall rate was 6.95 runs an over. Even in my inexperience I knew that this was unlikely to be sufficient. Aneurin Donald rushed to 44 of 23 balls, but James Vince, star player of Hampshire and England, could only manage 9 off 9. I could see that momentum and the intangible quality of self-belief were vital ingredients and communicated themselves more readily to the crowd than straightforward cricketing skill. However, I could also see for myself that skills in all departments, even if not of the traditional kind, were necessary.

The Gloucestershire innings was the reverse to that of Hampshire's. They started more cautiously, so that to my untutored eye after 3 overs they seemed behind the chase, but then they retained wickets, built partnerships and James Bracey's 64 off 48 balls was both bedrock and enforcer of victory. There was a clear turning point in the fourth over of the innings when Ryan Stevenson bowled a catastrophic first over: the first ball had Klinger caught behind, but the umpire gave it not out, possibly incorrectly as I learnt afterwards; a liberated Klinger then hit a six over mid-wicket, and then a three. We were halfway through the over when Stevenson, most likely thrown off his stride, bowled 2 wides. Bracey was now facing and hit 2 boundaries, but one of these was a no ball which gave him a free hit to which he hit a catch – and it was held – but it was not out! Gloucestershire rejoiced when Bracey hit another boundary off the last ball, making it 25 off the over, 21 runs and 4 extras. Gloucestershire, at a stroke or two, and thanks to a step too far (or two) by Stevenson, had decisively turned the match in their favour. Stevenson was stood down after that. This was worth being present for, as you could feel at first hand the reversal in fortunes – and the humiliation for Stevenson.

Hampshire struggled to rein Gloucestershire back, and around the fifteenth over, Sky TV at the ground were encouraging the Mexican Wave. Why do this? Because the game was over in practice if not in theory. I felt the tension drain right out of the match, with the power of crowds replacing the power of bat versus ball. I could not imagine how the players would cope with this. Another skill in cricket (and indeed in other sports) is blanking out what is going on around you and focusing solely on the here and now. What was new to me was the announcement of spycam – to reveal someone in the crowd behaving oddly, kisscam – a couple in the crowd embracing, dancecam – spectators ignoring the cricket to flaunt their dancing skills – or lack of them. If I was more used to this I could ignore it more easily, and then Sky announced the 'Fan of the Match' and my backstops were breached. Fortunately, the spycam did not pick out my putting my head in my hands.

And the noise! My failing ears had trouble hearing what other members of my family were saying. I had been looking forward to giving sage explanations of what was happening but in the racket this proved pointless.

One thing to credit was the way the bowling figures were presented on the scoreboard, since they did mention the number of dot balls for each bowler, but the really galvanising event was the biffed six. In the eighteenth over, Higgins hit a 6 to win the match:

up up and away

Bats-on-balls are the defining acts
but victory's best sealed with a six.

In my naiveté I thought cricket was the precious memory of the 'deathless hush in the close tonight', but there was no hush. And its absence was made excruciating by the apocalyptic nature of the flame-throwers (which reminded me of the *ignes fatui* in the dystopian film

Blade Runner), and the jolt of music over the PA switched on and off. 'Sweet Caroline' (Neal Diamond) erupted impromptu at the end; I would have preferred 'Satisfaction, I can't get no' (Rolling Stones). This struck me as another generational divide.

I could see afterwards that a really tight finish to the match could produce real sporting excitement, and perhaps Sky would pipe down in that case. I concede that being there provided something of that visceral atmosphere and thrill you can get in a stadium. But I also thought that watching it on television might be a better way of engaging with the ins and outs, the turns of fortune, the blasts and the blocks. I was to get an education in all this on Finals Day on 21 September, when four Blast teams would converge for a final shoot-out.

And yet my journey was not wasted. I had fulfilled a promise to my grandsons of presence at live professional cricket, and that was something valuable in itself. The event itself was painful to me, but not without several pleasures mixed in. What is more a B-movie was thrown in along with the main feature, and as can happen there was more pleasure to be had from this supposedly secondary event than from the main one. My ticket had given me free entrance to a match called Western Storm versus Loughborough Lightning. This was a match in the Women's Cricket Super League, so I had my first opportunity ever to watch a professional women's cricket match.

I had arrived around 4 pm so had missed the Western Storm innings, which had included a 29 off 17 balls by India's Smriti Mandhana, named by Wisden Cricket Monthly as their 'golden girl 2019' (as she had been in 2018), and 45 off 37 balls by the captain of the England team, Heather Knight. They had made 158 runs for 4 wickets at a run rate of 7.9, which I thought was an eminently gettable target for Loughborough. But it was not to be, wickets falling at 5 runs, 20, 37, 55, 98, 101, 106, 117, 117 and 118 all out in 18.2 overs at a run rate of 6.43. The last five batters could only manage 15 runs between them when a real push to victory was required. No doubt the top order needed to perform better. Again the tension leaked out of the game too early, and I was not sufficiently attuned to the attritional contest that does take place over 6 balls rather than over a session in slow cricket. New watching habits were needed.

My pleasure, it must be admitted, was enhanced by seeing this match in daylight, so I could see much better. But I thought the briskness of the proceedings admirable, and the crowd were well engaged without dominating proceedings as they did later. One intriguing footnote was that Mandhana's star quality attracted 135,000 viewers on a livestream of one Western Storm game, an indicator of one future for cricket on television.

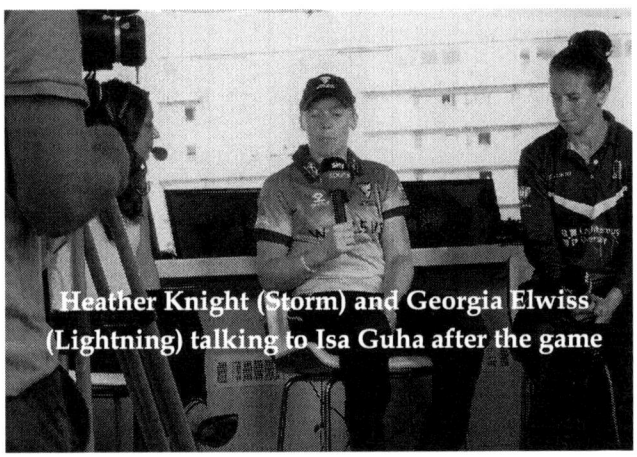

Heather Knight (Storm) and Georgia Elwiss (Lightning) talking to Isa Guha after the game

*

There was by now a blizzard of Blast games. Between 18 July and 13 August 80 games took place, and another 46 were scheduled up to 30 August (although the rain that had badly affected the Lord's Test meant that eight Blast games on Friday 16 August were abandoned). The four teams at the top of the North group and the four at the top of the South group would then go forward to the quarter-final games scheduled for 4, 5, 6 and 7 September. These were likely to be swept out of my mind by the Test matches and the little matter of a major operation at the end of the month to repair an aneurysm. Despite an ingrained scepticism about the Blast, attention to them would be rewarded once it came to Finals Day in September. Whoever arrived there, there would be good back stories.

Nor could I help noticing the rumours of cricket wars around the globe: India were touring the West Indies, and taking in the USA as well. Two T20I games were played at Lauderhill in Florida, a stadium which a month later hosted a Tri-Nation series between the USA,

Papua New Guinea and Namibia.

Then there was the Global T20 Canada; what is more Spain was touring Finland; and The Archbishop of Canterbury's XI played the Vatican's St Peter's CC in Rome; the Physical Disability T20 series had run in Worcestershire between 5 and 13 August; Canada beat Germany in the final of the Ahmadiyya Muslim Association Masroor International T20 in London; and the future (discuss) arrived at the La Manga Club in Spain when VOC Rotterdam won the inaugural T10 European Cricket League.

More arresting to the England-centred fan was the news that the Euro T20 Slam planned for the autumn had been cancelled. This was to be played in Scotland, Ireland and Netherlands, a Remain-fest of a kind. Teams would be involved from Amsterdam, Belfast, Dublin, Edinburgh, Glasgow and Rotterdam. County cricketers being touted for them included Roelof van der Merwe, Luke Wright, Paul Stirling, Boyd Rankin, Harry Gurney, Matt Henry, Ravi Bopara, Luke Ronchi, Samit Patel and Peter Trego. 13 matches were planned at Malahide in Ireland, including the play-offs, 10 at the Grange Club in Edinburgh, and 10 in Amstelveen, proposed to run from 30 August to 22 September. When I read about it, I instantly wondered whether this would affect the county championship in September, but there it was in mid-August being called off. I felt relieved, but sorry in a way, since the development of cricket in Ireland, Scotland and Netherlands felt wholly desirable and healthy for the long-term future of the game.
*

Amidst all this mind-stretching cricket, the **eleventh CC round** of Division One county cricket had been scheduled for Sunday 18 August to Wednesday 21 August. This was a sop to traditionalists who wanted, reasonably enough, to watch some red-ball cricket in August, as they had been doing for years. But a triple quart (Tests, Blast, county championship) was being squeezed into a pint pot since this was a competition too many. Some cricketers were being asked to shift focus from quick cricket to slow, something that surely needed some practice, and perhaps not all were up to it, to the championship's detriment. Indeed Sam Billings of Kent came out and said so, a feeling possibly exacerbated by the prospect of Kent having to rethink the timing of Canterbury Week, the world's oldest cricket festival. Cricket is on the edge, but I could see why this made people feel sore. Later in the year, James Hildreth, the Somerset batsman, spoke about the challenge of changing between formats, remarking that you almost had to take it as two different sports. "While batting in the championship is all about calmness, stillness and staying level, white-ball cricket is the complete opposite, with loads of stuff going through your head. Going back from white ball to red ball is challenging too, because it's hard to get back into the mentality of not premeditating."

Nor did this cramming of fixtures bode well for the addition of The Hundred to the mix, a quadruple pint pot when a triple one was hard enough. The draft fixture list for 2020 had the One-Day Cup and The Hundred running from mid-July until late August, with no room for the 4-day game. The sceptical part of me argued that, this being England, we would muddle through with much grumbling. Yet scepticism may not be the appropriate reaction: why mess things up? If the only answer is 'for money', this answer is, to use terms from philosophy, neither necessary nor sufficient. What is more, it has a squalid ring to it.

As it turned out, this isolated round of county championship games produced much fine cricket, with the Division One leaders taking part in two compelling games and achieving compelling victories. Warwickshire took on Somerset; Kent played Essex. At Edgbaston Warwickshire started with a score of 419, young-gun Rob Yates scoring 141, "Take that, Somerset." They replied with 308, 111 runs behind, which gave them three valuable batting points and meant they avoided having to follow on. Could Warwickshire press their advantage? No. In their second innings they were all out for 146, leaving Somerset 258 to win, a very reachable target. Tom Abell, their young-gun captain, having taken 4 wickets in the Warwickshire second innings, got them going with 25 runs, and young guns Banton (66), Bartlett (54*) and Bess (40*) – the last on 'holiday' from playing for Yorkshire in the Blast – got them over the line with 5 wickets to spare. Craig Overton had played, getting 4 wickets and hitting 36 runs, just before he got summoned to play for England at Old Trafford, a neat bit of scheduling. This was an old-fashioned jigsaw fitting a five-day cricket piece to a four-day one, making a perfect join.

Somerset were definitely in the hunt for the title. The drama at Canterbury was even more palpable. Kent scored 226 and then had Essex collapse to 114, the highest scorer being Mohammed Amir, who was the overseas bowler replacing Siddle. Essex looked affronted and possibly received a hair-drying pep talk from their captain or coach. If it was not that it must have been something since Kent were duly knocked over for 40 runs, 9 being the higher score. The damage was done by Essex's own young gun, Sam Cook, 'Little Chef' himself, who, having already taken 5 wickets in Kent's first innings, now took another 7. Essex only needed 153 runs to win, a stroll really, except that they only achieved it with 3 wickets left. At 82-5, it occurred to me that Essex's title challenge would be won or lost in the next hour or two, providing another entrancing long game to follow online. This was the match that triggered Billings's private blast about the difficulty of switching the mindset to red-ball cricket in the midst of all the white-ball fixtures. On the other hand, the same difficulty faced Essex, but by an act of will they seized the chance to assert their credentials for the top place in Division One.

After this round, with 11 matches played, Essex were on 188 points, Somerset on 186. 3 rounds more were to be played on 10, 16 and 23 September. I certainly wanted the weather to hold for the 2 Test matches in September but also for the very last round on 23 to 26 September, when Somerset were due to host Essex at Taunton. However, I felt very nervous that the weather might not co-operate, and the push-back of the County championship to the fourth week of September would prove to be a piece of mis-scheduling.

15 THIRD ASHES TEST:
22 to 25 August, Headingley

"You cannot win an Ashes Test if your side is bowled out for 67."
England needed to win, or at least draw this match, to retain a chance of
winning the series and bringing the Ashes back. The first day was affected by drizzle and poor light so that only 52 overs were bowled in
the day. Root, on winning the toss, opted to put a Smithless Australia in
to bat. What would have been the score he had in mind that he could
bowl Australia out for? Under a hundred would be a strong vindication
of his decision. As it was, Australia were all out at the end of the day on
179. This felt like a vindication too. 8 Australia wickets fell for 43 runs,
with only an aggressive partnership between Warner and Labuschagne
giving the score any kind of respectability. Their touch of aggression –
some 70 runs were scored in 11 overs after tea – might have offered an
indicator to England to go the same way if they were going to make a
score. Despite some ragged bowling, England won both sessions on
Day One, thanks to the role played by Archer taking six wickets in 17.1
overs. Unlike in the Second Test, he dialled the speed down to the 80s
(130s kph), and this ability to change speed was generously praised by
Warner. Warner of course had to play his cricket to a background of
booing, not just arm-wrestling with the bowling at the crease but arm-
wrestling in his mind not to be got down by the background noise. Both
parties could be said to be striving and not yielding, although there is a
considerable difference between striving against hostile bowling and
sitting on your backside mooing away.

On this day, as a measure of raggedness, Woakes bowled a wide
which went to the boundary. As I learnt from Michael Atherton in The
Times, before this match Woakes had bowled 5220 balls in Test cricket,
of which only 16 were adjudged wides, and of those 16 balls 13 were
from bouncers that had climbed too high over the batsman's head. So, a
Woakes wide was a significantly unwelcome event. Whether it signalled a deeper malaise I doubted.

The TMS team gave the impression of being keen to pounce on

Root for deciding to bowl, with an implicit tone, as I heard it, of, "Well, if it hadn't been for Archer, Root would have been very culpable." And yet Root must have chosen to bowl because he had talked tactics with Archer and others and realised that he was capable of being very destructive, so he should take some credit for what happened. On the other hand Woakes and Stokes bowled indifferently, so he should take some of the blame for this. How complicated; it is striking how friendless you can be when you are captain.

Worse was to follow for him, when in England's reply, he found himself at the crease after 3.5 overs, again having in effect to be an opener. On the second ball he faced, he nicked a sharp leg-cutter off Hazelwood to slip and was out for a duck, his second in succession. Like Woakes's wides, ducks do not come naturally to Root. I had had some business to attend to that morning so I had only checked the score at just before noon, to find England 2 wickets down, Nathan Lyon bowling, and Burns on 7 not out. In Burns I trusted, erroneously, since at 12.48 pm England were 45-5, soon to be all out for 67.

This was the third time in the year England had been out for under 100 runs. (First was 77 all out in the First Test against the West Indies in January; second was 85 all out in the Test against Ireland in July.) The horror may be partially gleaned from listing the fall of wickets: 1-10 (Roy, 3.5 overs), 2-10 (Root, 5.1 ov), 3-20 (Burns, 10.4 ov), 4-34 (Stokes, 14.3 ov), 5-45 (Denly, 20.1 ov), 6-45 (Bairstow, 21.1 ov), 7-54 (Woakes, 24.1 ov), 8-56 (Buttler, 25.1 ov), 9-66 (Archer, 26.4 ov), 10-67 (Leach, 27.5 ov).

On this occasion, the Australian bowling quartet was Cummins, Hazelwood, Lyon and Pattinson. Lyon in fact only bowled 1 over, and the wickets were shared between the other three, Hazelwood taking 5. The inclination is to trash England for their batting, but much credit needs to be given to the Australian bowlers, working as a unit, and bowling so accurately. My judgement that England had won sessions 1 and 2 on Day One had to be amended. Australia's 179 runs suddenly looked as if it could be match-winning.

It meant I could not bear to follow the progress of the Australian second innings on the afternoon and evening of Day Two. But I should have had more faith, because at close of play Australia were 171-6 after

57 overs. The sticking point was again Labuschagne, the Smith substitute who was acquitting himself extremely well. He had made 80 in the first innings and at close of play was 53 not out.

The Times on Saturday was scathing: the headline for the cricket section was 'No fight, no idea, no hope'. A headline says it all – except for the 50% it does not say. England had bowled well for most of Friday, but not well enough to restrict Australia to perhaps a 50-run lead rather than 100 runs. The headline was commenting on a particular day, and indeed a particular session, and unafraid to obliterate the way England had fought back in the Second Test to put Australia on the ropes, even if they did not quite deserve to win the match. Nor did it acknowledge that in the First Test, the match belonged to Steve Smith, the difference between the two sides.

The Australian Gideon Haigh, a doyen among cricket journalists, in his search for the killer hyperbole, overstepped the mark, linking the simple-mindedness of England's batting with the national predicament, as he saw it, facing the completion of the UK's exit from the EU. "This [the England innings] was cricket cakeism, everyone helping themselves, forgetful of the morrow, the match, the Ashes." I feared he was right, at least about England's batting if not about the exit negotiations, but I longed to see him eat his words.

Thinking about where England went from here, Australia having won all 3 sessions on Day Two, I concluded that England were going to have to win all 3 sessions on Day Three to retain a foothold in the match. Foreboding overtook me. After the first half hour, Labuschagne and Pattinson were still at the crease, so no wickets for England. And then Bairstow dived in front of Root to take a catch and dropped it. What is more Labuschagne had been dropped by Root when he was on 14, so each miss was adding a turn of the corkscrew to the heart. The air was seeping rapidly from my balloon of hope, and when there were four overthrows, I turned away too disgruntled to listen or even follow online. I want England to win, but not half as much as I want them to acquit themselves well. The latter did not seem to be happening.

And then they knocked over the last four Australian wickets so that they were all out for 246. Wickets had fallen at 10, 36, 52, 97, 163, 164, 215, 226, 237 and 246. The load was shifted from Archer (2 wickets in 14 overs) to Stokes (3 wickets in 24.2 overs). In fact Stokes's determination not to be a slave to probability was marked by his bowling from tea on Day Two to 12.25 pm on Day Three. And after the missed chances off Labuschagne, Denly and Bairstow brought his innings to an end with a brilliant run out. England's target to win was a mere 359, when I had thought Australia were going to take the game well beyond them with a 400-plus lead. The challenge was formidable, but the pitch and the conditions seemed to allow batsmen to get scores if they could survive long enough to get settled. A particular England virtue was that, despite the excellence of the Australian bowling and the poverty of the English batting, the bowlers had been compelled to perform again with barely any time to rest, yet had not flinched from the task.

In Burns I trusted again, but in the second ball of the first over, Cummins seemed to have seriously damaged his finger with a ball he took on the glove, so this trust felt misplaced. I had to go elsewhere at this point and so left the game full of foreboding. When I clocked back in, full of apprehension from memories of England collapses in the fourth innings, I found that they were 87-2, with Denly digging in and, even better, the embattled Root retaining his wicket and slowly knocking off the runs. This was red-ball cricket after all, in which time had no part to play, nor was the weather predicted to intervene. England had over two days to get what was needed, while Australia still needed to take 8 wickets. England seemed to be acquitting themselves well, and Test cricket was doing the same.

At 6.10, Denly was out for 50 (off 155 balls), and England needed 218 to win with 7 wickets left. It was the 60th over of the innings when Root was joined at the crease by Stokes, who needed to see the day out if English optimism was to be maintained. And so it was. At close of play England were 156-3, 203 behind their target with 7 wickets in hand. How would it end? Good weather was forecast for the last 2 days, but the new ball was due very shortly. Root and Stokes needed to get through that and beyond, and in particular Root needed to convert his 70 into 100, and go beyond. The Smith role, it felt, had fallen on him. Could he prove his mettle to his critics, including Geoffrey Boycott who had talked of Root having to resign should they lose the match. With a Yorkshire friend like this, who needed an enemy?

Before the next day, Sunday 18 August, even dawned, I lay awake borne along by a surge of optimism that England could win this match. If only Root and Stokes could get through the new ball, there were batsmen to come who were capable of taking England over the line or very close to it. What would a neutral want, I wondered? In terms of the series, one victory each would set up the last two Test matches very well. But that aside, an epic finish, say 30 or 40 runs to get and only 3 England wickets left, would be an enticing, no rivetting prospect. And what would the Aussie bowlers be thinking? They would be poised to strive, I did not doubt.

Anyway the sun would shine, and I hoped there would be a full crowd. It had been striking how much the spectators, the English ones at least, had got behind the efforts of Root and Denly on the Saturday afternoon, even though the scoring rate was a long way from one-day cricket rates, proof of a kind that dot-ball cricket can be an enthralling spectacle. On Day Two, the team were zero; on Day Three, they were being willed on to heroics. At 15-2 sunny optimism would have looked foolish. And yet 7 overs had been used up, and the captain was at the crease with a determination to wipe away his duck in the first innings.

Somewhere it is written already who will win and who will lose. So, fate? Destiny? Yet secondary to this mysterious process an effort from the human beings involved would be crucial. If you had asked an omniscient entity as to who the winner might be, on this occasion they might have replied that they did not know, since it was up to the individuals involved. On the other hand if you do believe that fate, chance, destiny are chimeras, since it is only down to the individuals involved and no one else, that would free you up to pass judgement on their performance.

And what was Ben Stokes contemplating for Day Four having scored only 2 runs in 50 balls on Day Three, I mused on his behalf?

Ben, you're the warrior
who's gone to war;
2 in 50? Do it again Ben.

When you have done, you have not done,
you must score more.

Stokesy's the man for master strokes.

    It was only at 12 noon on the Sunday that I was able to check the cricket score, hoping against hope that England were still only 3 wickets down, maybe having added 30 to 40 runs to the total. At 12.16, hoping for the best while fearing the worst, I found England 201-4, Root having departed for 77 off 205 balls. I wish he had not been out, but his application in the circumstances seemed to be admirable and in a way this was a real captain's innings. I did not want to see him replaced. Stokes was still there on 17 off 90 balls, and Bairstow was on 22 off 32 balls. The new ball was in play but was now 7 overs old. And then in the 87th over, Pattinson bowled 5 wides, and I had a touch of *schadenfreude*, such as an Australian supporter would have felt on Day Two when Australia were 6 wickets down, with England pressing, only for them to concede 4 overthrows.

    At 12.35 Stokes hit a six, and I noted that there were now 16 extras in the Stokes-Bairstow partnership of 70. At some point in the morning, England had not hit a run for 25 minutes and Lyon was getting very good turn. Despite this, I concluded at lunch that the session had been England's with 82 runs off 24 overs for the loss of 1 wicket. Stokes and Bairstow seemed to be building an impressive partnership. Stokes's forward defensive was immaculate.

    And so the afternoon session arrived, surely the make-or-break one for England, needing 121 runs with 6 wickets in hand. I was quite enslaved to the possibility of victory, especially when Australia appealed against Bairstow with gusto, and Bairstow reviewed with similar gusto, in Atherton's phrase, and was found to be not out. . . but then it started to go wrong. At 1.55 Bairstow was caught off Hazelwood for 36 runs. Next in was Buttler but at 2.10 he was run out with Stokes the culprit, so that England were 253-6, 106 runs behind. Stokes then reached his half century, off 153 balls, but when Woakes was caught at mid-off at 2.26 England were 261-7, and the 300 mark began to look some way off. Archer came to the crease, no slouch with the bat, at least in quick cricket, but was he the man for the hour now? At least he moved the score on a little, scoring 15 runs off 33 balls with 3 boundaries until succumbing to Lyon's spin, almost hitting him for a six but instead giving a catch to Head on the boundary. (The thought occurred to me that some time in the future Archer would perform some transformative heroics with the bat for England.) So Stuart Broad came in which immediately encouraged memories of his efforts with the bat as a tailender: surely he could help Stokes to get the score past 300, still of course a long way off, but maybe England would thus salvage some honour from the game. No. He fell to Pattinson 2 balls later. This was surely defeat and loss of the Ashes? Last man in and Leach came to the wicket. England's hopes were surely ended: Stokes would try to protect him from the Australian bowlers but he could only do so much, and in any case he had to score runs if England were going to get anywhere close to their target of 359.

Broad's wicket fell at 3.17, and an hour later England had won the match. Stokes was 135 not out off 219 balls, having batted for 329 minutes, while Leach was 1 not out off 17 balls.

Much has been written about that last hour and while analysis of its ebbs and flows provides a rational explanation of what happened, yet recalling the emotions of watching it in the tranquillity of the aftermath is difficult to do. Hyperbole probably helps: either, "This was the greatest Test match ever" (at least since the last great Test match) or, "Stokes's 135 not out was the greatest Test innings of modern times." One would want both to be true, except that only a few months previously in South Africa Kusal Perera had done something similar to help Sri Lanka beat the home team. South Africa were put into bat by Sri Lanka, and made 235, suggesting that Karunaratne, the Sri Lankan captain, had got it wrong, a view confirmed by Sri Lanka only scoring 191 in reply, leaving them 44 behind. South Africa then went on to score 259, so Sri Lanka had to score 304 to win. The probability was of a South African victory, but the notion was upset by a tenth-wicket partnership of 78 runs between Perera and Fernando. While Fernando held up one end Perera hit 5 sixes and 12 fours and cannily farmed the strike. What is more Dean Elgar missed a run out of Fernando. Thanks to these two, Sri Lanka made it to their 304 target to achieve a memorable victory for themselves and for Test cricket. What happened at Headingley on 25 August proved to be a remarkable echo of this narrative - and improved on it.

Analysis can offer a way into understanding what happened:

1) The partnership lasted 62 balls.

2) In overs 115 to 125, when the tenth-wicket partnership was in play, Stokes hit boundaries on over 116.4 (6 off Lyon), over 118.5 (6 off Lyon), 120.3 (6 off Cummins), he then went for Hazelwood in the 121st over – 4 on the first ball, 6 on the second, 6 on the third, 19 off the over in all. On 123.1 he sliced the ball in the air to deep backward point but Marcus Harris could not hold on to a very difficult chance. Stokes could not be any more emboldened than he already was, but clearly he must have been since he hit Cummins's next 2 balls for four. On 124.3 he hit Lyon for a six down the ground and on over 125.4 scored the winning boundary.

3) Stokes farmed the strike by taking a single on the fifth or sixth ball of the over in overs 116, 117, 118, 120, 121 and 122. In over 123 he took a single on the <u>fourth</u> ball, a gracious appreciation of Leach's defensive technique. In over 125, Leach reciprocated by taking a nifty single to leg to tie the match, bring Stokes on strike, and allow him to hit the winning four.

4) Australia only needed one wicket, but the running down of the runs required by England went like this: end of over 115: 73 needed, 116: 66 needed, 117: 62 needed, 118: 49 needed, 119: 48 needed, 120: 37 needed, 121 (that Hazelwood over): 18 needed, 122: 17 needed, 123: 8 needed, 124: 2 needed.

On the other hand a measure of how inadequate analysis is to explain what happened was that the TMS commentary, normally very good at explaining the scene for the listener who is not a viewer, and ensuring the match position is kept right to the fore, broke down. The most dramatic moment of the last hour occurred when on the fifth ball of over 124, Stokes reverse swept the ball to backward point, and Leach called for a run. Technically it was his call, and he will have been thinking that on the fifth ball of the over it was important to bring Stokes on strike. But there was not a run there, and Stokes sent him back, perhaps conscious of how he had done for Buttler earlier. Leach was well out of his ground when the throw-in came to Lyon, who then dropped the ball, allowing Leach to get back to his crease. The run out would have meant that Australia would have won by one run. How do you provide a proper commentary on such a drama? The answer was to jettison all decorum. When Leach was out of his ground and being sent back, three voices – I concluded they belonged to Agnew, Alastair Cook and one other – were shouting No No No No No, and then Leach got back, the run out had been missed, and order was restored. When the run-out did not happen when it should have happened, I envisaged a hand being placed on Leach's shoulder to remind him that he was mortal. Fortunately the other hand was placed on Lyon's shoulder to remind him that he was mortal, as if to say, "Back to your marks, both of you, we shall scrub that ball and start again."

Before the innings, the notion that England would chase down 359 runs was inconceivable until you reasoned that such an impossibility was there to be proved possible. After the game Tim Paine had a very good phrase to describe it, 'a game of inches'. Inches were involved when Lyon did not coordinate his eye and his hand sufficiently to take the throw-in and run out Leach. Inches were involved, perhaps calculated, when one or two of Stokes's sixes just got over the rope and not into a fielder's hand. Inches were involved when Harris did not quite move fast enough to take the catch off Stokes at deep backward point. Inches, perhaps millimetres, were involved when Paine went for a DRS review when the ball had pitched slightly outside the leg stump, thus wasting it. Inches had been involved earlier in the game when England dropped Labuschagne 2 or 3 times, until Denly and Bairstow got their hand-eye coordination - and the inches – right to run him out. Inches were involved in the fact that in their second innings in the field, Australia bowled 31 extras, including 7 no balls and 2 wides. England on the other hand managed 13 leg byes – was that calculated?

Stokes bellowed as *fortissimo* on reaching the winning target as he had greeted his century *sotto voce*. He's a straightforward character, and was straightforward about a dramatic moment on the last ball of the penultimate over, bowled by Lyon, when there was a loud appeal for lbw given not out, and Australia could not review it because they

had used all their reviews. The consensus seemed to be that he probably was out, but Stokes was clear afterwards: "It flicked my front pad
and didn't spin. I thought as soon as it hit me that it was sliding down
leg because there was no spin."

It was Ben Stokes's innings that rightly made it Stokes's match,
but a peculiarly quirky English hero emerged at the end in the person
of Jack Leach. He endeared himself to English supporters, and must
have riled Australian ones at the same time, by his practice of removing
his helmet and glasses to demist them with a cloth since in the heat of
battle they were regularly misting up. (Arguably it was their misting
up that had prevented him getting his century at Lord's against Ireland, although I think fatigue is the more likely cause. On the other
hand, he had learnt from it. He did not want misted glasses to enable
his dismissal in this crucial arena.) His name could have been zero if
Lyon had run him out, because the blame for the wicket that prevented
Stokes winning the match would have been laid on him, even though
the circumstances at the time were complicated. As it was, although he
only faced 17 balls, his defensive technique looked pretty sound, at
least by comparison with some of the batsmen who had preceded him.
However, this is misleading, since all the others were deemed to have
hitting capabilities against Australian bowling. What emerged so
brightly from the gloom of the England mini-collapse (Woakes, Archer,
Broad) was a batsman who realised his sole task was to preserve his
wicket and enable Stokes to do the hitting. It is an intriguing thought
that the Australians had bowling plans for all the England batsmen
except Leach, who as a comparative newcomer and a number eleven
would have escaped their scrutiny. One of the pleasures watching the
last hour was the way Leach faced his 17 balls with dignity and without fluster, doing it all in glasses. This was a sort of anti-celebrity cricket. When asked later in the season why he was popular, he said: "It's
probably because I look like a village cricketer out there in my glasses,
a bald head and maybe people think, 'That could be me!' All the others
looked pretty professional." Amateurism is quite dead in sport, but do
we have a nostalgia for someone who at least looks like an amateur?
The batting too was an unexpected compensation, and because unexpected therefore uplifting, for the fact was that he was in the team for

his bowling, but his skills in that department had barely been used, his figures in the first innings being pretty modest: 11-0-46-1.

Even in writing about the game, there is a temptation to focus on the highlight moments, but whether in words or in images, nothing can substitute for the experience of watching it all in real time, and not just later when you know the result, nor substitute for the sensation of seeing it unfold as it happened with all the suspense consequent on that, and feeling – even watching on a screen – that you were part of it.

One thing it was not was 'incredible'. After all, we witnessed it, we saw it happen, it did not require the suspension of credulity. There is more precision in calling the cricket on Sunday 'improbable'. On the other hand, Stokes's innings did seem to have a touch of the incredible: you could not comprehend what you were seeing. Like his catch in the opening World Cup game, you could not grasp how it was done, so how could you credit what was done? My particular choice was his turning a yorker from Hazelwood on leg stump – a ball in the manner Starc had undone him in a World Cup match – into a full toss hit for six, a champagne moment if ever there was one. He got his bat under it and flicked it to the boundary, not a four but a six. Superlative, and maybe barely credible.

There was one disappointment. I had wanted a massive Root century to get us over the line, so that when my father sent me a text from heaven, "How did Joe Root do?" I could send a heavenly reply, "He made a fine century." But it was Stokesy who struck the massive century, a detail I was not going to quibble with.

My immediate judgement on events was that it was the greatest game ever. But was it? It did have the magic ingredient of reversal of fortune as a result of England collapsing to 67 all out. And it had that essential ingredient of Test cricket, namely longueurs. Australia's first-innings had lasted 52.1 overs, to be followed by England's collapse in 27.5 overs. The Australian second innings lasted 75.2 overs, stretching the game out, but it really took the England fourth innings to pull it into proper slow territory. Their run rate was 2.8 an over, and the dot balls dealt with by Root, Denly, Bairstow and Stokes (more than any-one!) contributed to taking the edge off the Australian bowlers. They had bowled 114 overs when the last hour started and were entitled not to be at their sharpest; England's tactical nous in getting them to this position was a masterstroke. Thirdly, the image of Stokes with his Sancho Panza in the form of Leach will provide an enduring visual memory. As time goes on, this judgement that it was the greatest game will have to be tempered by mature reflection on other great games, not just in this country, but in other parts of the cricketing globe. The real pleasure will be in the debate, rather than the conclusion. After all, there had been the South Africa-Sri Lanka game in February. Perhaps personally was it my greatest game because I had only seen it in two dimensions? The greatest in my mind up to then was played at Lord's between England and West Indies in July 2000. On Saturday 3 July, I had attended with my father. England were one down in the series and were up against Ambrose and Walsh. England won the toss and chose to bowl, but West Indies scored 267, so perhaps not a good decision, which looked worse when England were bowled out if not for 67, then for a modest 134, 133 runs behind. Then the reversal happened: West Indies were bowled out for 54, so that England needed a mere 188 to win, but the pitch was sportive, and it was hard not to entertain a sinking feeling that defeat loomed. But they got there! Wickets fell on 3, 95, 119, 120, 140, 140, 149 and 160. There were no Stokes-type innings and top scorers were Atherton (45) and Vaughan (41). The hero of the hour was the number eight, Dominic Cork, who made 33 including three fours and a six, which I remember as certainly a precursor of Stokesian chutzpah. In classic fashion, the final runs were scored in singles by Cork and Gough until Cork hit the winning boundary. There was a pitch invasion (not including us) so unconfined was the joy, Courtenay Walsh ran a lap of honour to mark his last Lord's Test, and as we left, my father remarked, "We might see as good, but we shall never see better." But now I (at least) debated deliciously within myself whether I had seen better.

Thanks to Stokes, and a general England will to victory, the possibility of winning the Ashes back was still alive, hence the headline in The Sun: "Go urn, my son." The Daily Mirror, for which Stokes wrote a column over the summer, ran their story as "Mirror man Ben saves Ashes." Smith was likely to be back for the next Test at Old Trafford, which only made the prospect of something titanic more enticing.

The crowd were engaged, indeed they were a shining congregation in a way. On Day Four nearly everyone, 18,000 in all, was in their seats at 11 am for the start of play, and a ritual caught on in the afternoon, when someone shouted, "Shoes off if you love Ben Stokes," and the crowd went with him to wave their shoes in the air.

*

The day after the match ended, Monday 26 August, I went to Cambridge to undergo surgery to repair an aneurysm. Lying idly in a hospital bed at five o'clock that afternoon, I not only gave thanks that a fifth day of Test cricket had not encroached on my visit, an outcome finessed by the cricketing gods and heroes, but I experienced that oceanic feeling of pleasure which had first come to me the night before, enhanced by the knowledge that my hopes had not been illusory. My imagination and reality had not, as it turned out on this occasion, been so far apart after all. What is more, if Lyon <u>had</u> effected that run-out so that Australia had won by one run, if Australia <u>had</u> gone 2-0 up in the series and ensured retention of the Ashes, if they <u>had</u> posed a big challenge to England to square the series 2 games all, I would have experienced a chagrin of a kind, but only a mild one, since I had witnessed England performing at the top of their game. In fact, 1-1 in the series so far felt like a much truer reflection of the equilibrium between the two teams. It also kept the series properly alive. At one game apiece, there was still everything to strive for, which is how the best Ashes cricket is played.

*

"You cannot win an Ashes Test if your side is bowled out for 67." Was England's third under-100 innings in 2019 down to the bowling? Yes. Down to the batsmen? Yes, apparently. So damnation, but at Headingley salvation came in the person of Ben Stokes.

16 In search of lost cricket

Lying in a hospital bed in the week following my operation, time became indistinct. It was not just a matter of an inclination to fall in and out of sleep, which disrupts a sense of time, but the merging of day and night: sleep during the day, insomnia at night. The drugs were a source of mild hallucinations. Was I waking or sleeping? I constantly looked at my watch only to discover that hardly any time had passed since I last looked. Was this slow time, or just concentrated time in which the vividness of experience was distilled? At least I could replay the Headingley Test in my head, except my pixellating memory was already causing its details to become fuzzy, even forgotten. There came to my rescue a radio version of Marcel Proust's 'In Search of Lost Time', adapted by Timberlake Wertenbaker for BBC Radio in ten one-hour episodes. Thanks to iPlayer I could listen at will.

How did the BBC know that this was just what I needed, flat on my back? The narrator was Derek Jacobi whose articulate and confessional voice presses out the words as if he was pressing an orange to make orange juice. 'Courteous', *un mot Proustien* even in English, came out as 'qwertious', at least in my happily surprised mind.

Proust's novel is full of characters such as the Duchess of Guermantes, Charles Swann, Robert de St Loup, Mme Verdurin, Elstir, Albertine, The Baron de Charlus. I could go on. To read the novel is to form likes and dislikes, a process only heightened by this radio adaptation: who is the hero? Who is the slob? Who is vulgar? Who is oddest? The vividness of the characters' feelings is attractive, and so to my mind is their snobbishness: does it repel or does it humanise? Is it important for our self-esteem that we feel morally superior to the people we read about?

What really hit me was the fact that these individuals never went to a cricket match. That would surely have humanised them! Charlus, for all his graces, was never a member of Lord's. Marcel could never have sat through the greatest innings in Test cricket, even if it had been the one on the Sunday before. It was a case not so much of the characters' insincerity as their inauthenticity. Is that why the UK is Leaving not Remaining? The unexamined life is not worth living, and if it does not include cricket then it must be 'unexamined'.

And then I fell asleep, waking the next day to an awareness I had been hallucinating in the night, as if I had taken opium. Fled were those delusions.

17 FOURTH ASHES TEST:
4 to 8 September, Old Trafford

"You cannot win an Ashes Test if you only get Smith out off a no-ball."
To rate the Ashes as the pinnacle of Test cricket, and therefore of cricket, is to take a decidedly Anglo-Australian-centred view of the world. Even if it feels like it at the time, step away from it and you realize how inaccurate it is. Almost concurrent with the Fourth Test at Old Trafford was a Test played at Chittagong between Bangladesh and Afghanistan. In 2006 in Mumbai I saw a team wearing Afghanistan shirts visiting the stadium, novices maybe but a sight made heart-warming because they came from such a war-torn country. Since then the pupil has come on by leaps and bounds. In June they had run India close in a World Cup match. Now in Chittagong, playing Test cricket, they won a Test match against Bangladesh. Bangladesh, chasing 398 to win, succumbed to 173 all out. In both countries, hundreds of thousands would have been watching on television, pain for Bangladesh, ecstasy for Afghanistan. The star was the young (20 years) captain of Afghanistan, Rashid Khan, leg-break prodigy. "I can snap the ball from the top of my fingers," he said. "It helps me bowl more on a good length, every time, and I can spin the ball as I want." His figures for the match were 41.3 overs, 104 runs, an economy rate of 2.5, and 11 wickets. He also chipped in with scores of 51 and 24. Step aside, Ben Stokes. In Wisden Cricket Monthly for July he was listed as the top 'best young player in the world', and this match must have been a coming-of-age for him, not least because of the high regard in which he holds Test cricket. "It's real cricket. It tests your experience, your bowling skills, your patience, everything is tested. That's why I'd love to play a lot of Test cricket." Added to this was a strong dose of melancholy realism. Asked whether Afghanistan would be playing regular five-day Test cricket in the next five years, he said that they would hardly play many Test matches. One can only hope that as many as possible are found. Put the Ashes on one side for a moment: England need to play their part in this process.

Cut from Chittagong in Bangladesh to Arbroath in Scotland. In an ICC Women's T20 World Cup qualifier, Papua New Guinea women (133-3) are playing USA women, who have been set a truncated target of 117 runs to win. When I checked later they only got to 94-7 in their 17 overs. *Sic transit gloria?* Hardly. But is there glory to come, a women's fixture of a similarly esoteric nature in fifty years' time that grabs everyone's attention? If Afghanistan can do it, so can a lot of others . . .

*

I had returned home from hospital on Sunday 1 September, with instructions to take the next two weeks very easily. If you wanted to find an activity, one might call it a 'passivity', that would rest the body without inducing boredom, a suggestion in my case would be to watch two Ashes Test matches from start to finish. And that was how it turned out. I subscribed to Now TV for a month, so I could sit back and watch wall-to-wall cricket, and not just any old cricket. It was a mysteriously felicitous arrangement of the calendar.

Old Trafford was to be a crucial test in the arm-wrestling: 2-1 Australia if they win, and that would mean that they retain the Ashes, or 2-1 England if they win, with the prospect of going for a second win at the Oval in order to get the Ashes back. Or would rain in Manchester bring on another drama, with the series to be decided at the Oval?

We seemed to be in for a pace-fest, Archer versus Starc. Curiously Woakes was dropped in favour of Craig Overton. I am well inclined towards both bowlers, but it puzzled me that Woakes was not included. Did Woakes's loss of batting form have something to do with it? And what role might spin play? Lyon versus Leach? Denly and Labuschagne both did leg-spin, so would this be used to break up the quicks? Questions only at this stage, but I found that anticipating the answers is one sort of suspense. One question was more urgent than all the others. Smith was back in the side, so how were England to get him out twice?

Another question was that of the toss. Would Root be keen to win it so England could bat first? After all, Australia had batted first in the other three Tests. Paine did it yet again, as good at winning the toss as he is indifferent in handling DRS, and chose to bat. First blood to them, but then second blood to England when Warner was out on the fourth ball of the innings, to Broad naturally. As I watched, I thought the television had slipped in a replay of his dismissal from the Edgbaston Test, and then I realised the wicket was in real time. This was promising. Promising also were the views across Manchester, with the hills beyond. This was the green and pleasant land, free, at least in this view, of dark satanic mills. And then the clouds rolled in. The television commented that the Australian batsmen were too comfortable. Archer was bowling within himself, presumably saving his fastest for when Smith came in, and perhaps making trial of the Old Trafford pitch where he had never played red-ball cricket before.

At 11.32 Broad had Harris lbw, which Harris reviewed unsuccessfully – again it was curious how poor Australia were at DRS – and Smith came to the wicket. One challenge for Root was how to husband Archer's energy to best effect and not overbowl him. Root seemed aware of the fact, and when Archer was unsuccessful in getting Smith very early on, he replaced him with Stokes. And then at 12 o'clock Leach came on to bowl and was extracting 'gentle turn', a phrase which sounds distinctly unthreatening. When the drizzle and lunch arrived at 12.54, Australia were 98-2, scoring at a run rate of 3.77. Never mind Smith, Labuschagne was going well at 49 not out, to the Test arena born.

After lunch I went straight to an armchair to sleep, and did not wake up until 2.35. Dare I look at the cricket? When I did so, I found that rain had stopped play, and I had to wait until 4 pm for the restart, when the rain came again, and the restart was restarted at 4.19. Conditions were unpleasant for both sides, but England were more up against it. There was now a very stiff wind blowing across the ground, enough to bring crisp packets whizzing in and across my screen, and even at one point removing the bails. 'Gale stopped play' is not in the lexicon, but there was no pleasure to be had in watching. I did not care to think how many layers the spectators needed to be wearing yet had failed to bring, and Broad bowling into the wind was not finding it pleasurable. There were regular delays, and the proper intensity of high level cricket seemed to drain away. At 5.02, it was remarked that Overton looked like taking a wicket, which he did soon after when he bowled Labuschagne for 67 off 128 balls, although not before Smith had hit a boundary from a virtual wide off Stokes to bring up his 50. When further rain finally brought the day's play to a close, Australia were 170-3. It felt far from being a pushover for England, but then desire rather than reason was fathering the thought that it might be.

There was a certain irony in the fact that Smith's felling at Lord's brought in a concussion substitute, who was turning out to be a concussion partner, as if this unkind act should require Fate to compensate Australia with gifting them a good new batsman. Conditions on the first day were extremely trying, and the cricket consequently suffered, although Australia held their composure to capitalise on it. In the afternoon, after the rain had stopped but the wind was at its strongest, the bowlers' run-ups were being affected. According to Overton, quoted in The Times: "You feel like you're getting to the crease and all of a sudden the wind hits you and it pushes you forward and you have to shorten your stride or it pushes you back and you have to jump back . . . We all tended to struggle with the wind." So the question for the next day was whether conditions would be more settled and allow Archer to bowl faster at Smith. The Times, in its headline, called Archer 'tame', a good example of the media's 'must grumble' approach to life. Was there a reason for Archer not bowling much at Smith in the morning that we were not told about? I presumed that it was a deliberate tactic of not overexerting him for fear of burning him out. The commentariat was going on about this, as if they wanted it both ways: don't underbowl him but don't overbowl him, and we are the best judges of that. It also occurred to me that Archer's gifts show a variety of skills and not just pace.

On Day Two, the wind was still there, but nowhere near as strong. Although it was cool, at 11 am it was sunny. 'Jerusalem' was just audible from the crowd. Expectation was everywhere. In the second over Archer induced a play and a miss by Smith, conceded a boundary, almost snaffled a caught and bowled chance – very sharp but holding it would have turned the match – and then got Smith close to a drag-on from which he took a single. That brought Travis Head to face. He defended the fifth ball, but the sixth went past his outside edge. The over felt like an England-Archer victory, but nine runs came from it. England continued to fight to stay in the game: Head went at 183, and Wade at 224. At 11.37 Archer bowled a 146 kph / 91 mph ball. When Leach went past Smith's outside edge, Smith seemed to mouth 'well bowled'. Shane Warne commented, "I would hate that. And say, 'You worry about your batting mate.' Or words to that effect." I preferred the way Smith observed some discussion protocol on the cricket field. Leach was exerting pressure so that at 12.29 Wade holed out to long off. This was a pleasurable wicket but you needed to witness the whole passage of play to truly relish it. The morning session of 25 overs had brought 2 wickets and 75 runs at a run rate of 3.0, so evens in a way. Just before lunch Smith reached his century, and I distinctly failed to hear any booing.

Checking in after a post-prandial sleep, I was filled with foreboding. Australia were 305-5, with Smith on 138 and Paine on 29. Paine I learnt had had a let-off when Roy dropped a catch, and worst of all Leach had had Smith caught in the slips only for it to be judged a no ball. This was either heart-breaking or the ultimate *faux pas* for a slow bowler, depending on your mood, distress preceding annoyance and anger. At 3.32 Smith reached his 150, and Curran on the field in the place of Stokes dropped Paine on 49. This session brought 124 runs with no wickets. After tea, Smith went to his 200, Starc hit Broad for 4 fours with a tail-ender's licence, and when Smith was finally out caught Denly bowled Root for 211, Australia declared on 497-8. Leach's figures were 26.1-3-83-2, with 1 no ball, but what a no-ball.

A big task faced England. They had a tricky 10 overs to negotiate before the close of play, and Denly went in the seventh over. On this occasion, Root did not come to the crease but the task was handed to Overton as the nightwatchman. He survived. Every England run was being cheered, but Michael Holding commented sagely, "Can they keep this up for three days?" This last session was emphatically Australia's since they took the game right away from England whose first challenge would be to score at least 297 runs and thus avoid the follow-on.

On Day Three, Friday 6 September, the start had been delayed by rain, and when I checked in at 3.10, Overton had gone but Burns and Root were still there with Burns on 53. The run rate was 2.71 an over, significantly lower than Australia's had been but then batting through the overs was more important than run rate. This session produced 102 runs for only one wicket, and England were 125-2. Might this be called England's session? Australia needed to take 2 lots of 10 wickets, and so far had only taken 2. However England were only 125 runs towards the immediate target of 297. Could they get within striking distance by the end of the last session, while still retaining some wickets?

At 5 pm, Root reached 50, and then nicked Cummins between wicket-keeper and first slip, giving him a life. Even an ascendant Australia can nod. At 5.10, Australia lost a review on an lbw appeal, and shortly after the crowd, wearing their beanies and hoodies to mark the end of summer, were rowdy and in Mexican-wave mood, always a sign of boredom, in this case possibly at the lack of free scoring, possibly to warm themselves up. Both teams were in fact engaged in attritional cricket. In due course Burns and Root lost their wickets, and Roy was bowled by Hazelwood for only 22. Soon after the umpires were chatting about the light with Paine, explaining, as far as I could gather, that the quick bowling needed to be replaced by Labuschagne's leg spin. Paine declined to do this, so the umpires took the players off: bad light stopped play with England on 200-5.

The last session really belonged to Australia because those late wickets gave them the chance to enforce the follow-on. The challenge to England to bat out the game to the end of Sunday was immense, and it was very clear that the 100 runs Smith scored after losing his wicket to a no ball were making a devastating difference in pushing England right onto the back foot.

Day Four dawned, even a bit warmer, with a capacity crowd. Stokes and Bairstow started okay, looking to build a significant partnership. The surface was good and I wanted them to get to 250 without losing a wicket. However, at 11.48 a big inswinger by Starc bowled Bairstow. England 228-6. At 12.10 Stokes was caught in the slips off Starc for 26 from 62 balls in an example of his new restrained style. England 243-7. The air was sliding from my lungs, the head slumping on the chest. Despite the Aussie stranglehold, the crowd were giving England full support. When Archer was casual on a single, he was lucky not to be run out. Buttler was engaged in a private battle to get a score of some kind. At 12.25 Lyon was on to mop up the tail, with

Cummins at the other end. At 12.34 Archer wafted at a ball from Cummins, out for one run off 19 balls. England were looking very uncomfortable, getting lucky until Australia made them get unlucky. The crucial figure was Jos Buttler. The commentators were urging him to play his natural attacking game. This may be red-ball cricket, to which Buttler was rightly adjusting his mindset, but they seemed to ignore this point and wanted a bit of white-ball cricket. He had to farm the strike as well, but was finding it difficult. The important score of 297 was looming out of the fog of 'what next?', when a Cummins no ball went over Broad's head and was given as four wides. Broad then nicked a single because backward point seemed to be asleep. England now needed only 22 to avoid the follow-on. Buttler then played a yorker well, which was a good sign, and what is more Cummins was bowling no balls to Broad. 78 runs were scored in the session for 3 wickets at a run rate of 3.25.

After lunch, I delayed my sleep to 'enjoy' the excruciating spectacle of whether England could or could not avoid the follow-on. At 1.55 the run rate had slowed to a trickle, dot ball succeeding dot ball, and yet it was absorbing. Broad was then bowled for 5 (off 29 balls) and England needed 15 more to avoid the follow-on. Last man in was Leach, who received a sterling reception. Would he burnish his reputation or tarnish it? When he hit a boundary, a great cheer went up. Only 7 runs to avoid the follow-on. A big lbw appeal followed, given not out, and the Australians could not review it because they had burnt both their reviews. Hawkeye seemed to suggest that it was in fact out. Trust the umpire, I told myself. At 2.13 Buttler hit a boundary to prevent the follow-on and take England to 300, but soon afterwards he was bowled for 41 (off 65 balls) and England were all out for 301, still 196 behind. There was something pleasing in not having to follow on, which in any case may not have been enforced, so it was really an illusory pleasure. Time to take my sleep, and get away from this slow-motion car crash.

When I looked in an hour later, Australia were 28-3! At 3.36 they were 44-4. In the over in which he bowled Head, Archer's speeds were 90 mph, 90, 89, 90, 93 and 92. Head hit a boundary on the fifth ball, and on the sixth was bowled. There was a shot of Head in the dressing room wiping his face, and looking as if he wanted to have another go. There was undoubtedly something compelling about watching Archer bowl. Just after four o'clock Leach came on, and I watched forgetting the rest of the match, and instead just thinking that England was right on top. At tea, I noted that it was England's session, but unless they could dismiss Australia for a very small total, the risk was that the game was being taken from them once again by Smith.

After tea, could Overton and Leach exert pressure? The television showed the passage of a beachball among the crowd, which must have been fun, possibly even superb fun, provided you were not trying to concentrate on the cricket. At 5.08 Smith reached his 50, and with Wade began to take the match away from England. The lead was now 327, and England needed 2 quick wickets. And then Smith got out, holing out to Stokes off Leach, and soon after Bairstow took a fine catch off Archer to get rid of Wade. Australia were 158-6, but Paine shepherded the score, with a run rate up at 5.4 an over, all the way to 186-6 declared, a lead of 382. Broad and Archer had taken the wickets, and it idly came to my mind, what if Woakes had been bowling as well? But he was not, and the Aussies strongly sensed the chance to seize the prize of winning the match and thus retain the Ashes. It would be an immense challenge for England to stave them off.

Right at the end of the day, England had a difficult passage to negotiate when difficulty turned to disaster. On the third ball of Cummins' over he induced a leading edge from Burns so he was gone for 0. Root, having to play the opener again, got an unplayable delivery and was bowled. 'Unplayable' I doubt is in Root's mindset, but to ordinary mortals it looked that way, possibly the ball of the series in view of the importance of the wicket. Roy came in at number four, with England's plan to keep him away from the opening slot in tatters. However, he survived the hat-trick ball, and was still there at the close of play. His hands seemed to hold the bat too firmly. Was this natural for him or nerves? I had observed that in the field he is a nail-biter.

At the end of the day, 82.5 overs had been bowled, 305 runs had been scored, and 13 wickets had fallen at a run rate of 3.68. England might be in dire straits, but there was no denying the entertainment value of this intense cricket.

On Day Five, I awoke finding it hard to imagine that England could bat through the day and live to fight the next Test and win the Ashes: only the result in the Third Test challenged deterministic predictions of a victory to Australia. A draw felt beyond England, not just because they were 2 wickets down, and because of their batting frailties, but because the Australian bowling quartet had been so good. Maybe Lyon, after a strong and threatening First Test, had been the weakest link, but he still exerted a stranglehold which aided the quick bowlers. If Starc were to fire, they had a bowler who could knock over a tail of batsmen. Would it be all over by lunchtime then? And if it was not, what difference would that make? This was a gloomy prognosis. I resolved to watch with the England batsmen and feebly add my will to theirs.

When play began it was a lovely day in Manchester to help the batsmen and there was a good fifth-day crowd. As part of the introduction of my grandsons into the mysteries of Test cricket, my daughter told them that people would have come to the ground wanting nothing to happen, at least certainly not wickets.

Shane Warne remarked that Roy in the World Cup had been capable of calm defence, while in Tests he had hard hands, which suggested a certain brittleness. However, Roy and Denly got through Cummins's opening spell, Lyon came on, and Denly swept him for four, a little victory. At 12.27 England were 67-3, when Roy was bowled, with Denly on 36 off 86 balls. Their partnership was worth 64 runs, and I mused that if England could only lose one wicket every hour they would get through to the end of the day. And then at 12.42 Stokes was caught behind off Cummins, the ball having feathered the bat on its way through. Stokes walked off so quickly that the umpire was not required to adjudicate nor Australia to review it. This was deflating but also honourable and uplifting. At the end of the session, England had scored 69 irrelevant runs and only lost 2 wickets.

Returning to the screen after my sleep I found England on 139-6 with Bairstow just out. Buttler was battling again at 18 not out off 53 balls. It felt hopeless but there was still value both in entertainment and in honour to be had from resistance. At 3.17, 48 overs remained for England to see out the game, and a ray of hope offered itself in that Lyon's spinning finger seemed to have a split callous. Then in the 57th over of the innings, the ball was changed again for some inscrutable reason, and Cummins got it to swing away extravagantly. There was a shot of Smith looking at it and seeming to say, "We"e got a good one here." The ball moved from reverse swing to conventional swing, with more bounce and zip. Ricky Ponting remarked that Buttler had to start all over again. By this point he had been in for 70 balls, so he should have been seeing it reasonably well, and not playing and missing. Before the change, Cummins's pace had been dropping off, but the 'new' ball seemed to revive him. England tried to show some resistance. Overton overturned the umpire's lbw decision against him, and he was dealing satisfactorily with Lyon, possibly helped by all that practice on Somerset pitches against spin bowling. He was now 11 runs off 35 balls. 38 overs were left, so there was still much arm-wrestling to do. In this session only 2 wickets had fallen, and Buttler had been at the crease for 130 minutes. But then after tea it was 172-7 when Hazelwood bowled Buttler for 34 (off 111 balls) and Lyon had Archer lbw with one that kept low. 173-8. Shortly after 5 pm Australia lost another review. Would this haunt them in the way that lost reviews had haunted them at Headingley? 28 overs were left, and at 5.20 the new ball was available, with Overton on 20 and Leach, who in acknowledgement of his defensive technique had moved a step up the order to number ten, on 8. Earlier the commentary had quite rightly been about the quality of the bowling, but suddenly it was switching to the way these two batsmen were performing. At 5.45 20 overs left. At 6.01, 16 overs left.

Tim Paine was constantly rotating his bowlers, indeed there were more than 30 bowling changes in the whole innings, and then he produced an Australian masterstroke. Labuschagne was brought on to bowl at Leach, his leg-breaks becoming off-breaks to the left-hander, and getting bounce from the footmarks: in the 90th over he had him caught at short leg. Only 1 wicket was needed by Australia when at 6.09 the final hour arrived with Overton and Broad at the crease. When Overton fell at 6.14 lbw to Hazelwood, the survival of only (only?) 81 balls was needed to save the match. In the end, England spent 1,838 minutes at the crease compared with 1,588 for Australia,

513 of which were by Smith.

The Australian bowlers were admirable. Hazelwood took 6 wickets in the game, having been rested for the World Cup and being perhaps fresher as a result. The effort to get experience of English conditions before the series began seemed to have paid off. Australia had shrewdly played an 'in-house' match of a Haddin XI versus a Hick XI before the series began, either because they held county cricket in low esteem – for once the tour had no Australia-county match – or to develop their strengths out of sight of England. The plan paid off well, since it was 18 years since Australia had won a series in England, which would motivate them to finish the job in the final Test, due to start in four days' time.

*

Imitation is the sincerest form of flattery. In The Times a day or two after the match ended, a comic story ran about how after the game had finished Australia took to the outfield to celebrate retaining the Ashes. Steve Smith took a pair of spectacles, wiped them before putting them on and started shadow-batting left-handed. The team were then heard shouting 'no-ball' and 'Come back Smithy.' Leach had truly arrived, for what greater compliment could be paid to his character and to his bowling skills?

18 FIFTH ASHES TEST:
12 to 16 September, Oval

"It helps to win an Ashes Test at the Oval by batting first, provided you can put together an opening partnership . . ."

. . . and provided the weather co-operates. Here we were in mid-September, still playing Test cricket: might it not be a washout? It was unclear whether the heat dome happened in the way that was forecast earlier, but certainly in this Test no play was lost to rain. 328 overs bowled, 40 wickets taken, and 1111 runs scored. Yet another Ashes Test to give us our money's worth.

First up, in the necessary ritual, was the toss which was won by Australia who chose to field. If it was my decision, I would always be choosing to bat first, so I would certainly make a mess of it, but on this occasion, surely Tim Paine had made a mistake. Yet I only have an uninformed point of view; he had studied the pitch in close-up, and trusted his bowlers. Cummins, Hazlewood, Siddle, Marsh and Lyon were capable of knocking England over quickly, allowing Australia to post a big score, no doubt courtesy of Smith, and then knock England over again saving Australia the trouble of having to do much batting in the second innings. If they did have to make a good score in the fourth innings, perhaps they considered Leach a decent but perfectly manageable spinner. The flaw in this promising scenario was that the Australian bowlers had been going flat out only four days before. Another ridiculous train of thought went through my head: in the four tests played so far, Australia had won the toss in three of them, so the decent Tim Paine, in kindly mood, thought he would do England a good turn by letting them bat first (and Root commented immediately after the toss that he would have preferred to bat first anyway). This delusional train of thought was made odder by the fact that Australia had won the toss in the Second Test, had then chosen to field, and while drawing the game had their backs to the wall at the end of it.

As the England innings began, we were informed that the opening partnership for both teams in this series had never been more than 9 runs. The tale seemed to be continuing when on 7 runs, Burns was adjudged lbw. The umpire had a long pause before raising the finger, as if he was in two minds to give it out. There was no such pause by Burns in reviewing it, and the ball was shown by hawkeye to be going over the stumps. Did the umpire make his decision with the thought that the batsman could at least review it? As if to say, "I'm not absolutely sure, so what do you think, Mr Burns?" The indecent thought perished in my mind.

And then at 11.23 England reached 11 and had gone past the figure of 9 for the opening partnership. In fact Denly fell when the score was on 27, by comparison a positively ample figure. That was in the ninth over, so when Root walked to the wicket perhaps he was consoling himself with the thought that at least it was not the second or third over. He started in his normal manner of taking runs when offered and finding runs when he could. However, in the 21st over he offered a dolly catch at fine leg, and was dropped, and two overs later, off the same bowler, Pat Cummins, he was dropped by Paine. When they went to lunch England were 86-1, with a run rate of 3.44 an over. It felt like England's session.

In the afternoon, Root batted right through the session, going from 28 runs to 57 runs, far from an express pace but his fixity helped to build the innings – thanks to being dropped three times before he was out. Apart from Burns, Stokes fell in the session, so England were 169-3 at teatime, their session despite themselves. One did have the impression that Root was somewhat out of sorts, while Paine's decision to bowl cannot have been welcome to Cummins and Hazlewood, who had taken Australia to victory 4 days earlier, yet were entitled not to be right at the top of their game. Mitchell Marsh was the Australian bowler doing the damage, getting good swing and good pace.

Root was out immediately after tea, Bairstow followed him, Sam Curran was out off a no ball and then out properly caught in the slips playing in a way that gave Australia another unnecessary wicket. Woakes went quickly, as if the Australians had well worked out how to get him out, and we were treated to a shot of Archer at the crease wearing a very expensive-looking watch (surely it needed its own mini-helmet?). And with the score on 226 he fell to Hazlewood. At the other end, Buttler, who had come in at number six, was fighting to keep the innings afloat and suggesting that, even if he did feel jaded at the end of a long season, he was not going to allow that to affect his batting. Indeed, the situation allowed him to play the Stokes role, slipping when necessary into one-day mode. The bowlers were likely to be tiring, while at the other end Leach was his partner, perhaps the perfect foil by concentrating on his defence and co-operating with Buttler in letting him farm the strike. Marsh was off the field briefly with cramp, and at 6.05 Buttler hit Hazlewood for 6 to reach 52. At 6.10, with 3 overs to the new ball, Labuschagne, Leach's nemesis in the previous Test, came on to bowl his leg spin, except that Buttler was cleverly keeping Leach off strike. At 6.15 a sort of peace seemed to have broken out when we were shown Warner signing mini-bats on the boundary. Marsh was back on but bowling at 80 mph, feeling it in the body, and at 6.23 the second new ball was taken. It felt very important that Buttler and Leach survived until the close of play. Then, at the end of the 81st over, Buttler failed to take a single from the last ball, leaving Leach to the tender mercies of Cummins for the last over of the day. Could Cummins' skill and the new ball do for him? In the months after the cricket season has ended this gave the look of a dry, even dead, passage of play, but to experience it in real-time was to feel the intensity of it. In a way both sides will have been disappointed with their performance on Day One, and England would be fighting to take their score beyond 300 without losing a final wicket for the day. Leach had six balls to survive, and on the second ball of the over, the ball hit his forearm, flew to gully and was held. I could not tell whether the ball had hit his bat so my heart was in my mouth, and then I felt the small flood of relief when it was given not out and shown to be not out. Despite a blow to the forearm, Leach survived the next four balls. The session had been going Australia's way until Buttler and Leach pulled it back: Buttler was 64 off 84 balls and Leach was 10 off 31. By now, Paine was getting a lot of stick for inserting England, a point of view I was inclined to agree with, while Root, to whom at that moment I felt lenient, was being criticised for looking and batting jaded. What does the commentariat want? Superman? Still, the criticism would have had real force if he had been out when he was dropped first time. So, England were 271-8 at the end of Day One.

Root was among those captains for whom the burden of the job was affecting their batting. Part of Smith's success in this series I was inclined to put down to his release from the burdens of captaincy. There seemed to be sense in Paine taking the job on: he was not Australia's best player, yet he was a good ambassador for his side, and even if this day was not his best he had captained well at certain stages, helped of course by certain individuals, notably Smith, Cummins and Hazlewood. Now, Rory Burns had the experience of being captain at Surrey, so why not let him captain England? And thus release Root from his supposed demons – maybe only to heap them on Burns. Yet the rule that the best player always captains looked and felt jaded. Cricket is changing, and another new feature of the game was the value to be had from partnering a cavalier, attacking batsman with a roundhead, defensive one, so that the partnership is greater than the sum of the two partners. This had proved match-winning at Headingley, and was possibly going to prove match-winning here.

What were the omens on the next day, Friday 13 September? The Australian bowlers had been rested; Buttler and Leach would have to get their eye in again. Australia would want the last two wickets very quickly, while England, as I feverishly imagined in the night, could go beyond 300 before being all out. The initial passage of play would have its own quality of excitement.

It all started more comfortably, since the humidity on the first day had apparently been at 60%, perhaps accounting for the bowlers feeling weary, whereas it was only 37% on the second day. The two batsmen tried to get things moving, helped by a Cummins bouncer going for 5 wides in the third over of the morning, but at 11.18 Buttler was bowled by Cummins for 70 (off 98 balls), and at 11.25 Leach played on to Marsh for 21 runs (off 43 balls) so that England were 294 all out. There was a sense that it took Australia a few overs to find their radar, and in the end Marsh proved the pick of their bowlers: 18.2-4-46-5.

Now it was Australia's turn, but the opening partnership did not even make 9 runs when Archer got Warner in the second over, and Harris in the sixth. Labuschagne and Smith were at the crease, and their 2 wickets felt crucial for England's success. At lunch Australia were 55-2.

After lunch, the ball did not seem to be doing anything much at all, while Archer was in full flow and constraining the batsmen. There was a shot of Teresa May at the ground, released from the burdens of captaincy, and there was a sense of absorption in the crowd, which I felt must communicate itself to the players and help to raise their game. And then at 2.30 Archer had Labuschagne lbw for 48. The previous ball Labuschagne had just worked away to leg for 2. The next one was similar but very slightly fuller and bowled at 88 mph. Was Labuschagne eyeing his 50 and therefore getting impatient? Whatever, he had proved a very doughty opponent to the England bowlers. His five innings so far had produced scores of 74, 80, 67, 11 and 48.

Shortly afterwards, there was a comic incident when Bairstow gave Smith the impression that he was about to run him out coming for the third run so that he had to dive frantically for the crease. It turned out that this was a little joke on Bairstow's part. Gamesmanship of a kind, but somehow enjoyable even if you were an Australian. At the end of the session England had only 2 wickets but the runs were being contained even if Australia were halfway to the England total.

After tea the cricket continued to absorb. Smith was looking uncomfortable against Archer, cutting it and almost giving Root a catch, then the ball opened up from the splice but no one was there to take the catch, then he did a play and a miss. The crowd was probably well-tanked by now but there was an absence of uproar which I interpreted as a sophisticated engagement with the game. In the 54th over, Curran bowled a magic 6 balls: 132 kph / 82 mph, 84 mph, 80 mph, 80 mph: wicket - Paine caught behind for one run, 85 mph: wicket - Cummins lbw for nought, Curran on a hat-trick, so the sixth ball was fastest of the lot at 141.6 kph / 88 mph but Siddle survived. Smith was in an awkward position in a way, wishing to proceed in his own manner and in his own bubble, yet sensing that he must not get stranded at the end of the innings. Even he was tiring. Curran's in-swingers were causing him slight discomfort, and there was a certain twitchiness about his dealing with Archer. He gave the impression when Woakes came on of slightly relaxing his guard. What happened next was credit to Woakes, but also credit to Root for the bowling change. For some reason at 5.25 Smith lost concentration, missed a straight ball from Woakes, and was lbw for 80 runs. Maggie remarked in an offhand manner, "You can retire now, Woakesy." Perhaps he should have because Lyon hit 10 off one of his overs until he was bowled by Archer with a ball that dipped in at 121 kph / 75 mph, that seemingly new invention, or perhaps it is a new name for the slower delivery, the 'knuckle ball', known to Cricinfo as the 'doodlebug'.

Catches can have a galvanising effect. When Burns took an outstanding gully catch diving to his right to dismiss Siddle off Archer, Australia's innings came to a close at 225, 69 runs behind. England seemed galvanised. And when England batted, Harris dropped Denly in the slips. Australia less galvanised. On the last ball of the day, Burns was given out lbw, which he reviewed immediately and successfully. Also galvanising in its way. Perhaps like some of the players, the umpire was losing concentration. 257 runs had been scored in the day, and 12 wickets taken at a run rate of 3.29 an over, a day for the bowlers but still tremendously exciting. 78 overs had been bowled which was 7 overs short apparently of the full complement. I had no sense of being short-changed.

The outstanding performance came from Archer, bowling with a quality of line, a quality of pace, and a quality of variation. He bowled in four spells: first, 7 overs, 7 runs, 2 wickets; second, 6-23-1; third, 7-19 -1; fourth, 3.5-13-2. Root was deploying him in spells that allowed him to be at his most effective. He ended up with figures of 23.5-9-62-6 at an economy rate of 2.58. But what gave real spice to the day were the catches missed and taken. First of all, Root dropped Smith off Curran, getting his hand to a ball flying above his head but not holding it. Was he distracted by the proximity of Stokes's big hands going for it but not going for it? Were they too close to each other? As it happened, the camera showed an advertisement for Hardy's Wine visible behind them and the slogan 'a drop to enjoy'. Aimed at the Australian rather than the English spectator, I thought.

Secondly, Leach dropped Lyon in the deep. He ran forward, got his hands underneath it, but the fall jarred his elbow so the ball popped out. In the unequal light at the end of the day did he pick it up quite as early as he should have done? You don't just need to practice catching but practice catching in September conditions at 6 pm.

So, misses seemed the order of the day until Burns caught Siddle with a screamer. Suddenly England looked like a winning team. Burns must see the red ball in these shadowy conditions very well, as witnessed by his batting out the close in the gloaming, ducking and twisting for 4 runs in 15 balls.

And then Harris at third slip dropped Denly and damaged the webbing on his hand so that he needed 7 stitches. He cannot have seen the ball until it was too late, a red ball rocketing straight at him at 6.30 pm in September out of a darkish background, even with the lights on – a white ball would be so much easier. No excuses for him but there are reasons.

*

The third day arrived, with the game half over and very much in the balance. Shane Warne commented on the value to a fast bowler of a second night's sleep after a long day bowling. Could England bat all day and give Archer that second night in readiness for the final effort of the season against Smith et al. in Australia's second innings? And could Cummins, Hazlewood and Marsh shake off their weariness in having to bowl again so soon after the England first innings and run through them for a low score on an Oval pitch? Once again, more striving from both captains, both teams.

This third day, Saturday 14 September, also happened to be the last night of the Proms at the Albert Hall, of which we were getting an early preview by the playing of 'Jerusalem' over the PA.

The challenge for Burns and Denly was to beat the 27 runs they scored in their opening partnership in the first innings. They were obliged to Lyon bowling at 11.36. Three minutes later England were 31 for no wicket and had gone past the 27 partnership in their first innings. Denly then hit Lyon for six, England's tactics being to knock Lyon out of the attack so that Australia would have to bowl their quick bowlers. His first two overs went for 15, nearly all scored by Denly, except he then had his revenge when Paine snaffled Burns for 20. Still the opening partnership was 54 runs, the highest of the series so far by some distance. And then there was one of those obscure incidents, murky even on television, when umpire Erasmus seemed to be impressing on Paine that his side were not to talk to the opposition. Was sledging about to be banned? If only. It did not seem very likely.

Australia continued to strive mightily with the ball, and perhaps less with the mouth. Cummins and Hazlewood were pressing for the breakthrough, and Cummins's 86.4 average speed was quicker than in any other Test in the series, Cummins being the only Australian quick to have bowled in all five matches. At 12.30 Marsh was on and getting it to swing, but the Australian field was slightly more defensive. And then Lyon struck again having Root caught in the slips for 21 (off 26 balls) so that England were 87-2. However, the run rate was 3.04 an over, and they had a good platform for the rest of the day in batting Australia out of the game. I had my usual sleep after lunch, and woke just before 3 pm to discover that England were still only two wickets down, imparting that pleasurable sense of relief coupled with the impression that England had a real chance of winning the match. Around 3.30 the Denly-Stokes partnership of 100 was reached and when England went into tea they had scored 105 runs in the session at a rate of 3.5 an over. I thought this would do very nicely. However, they then wobbled. Stokes went for 67, and at 4.30 Denly was in the nervous 90s. It was commented on the television that it would be amazing if he got to his century, and lo and behold next ball he was caught in the slips off Siddle for 94 runs off 206 balls, a very sedate rate of progress but then that was quite trumped by the sight of an England opener still at the crease for so much of the day.

As on the previous 2 days, the bowlers were getting swing. Paine was constantly changing them, as if the bowlers were capable of only delivering very short spells. This made me think that it was a deliberate tactic of Australia's worked out between the captain and his bowlers and that, in the light of it, Paine had the confidence to field first after winning the toss. This did not necessarily seem to be poor captaincy. When Bairstow went at 4.58 and England were 249-5, it suddenly seemed possible that England would be all out by 6 pm with a lesser lead than they would wish. Once again the initiative seemed to be in the hands of Buttler, who with the aid of Curran, batted sensibly for a 30-run partnership, and then had a 26-run partnership with Woakes. At 5.56, the 300 came up, with the lead 369, and England looked to take it beyond the magic 400. A brilliant catch by Smith saw Woakes gone, and England were 305-7. Australia were keeping in the game, and immediately afterwards Buttler was caught in the outfield by Labuschagne running in and keeping his elbows from hitting the ground hard that might cause the ball to jump out of his hands. Cummins was now bowling hard at Archer and Labuschagne was on to get Leach. Yet England survived to the close to reach 313-8, 383 runs ahead, only 17 short of the 400-run target. The run rate for the day had been 3.49, and 8 wickets had gone down for 304 runs. This was a real fourth-day moment with one side seeking to secure their dominance ready for the fifth day. Australia had done it at Old Trafford, now it looked like England's turn.

I watched the Last Night of the Proms at the end of the day, but had to wait until after 10 pm for 'Jerusalem', a satisfying complement to the events of the day at the Oval. The latter has a capacity of 24,500, and also a very substantial television audience, while for the Proms the capacity of the Albert Hall is something over 5000, and there were 40,000 in Hyde Park for the Prom relay there. At the same time, there were League football matches going on in London and other parts of the country. The icing on the cake came with the discovery next morning that Norwich City had beaten Manchester City 3-2. It felt inevitable that Manchester City would beat Norwich City until it failed to happen. All in all this offered a surprisingly benign picture of the country enjoying itself – when at the same time the Parliamentary situation had Britain engaged in its own slog through the mud, its own Passchendaele.

At the beginning of Day Four, I learnt on Cricinfo that England's bowlers had 21 LBWs for the series to Australia's 10. Was this because they are natural lbw bowlers, or because they were making better use of DRS?

"The old order changeth yielding place to new." Tennyson again. Gower and Botham were standing down as presenters for Sky, and rumour had it that Isa Guha, a TMS regular, was lined up to come in as the Sky anchor.

I also learnt from the media that a certain scratchiness seemed to have crept into the on-field relations yesterday, not that I saw much of it, except umpire Erasmus telling Matthew Wade to pipe down. Apparently too Warner's verbal abrasiveness was less under control than it had been. Pity really. Poms whinge according to the cliché, Aussies sledge. Yet it doesn't have to be that way.

My first hope for today was that Archer and Leach could get England over 400 runs ahead, and then lead the charge in taking 10 wickets, all in approximately 85 overs for the innings. At 4 runs an over that is 340 runs, not quite enough for the Australians to win but getting close. They might do better with 2.5 runs an over for 160 overs spread over Sunday and Monday. Smith is the barrier to be surmounted, and if he resists, it will be the greatest Test innings since . . . since . . . Stokes at Headingley. However if that fortress falls, England can surely press through the breach.

I had six other hopes for the day: that Archer had had 2 good nights' sleep, that Leach could get turn not just out of the rough but out of a dry track, that Broad could bowl as well as he has all series, that Curran swing would have its moments, that England's catching was match-winning, that a brilliant run out, largely absent up to now, might be the icing on the cake.

When play started, Lyon, bowling to Leach, got plenty of spin. However Leach threaded a boundary through the offside fielders, but when he tried a sweep, he missed. At 11.05 Archer was out caught behind, having being given not out. Paine reviewed the decision on his own initiative, and ultra-edge showed a feather off the glove. I daresay Archer did not feel it at all. Paine was congratulated by his team-mates for having got one right. Yet there were advantages to England since Archer was able to return to the pavilion and gather his strength. Broad was last man in, and with Leach they went into cavalier mode. Broad hit Cummins for two sixes, but when Leach tried to do the same he holed out to Hazlewood off Lyon. The innings ended only 12 minutes into the session, but England had left Australia needing 399 to win. To help them reach this target the heavy roller was brought on, but England had their own heavy roller in the person of Jofra Archer.

The Australian innings opened with Broad bowling to Harris, and from the first ball Australia ran a bye. Since this brought Warner to face Broad, I wondered idly if the bye had been a deliberate move by England. Warner survived perilously, demonstrating his own demons in the process. Yet at the end of the fourth over, Australia were on 13, their highest opening partnership of the series. It was not to last: at the end of the next over, Harris was bowled by Broad with a ball that moved slightly off the seam, ripping through his defences and causing the stump to cartwheel away. Like all sport, cricket is primarily visual, and this sight fired up the team and fired the crowd. Australia's okay start then became a poor one when at noon Warner was caught in the slips off Broad for 11 runs off 22 balls. 2 wickets down, 8 wickets to go for England, except that Labuschagne and Smith were now at the crease. At 12.25 Leach came on in place of Broad, and at this point there was a Spitfire and Hurricane fly past in a reminder that it was Battle of Britain Sunday. Was this an omen of victory? Leach then almost wrote himself into the history books when in his first ball at Smith, he bowled a length ball just outside off, spinning in. Smith left it alone, and the ball fizzed past very close to off stump. Leach leapt, I leapt – "You can retire now, Leachy" – but it was in fact a plain dot ball in the scorebook, and probably one in Smith's mind: he left it alone because he knew precisely where his off stump was – and that it was in no danger of being hit.

But 15 minutes later, Leach had Labuschagne stumped by Bairstow for 14 (off 39 balls) putting Australia 3 wickets down. The appeal for out was referred upstairs, which added to the theatre of the incident both in the ground and at home. There is palpable suspense in waiting for the verdict on the big screen. At lunch therefore Australia were 68-3 from 21 overs, and the run rate was down to 1.9 an over for the last 10 overs before lunch. A minimum of 62 overs remained for the day.

After lunch I went without a sleep, since I could not bring myself to answer the question, "Where were you when Smith was out?" with the answer "asleep". My vigilance was rewarded when Broad had Smith caught by Stokes, Broad working to a plan of putting Stokes at a fine leg-slip position and Stokes making a very good catch diving to his left. This had the feel of a winning wicket, except I also had the curious sensation that now that Smith had gone, something had gone out of the contest. In partial recognition of this, as Smith returned to the pavilion the crowd stood for him.

Soon afterwards, Burns took a brilliant catch off the bowling of Woakes to dismiss Marsh – only it was a no ball, so not out. We then learnt that officially this was the first no ball Woakes had bowled in 5000 deliveries in Test cricket. Like wides (see p. 138) no balls were not his thing, yet it was also revealed that the ball before that one was a no ball, only not called as such. Woakes, perhaps disappointed that he had not made more impact in the series as a whole, was striving mightily. A few minutes later Woakes got the ball to fly off Marsh's bat to Burns but it would not stick. The partnership between Marsh and Wade was beginning to build when at 3.25 Root put himself on in place of Leach and promptly had Marsh caught sharply at forward short leg. Good captaincy, never mind the bowling. Australia 148-5. What was more, Wade was finding it harder to get Root away, and in attempting to break the shackles was not far from holing out to Broad. Root seemed to be getting better speed on the ball and better revs than Leach. However, Leach came back on for the last over before tea and Wade hit it high to Curran at deep mid-wicket, only for the ball to drop just in front of him. It was a pity that Curran is not taller. Wade was going after Leach, but living dangerously in doing so. In this session 99 runs had been scored for 2 wickets, so Australia was holding out.

After tea, at 4.42 Paine was lbw to Leach, Australia 201-6. Matthew Wade remained the locked door, so Root brought Archer on not to pick the lock but to break the door itself down. He proceeded to ramp up the pace and in the seventh over of his spell hit 153.9 kph / 95.6 mph, the quickest ball of the match. To his credit, Wade was not to be moved, and just after five o'clock only 21 overs remained for Australia to see out the day (leaving another whole day to bat), which meant a wicket every 5 overs if England was to finish the match by the close of play.

At the 63-over mark there were only 17 overs to the new ball and at 5.35 Wade reached his century. Cummins went very soon after, leaving Australia 7 wickets down. What was Wade to do? He was finding Root difficult, and indeed his impatience with Root's bowling suggested that his nerve was failing him. Just after six o'clock Root had Wade stumped by getting good turn out of the rough, away from the left-hander. 2 wickets for England to get with 10 overs remaining. And then the door collapsed when in the 77th over, before the new ball was required, Leach had Lyon caught at square leg and, next ball, Root took an even better catch diving to his left off Leach to dismiss Hazlewood.

England had won by 135 runs. And yet, in a way, everyone had a prize: both sides had played some very good cricket, the series was drawn, and Australia kept the Ashes. In view of the equilibrium between the two teams this felt a very satisfactory conclusion. In any case there is no better sort of Test cricket than two teams striving in an even contest. Test cricket, not just over 5 days but also over 25 days, is like a flywheel that stores rotational energy just when longueurs – and an apparent inertia – creep in, only to release it later, especially on intense final days.

Later in the year (October) I came across a letter from Paddy Briggs in the Cricket Society Bulletin: "Test cricket is like [the music of] Bruckner in that it takes a while to play but can reach a climax that no other format of the game can achieve." To appreciate it you just need to discern its architecture.

Part 4 EMBERS

19 The everblasting arms: 14 August to 21 September (Finals Day)

'Cognitive dissonance' is a phrase from social psychology that has gained common currency. It is possible that I was guilty of it; I rated slow cricket much higher than fast cricket, and yet 2019 had shown me how enjoyable the latter could be. I was therefore being inconsistent. My head was shouting, 'Make a choice!'

Yet 'guilty' is possibly the wrong word. Instead the heart should embrace both versions as meritorious in themselves – an attitude which would still allow me to rate slow cricket higher than the fast version – and enjoy both when they presented themselves. An Ashes series juxtaposed with the T20 Blast enabled me to do just that.

*

Finals Day, as the Blast climax is called, brought together 4 teams at Edgbaston on 21 September: Derbyshire, Essex, Nottinghamshire, Worcestershire. Since I had not been following it closely, I was not clear how these 4 teams had risen to the top of the heap. The other 4 contenders to reach the quarter-finals were Leicestershire, Middlesex, Sussex and Gloucestershire. Top of the North group was Lancashire with 20 points, 4 more than Notts in second place, so a clear candidate for Finals Day. In the South Group, Sussex were hardly different, with 19 points from 8 wins, and Gloucestershire 1 point behind them. The finals therefore looked as if they would be contested by Lancashire, Nottinghamshire, Sussex and Gloucestershire. If achieved, this would mean that there would be three Division Two teams in the mix.

Essex, by comparison, were comparatively lowly. They only won 2 out of their 10 games in the first rounds, with 4 rained-off games. From 22 August they won a series of games by tight margins, beating Sussex by 9 runs, Surrey by 19 runs, and next day Kent by 10 runs. In between those games, on 25 August they had tied with Hampshire, which would have been a sporting spectacle well worth being present at, although minds must have been elsewhere earlier in the day when Stokes triumphed against the red ball at Headingley. Needing 31 off the last two overs, Hampshire reduced the total to 11 off the last over thanks to 3 wides bowled by Beard, which is perhaps not such a sin when the margin between a wide and a dot ball is so tight that it is well worth striving for. In any case it was quite eclipsed by Northeast's skill in taking balls 3 to 6 for 4 4 2 and 4. The last over was down to Amir which he delivered with considerable skill: 1 wide 1 4 (Northeast) 1 wide 1 0 1. On the last ball, with Hampshire needing 1 run to win, Northeast was run out making 73 off 56 balls, almost a hero but not quite since Hampshire ended 139-6 to Essex's 139-7. The upshot of all these close-run affairs was that Essex sneaked through to the quarter-finals.

Again, the quarter-finals took place without my paying them due care, but then they looked tame: Essex beat Lancashire by 6 wickets, Notts beat Middlesex by 10 wickets, Worcs beat Sussex by 8 wickets, Derbyshire beat Gloucs by 7 wickets. The standout result seemed to be at Trent Bridge where Middlesex scored 160-8 with Morgan chipping in 53 off 31, but when Notts batted it only took Chris Nash (74) and Alex Hales (83) 98 balls to demolish this total. But the game at Hove sounded pretty remarkable too: Sussex made 184-6. Worcestershire lost their first wicket with 2 on the board, which brought their captain Moeen Ali to the crease and he promptly dispatched Sussex to the dustbin of Blast 2019 history by clubbing 121 runs off 60 balls, 65% of the runs needed.

To the neutral spectator the defeat of Lancashire was the best story. Normally, the match would have taken place at Lancashire's home ground of Old Trafford, giving them a certain advantage because they would know the conditions so well. But the fourth test being played there had put paid to this, and so Lancashire had to find another venue to play their game. TV rights meant that it had to be played under floodlights so they stayed north but the other side of the Pennines by going to the Riverside at Chester-le-Street in County Durham. Although this is a tricky place for T20 I learnt later, in scoring 159-5 they must have felt that they were strongly in the game. But were conditions right for cricket, I wondered? The date was Wednesday 4 September, the day a gale was blowing at Old Trafford when England laboured in the field, and at Chester-le-Street they were playing in the evening of the coldest day of the summer. So, which side could stiffen its sinews, and even more importantly summon up the blood?

When Lawrence was out for 15 in the fifteenth over, 5 overs to go, Ryan ten Doeschate on 24 was joined by Ravi Bopara. At the end of the over, 51 was required from 30 balls at a required run rate per over of 10.20. Up till now the run rate had been 7.26 so to an untutored eye like mine, Lancashire had victory firmly in their sights. It was no better at the end of over 16 when only 5 runs had been scored. The rrr was now 11.50. Lancashire supporters, who had provided some of the best attendance throughout the Blast, must have started to feel a warm glow inside provided they had wrapped up well enough. Essex supporters (were there any? Chester le Street is a long way from Chelmsford; better to watch on TV?) must have wondered whether they faced a long and dreary return home.

And then things perked up for them. In the 17th over, Liam Livingstone went for 11 runs, so the rrr was kept in check at 11.66. Next over, bowled by James Faulkner, went for 12 runs, rrr still in check at 11.50. Livingstone had bowled three overs for 25 runs; could he keep his fourth to under 10 runs, leaving the challenge of winning to the death bowler at the end? No. His over went for: 1 (ten Doeschate), 6 (Bopara), 6 (Bopara), 1 (Bopara), 2 (ten Doeschate), 6 (ten Doeschate) – 22 runs off the over so that now only 1 run was needed by Essex to win. Matt Parkinson was chosen to bowl the last over, but Bopara unceremoniously sent the second ball for six. Lancashire had gone from hope to deflation, Essex from melancholy to elation. They had completed their sneaky route to the finals.

One statistic to dent my one-dimensional understanding of the Blast was that the top three run-scorers in the competition so far were Azam and Banton from Somerset with 578 and 549 runs respectively, and Malan from Middlesex with 490, yet none was figuring in the Finals, whereas two top wicket-takers – Rampaul of Derbyshire (22 wickets) and Gurney of Notts (20 in 11 games) -- were. So maybe the bowlers made a bigger contribution than the batsmen?
*

Then it was Finals Day on Saturday 21 September.

In some ways, watching Finals Day was purgatorial. It started at 11 am, and finished at 9:30 pm. All that television made me punch-drunk, and I was lucky that my medical condition gave me permission to be so passive. The wheels were coming off at the end too. In the last 30 minutes, the livestream was breaking up. This felt as if it was a result of the frenetic cricket but no doubt was the fault of my broadband. Anyway it was the wrong moment for this to happen, it had worked for much of the day, so why be difficult now, I reasoned irrationally.

As difficult to handle were the adverts, but I have a strategy for this: kill the sound, turn the head away, lie back and think of the cricket I've been seeing. This works, but there was a third difficulty, which was much harder to handle because so unpredictable. It turns out there are two spectacles on Finals Day. One is the cricket, which lures the punters in. The other is party-time in the stands. I am able to enjoy this in moderation, but moderation is not part of the Sky *modus operandi*. And so it was that we got to see much flaunting, and the camera joining in, sneaking its way among the spectators. There is an aesthetic problem here: parties, revelry, orgies have been the stuff of movies from the beginning. The trouble is they look great to be part of, but at one remove from reality they pall and pall quickly. Hence the need for moderation, the one thing Sky cannot deliver.

It is a commonplace for managers, players and commentators to describe the crowd as 'absolutely brilliant'. And indeed the good humour of these big occasions can be uplifting. But to go to Edgbaston to party looks like a confusion: surely you go to watch the cricket? Well, you can do both, and some clearly do. But could you go to Finals Day, and choose a seat on the opposite side to the raucous Hollies stand, committing yourself to 'quiet enjoyment' of the spectacle – to use a phrase from residential leases to mark the tenant's rights. If this was the case, then that was of no concern to Sky who were anxious to paint a Hollies-stand version of existence.

This does not matter much except when it gets in the way of enjoying the cricket, which it began to do seriously when around the seventh over of the Essex chase in the final game we had to endure Robert Key going into the Hollies stand with a selfie stick – nor did his sheepish expression suggest that his was a particularly enjoyable existence at this point. Yet tight run chases rely on ratcheting up the suspense – and at that point Essex's powerplay in its way had been disappointing. Were they going to fail in the chase? It was vital for the spectator to engage with this question, without diversions. Briefly, tin-eared Sky could not deliver, although in their defence things came right as the overs clocked off, the Essex runs-per-over rate began to climb, and the spectator watching at home was put right there in the middle, I am sure more compellingly than a spectator in the stands.

*

At 11 am we were away with the Notts v Worcs game or, if you prefer, the Nottinghamshire Outlaws versus Worcestershire Rapids. The Outlaws won the toss and made the Rapids bat first. The batsmen started rapidly enough, taking 9 off Luke Wood's first over, and his bowling was rapid too, the last ball hitting 145 kph / 90 mph. Another thing that went rapidly were the slip catchers who lasted just two balls. As I kept being told through the season, not having appreciated it sufficiently, there was no swing with the white ball. Matt Carter's right-arm spin came on in the second over, and induced Rutherford to be caught by Hales tracking back and using his height with great athleticism. Moeen was wanting to pick up from his innings at Hove. In Wood's second over, his second and third ball were hit for six, while Wessels stroked an elegant drive for four, threading the fielders, a more luscious sight in its way then Moeen's sixes. Then in the fifth over Moeen was bowled trying to sweep across the line (21 off 9 balls), and when Wessels was out in the thirteenth over for only 34 off 38 balls, Moeen's aggression looked the more effective. Parnell at number 4 tried taking up the cudgels but fell for 15 off 14 balls. Notts were doing well, until Worcs was rescued partially . . .

-- But then I had to endure the sight of beach balls in the crowd. More uplifting was a sideshow of Mexicans carrying a wall along with a Trump inflatable. I was reminded of the gravedigger's logic concerning Hamlet being sent by the King of Denmark to England:

Gravedigger: It was the very day that young Hamlet was born, he that is mad, and sent into England.

Hamlet (incognito): Ay marry, why was he sent into England?
Gravedigger: Why, because he was mad; he shall recover his wits there; or if he do not, it's no great matter there.
Hamlet: Why?
Gravedigger: 'Twill not be seen in him there, there the men are as mad as he. --

. . . by Whiteley hitting 36 off 24 including three sixes. With 12 balls to go, there was a question to be answered, namely could Whiteley get Worcs over the 150 mark? Wood bowled the nineteenth over for only 5 runs. Worcs 137-7. Last over up, bowled by Gurney. 1 run (Mitchell) to 138, 1 wide to 139, dot ball – a slog and a miss from Whiteley, 1 wide to 140, Whiteley out at deep midwicket to slower ball – great spectacle, 6 (Mitchell) to 146 – even better, Mitchell out to extra cover off another slower ball – great bowling, last ball: 1 bye to 147-9. Thwarting the 150 looked like a Notts victory. It should have been easy for Worcs to get these surely?

But what do I know of the Blast's 'game of inches'? That is what we got. Moeen's fourteenth over had Hales, who had been going well on 52 off 42 balls, well caught by the wicket-keeper. The second over had gone like this: dot 4 4 4 dot 6, all from the bat of Nash. Hales was going especially well, piercing the field skilfully. After 5 overs they were 44-0. At the end of the powerplay they were 52-1, and Notts would reach their target in 18 overs. After the 60-ball (10 overs) tipping point Notts needed 62 from 53, and then 'Brother Mo' got Hales. The game had something left in it after all. Duckett took up the cudgel, or rather the ramp and was almost caught when Cox got a hand on a ramp shot but could not quite hold it. Then Duckett hit a boundary to console himself. Only 35 needed from 24 balls, and then 26 from 18 balls. Notts were 112-2 when at this stage in their innings Worcs were 125-7. Wayne Parnell's third over then went like this: 6 (Christian out of the slot), 1, 4 (inventive ramp shot by Duckett off a wide), 2, 1, 1. So 15 runs from the over, and 11 needed from 12 balls. The penultimate over went to Dan Brown, yet another name quite new to me, who had Christian caught by Moeen at mid-off timing his jump to perfection and taking it one-handed. This was a captain's team-motivating catch. 2 balls later Tom Moores holed out at long on. Then came a moment of weakness, of pressure, of panic: Duckett hit a single but Stephen Mullaney wanted a second, Duckett sent him back, reasonably in the circumstances – get 'em in singles after all – and that's Mullaney run out. As he tramped off the two batsmen exchanged winged words. A collapse – and a collapse of nerve with 4 runs and 3 wickets off the over.

Now 7 runs were required from 6 balls, and by this time the camera was focussed entirely on the cricket so it must have been exciting. Parnell is to bowl the last over. Come on Wayne, this is your moment. Ball 1) He starts with a dot. 2) A single from Samit Patel brings Duckett on strike. Come on Ben, this is your moment, you know you only need 6 from 5 but since in a tie Notts would win by virtue of having lost fewer wickets, actually 5 from 5. 3) He can only take a single. Then Moeen is taking time setting his field, an example of how coolness can create its own pressure. Does the batsman chill out, or psych himself for battle? Moeen is not offering him any advice. 4) Patel hits 2, playing his part even if it is pretty frantic since the 'Jason Roy gambit' (a straight throw-in on the bounce) might have done for him. 2 from 2. Message arrives from the dressing room which we can only guess – Samit, a tie is OK for us, perhaps? 5) A single brings Duckett on strike, and another message from the dressing room is delivered in person, a tactical delay, except Moeen is taking so long to set his field that no advantage is gained. The PA is pumping out 'We will rock you' in case anyone had not been following events. And then we are ready. Only a single is needed for the tie. Parnell runs in and then stops to warn Patel not to leave his crease too early or he will be 'mankad-ed' (see Glossary). (Had he spotted this himself? Or had Moeen, or another Worcs player, advised this? Very good tactical move to keep the psychological advantage.) 6) A dot ball, so Worcs win. But 'dot ball' speaks a whole history: Duckett swiped and missed! A dab would have been enough! I thought he had been bowled, no, stumped since Cox is standing up to the wicket, no, not out, the wicket-keeper had merely stopped it with his pads. Why had the stumps lit up? Was there another ball to come, I wondered? The over had taken so long I had lost track of where we were. Dim. The

Outlaws had been sent to the gaol of defeat; the Rapids were in the final Final.

Next up Eagles versus Falcons, or rather Essex versus Derbyshire, a game in which the Essex names were as familiar as the Derbyshire ones were unfamiliar. I needed to recover from the excitements of the first game, so I took a break from watching, and when I tuned in Essex were on 99-3 after 12 overs with a projected score of 165, scoring at 8.25 an over. As I understood it, the pitch was slow, prompting a forecast from David Lloyd that with dew on the pitch in the evening the final Final would see the ball skid on. Essex were scoring in singles, and first it was 24 balls since the last boundary, then 31 balls. For instance the nineteenth over went: 1 1 1 2 1 dot. When Wheater hit a four off the third ball of the last over, it was the first boundary in 37 balls. Essex finished on 160-5 at a run rate of 8 an over. Was there a hint of disappointment in the air? Not what the punters came to see?

But they did get a spin master class. First the seamers came and went: Porter's first over went for 15, Beard's second over for 6 with one good wicket, Porter's second over for 9. Time for spin so Harmer, who is captain, brings himself on and takes a wicket first ball, a harbinger of things to come. The next over is bowled by slow left-armer Aron Nijjar in his second T20 match. His first four balls went for 4 6 dot 4. A harbinger of Derbyshire victory? No, since on his next ball he bowled Wayne Madsen round his legs, and Essex had found the formula to take charge. When Ravi Bopara bowled in the fifteenth over the speed was 97 kph / 60 mph, and Cameron Delport's pace in the seventeenth over was described as 'very gentle', with 'no pace for the batsman to work with'. Thus the match ended with an Essex victory, Derbyshire all out for 126 with 8 balls left in their innings. 8 wickets had fallen to spin and 6 were bowled. It helps to have Harmer in the team: his figures were 4 overs-14 dots-19 runs-4 wickets, economy rate of 4.75 an over, figures tarnished by Ravi Rampaul mowing him for a six, but only slightly.

It was just after 6 o'clock and I realized I still had one more game to go, Essex v Worcs. Essex won the toss and chose to bowl with Harmer being engagingly unspun: "We're hoping that dew's going to come into it later – pretty buggered if it doesn't! I guess it is a bit of a gamble but the batters will have to deal with it." Worcestershire were unchanged, but for Essex Sam Cook was favoured over Porter.

Harmer opened with Dan Lawrence's twirlygig spin and the third ball pitched on the middle stump and hit the top of off. That brought Moeen Ali to the crease. The second over, bowled by Cook, went for 4 dot 1 4 dot 4, taking Worcs to 23-1. Then it was Beard's turn, Beard to beard, and his over went for 7 runs, 3 of which were wides. Cook's fourth ball of the third over went for a six, and that was the end of the quicks, except that Cook was bowling at a slower pace than normal, no doubt under instruction. At the end of the powerplay, Worcestershire were 47-1. This brought a juicy contest to the fore with Harmer bowling to Moeen, captain versus captain, one good spinner against a batsman good at spin. In the ninth over, Harmer had Moeen caught and bowled, Harmer diving forward to take a catch just above the ground. Moeen was gone for 32 off 26 balls, and then Cox fell lbw to Harmer, a great strike for Essex except that replays showed that Cox had hit the ball before it hit his pads. It did seem odd that there was no DRS in use for lbws so it remained out. Worcestershire had to fight still harder having only taken 2 runs off that 2-wicket over, but then Nijjar came on and they took 13 off the over, getting back in a groove. The thirteenth over was Harmer's fourth, ending with Parnell's wicket and Worcestershire on 91-4. Bopara was playing his own particular part: his first over (sixth of the innings) had gone for 9 runs and his second (the eighth over) for 6. I was learning that to be successful in T20 you had to be able to come on and go off, performing with every ball, and there was no question of trying to find a rhythm. Bopara, as a seasoned campaigner, was a very useful bowler to have. His third over, the fifteenth of the innings, went for 9 and Worcestershire were still only 107 -4. Then another match-turning moment occurred. Paul Walter, squarish on to the stumps, brilliantly ran out Mattheus Wessels, a decision which had to go to the third umpire since it looked as if maybe Wessels had made his ground, but the decelerated replay showed he had not dived and so was given out by a tiny margin. Lawrence bowled the seventeenth over at the end of which his figures were 4-0-26-2, a pretty good contribution. The eighteenth had Delport bowling his dib-bly-dobs, proving so hard to get away. Whiteley did hit him for a low six, but he then holed out to Harmer deep on the leg side. 130-7. 2 overs to go. Were they not going to make 150 even? Nijjar bowled the nineteenth over: 1 2 1 dot 1 dot, 5 runs in all, which was very niggardly in the circumstances. 135-7. That left the last over, for which Bopara seemed the natural choice. I was not sure whether Essex or Worcestershire came out on top but it was massively exciting. Ball 1) Single run. 2) Ed Barnard scooped and failed, out caught at short third man. 3) 4 byes! A ball for the dustbin except that it won't be if Essex lose by 3 or 4 runs. 4) Single. 5) Boundary struck by Brett D'Oliveira, a familiar name to me but it is Basil's grandson. 6) D'Oliveira picked out deep midwicket and was out. And here endeth the Worcs' innings at 145-9, scored at a run rate of 7.25 per over.

Like Notts in the first semi-final, Essex might have felt it was in the bag, except there was the little matter of dew on the pitch and how it would affect matters. Would it make the ball skid on later and fly off the bat? Moeen takes the first over and only concedes 1 run, leaving him 3 overs to bowl later in the innings. In the third over, bowled by Parnell, Delport hits a full toss into the deep but unfortunately for him Moeen has just changed his field especially for this ball, and he is caught. At the end of the over Essex are 16-1, needing 130 from 102 balls. Suddenly I realise that T20 is not all about blast, but also about nurdle, and cunning is required from both batsman and bowler. In the fourth over Pat Brown is bamboozling the batsmen with 'doodlebugs', balls that die on the batsman. At the end of the powerplay Essex are 36 -1, scoring at only 6 runs an over against an rrr per over of 7.86. In the eighth over Darryl Mitchell bowls Wheater attempting a sweep, so 49-2. In the ninth over Dan Lawrence hits a six and at the end of the tenth over, halfway through the innings, Essex are only 63-2 against Worcestershire's 75-3 at the same stage. Although Tom Westley is building an innings, in the eleventh over he top edges Parnell and is caught at midwicket for 36 runs off 31.

Time for the captain to tighten the screws so Moeen comes on for his second over. Although Lawrence manages a reverse shovel for four, ten Doeschate hits the ball hard straight to a fielder and is out for 1 run. Only 7 runs came from the over for one wicket. I was wondering if the game was slipping away from Essex in terms of their losing firepower but then I realised that the new batsman was Ravi Bopara. Bopara is now in and with Lawrence attempts some big shots, but they do not connect. Essex now need 64 from 42 balls when Lawrence hits Moeen hard and high and is caught, when an armchair critic like myself knows that he needed to hit it less high, with less of a parabola, and then he would not have been caught. The required run rate is now 10 an over but Bopara is keeping Essex in the game with 2 boundaries. On Moeen's fourth over, the sixteenth of the innings, Bopara hits a six and 10 runs come from the over. The score is 107-5 and Bopara has 22 off 13. 38 runs are required for an Essex victory. In his penultimate over, the eighteenth, Brown continues to be clever with his deliveries that decelerate on their way into the pitch. Paul Walter misses a six because he cannot get the pace of the pitch. No sign of the desired dew in operation here. Are Essex 'buggered'? They now need 30 off 18, so the rrr is down to 10 again. Parnell's penultimate over sees Bopara being starved of the strike, so that with 12 balls left 23 runs are still needed. For the nineteenth over Brown sets his own field and concedes a boundary, but then has Walter out cross-batting it and playing on. Essex are now 129-6 and sliding out of the game. But the man who comes to the wicket is Harmer, unafraid to cross-bat Brown for a four on his first ball in absolutely the incorrect way. Who dares, wins. The mean thought crossed my mind that it was a boon for Essex to have Harmer for the showdown in place of Walter since if anyone's confidence would take them over the line it would be Harmer's coupled with Bopara's.

The last ball of the over brings Harmer on strike for the final 6 balls when calculations might have suggested that they were better faced by Bopara. For the last over Parnell has to be Worcestershire's man. Technically 12 runs are needed by Essex, although 11 for the tie will do since they are fewer wickets down. By now, I had been gripped by the possibilities of Blast cricket, since clearly blasting is not enough. What is more, considerations of being buggered by the lack of dew were irrelevant, since now it was simply a case of winning by daring. Harmer takes a single off Parnell to bring Bopara on strike. Good plan. But Bopara can then only get a single off the next ball. No problems: Harmer gets 2 runs off the third ball leaving 7 runs required off the last 3 balls. Another 2 runs brings it down to 5 off 2 balls. The wind is in Harmer sails and also behind the ball. He cross-bats a boundary - incorrect again! – back over the bowler's head, leaving himself one run to win off the final ball. Go on, Wayne, rout the inevitable, strive! The fielders are brought in to prevent a single, but completely composed, Harmer, the better striver, square drives it for a four to win the match. How could it end otherwise?

I slept fitfully that night, my sleep punctuated by images and thoughts from the Final. The image I savoured was that of Bopara coming off the field and wagging a victory finger at the camera with a Mona Lisa smile on his face. In comparison with Harmer running about the field demented having hit the winning runs, I thought this was admirable. Admittedly, Harmer calmed down pretty quickly, and he was entitled to be pleased with himself: 3 wickets, 3 boundaries at the end, astute captaincy, even calling the toss right as it turned out though it was a very close-run thing. Perhaps because sporting triumph is so ephemeral, players are entitled to milk the moment.

20 County Championship: endgame . . .

How do you make a long story short? Sometimes you cannot.

In the gap between the Fourth Test and the Fifth Test, which was only three days long, the County championship started up again on Tuesday 10 September for the final three rounds, **the twelfth, thirteenth and fourteenth**. Essex and Somerset were fighting for the Division One crown; in Division Two Lancashire were well out in front but the scrap for second and third places was between several teams. There was much cricketing spice to be savoured.

The two big games were Warwickshire versus Essex at Edgbaston and Somerset versus Yorkshire at Taunton. At both venues the toss was uncontested with Essex and Yorkshire both electing to field first. Warwickshire immediately started to build a big innings, with Sibley to the fore. At the end of the day they were 269-3 and both Sam Hain on 77 not out and Matthew Lamb on 69 not out had eclipsed Sibley. Did this mean that Essex had made a mistake in fielding first?

At Taunton on the first day, it looked as if Yorkshire had made the right decision – until it didn't. Initially there was no livestream at the ground, apparently because someone inserted the cable in the wrong socket, but it was back on track for the afternoon. Somerset were in big bother at 107-6, and around 3.15 they were 173-8, 27 runs off a batting point, so crucial to them, and their captain Abell was on 59 not out. He got them to 199 before he was lbw to Maharaj (having patiently got to 66 off 193 balls), so 9 wickets down, but if Davey could survive the 3 balls left in Maharaj's over, Jamie Overton at the other end, on 40 not out, could surely get them to the magic 200.

Alas, Davey fell 2 balls later, lbw to the said Maharaj who finished on 23.5-7-54-5. Maharaj, the South African Test spinner, is another top player to have been drawn into playing county cricket, so the Somerset batsmen were being tested significantly, against their will no doubt because in the 3 matches he had played against them, one in 2018 and two in 2019, he had taken 26 wickets in 5 innings at an average of 10.88. The wicket seemed to be living up to its 'Ciderabad' reputation, an impression not dispelled when Yorkshire batted. They were 70-3 at the close, following the curious sight of Bess, the Somerset warrior, who had been hired out to Yorkshire as a mercenary earlier in the season, getting the significant Yorkshire warrior of Ballance for 35 runs with 10 balls left in the day.

The next day, 11 September, after half an hour Yorkshire were 94-6, and there had been 4 scoring strokes off van der Merwe in his 8 overs (8-4-10-2, 1.25 economy rate), and at 11.20 he took the last wicket so Yorkshire were 103-9, but Ben Coad being unable to bat, they were in effect 103 all out, giving Somerset a 96-run lead.

Warwickshire were ploughing on at Birmingham and had got to 310-6 when Somerset started its second innings. Of the Yorkshire players, Maharaj must have been enjoying the prospect most, and came on from the beginning. When he had Murali Vijay lbw for nought in the third over, bowling must have been pure pleasure. Should Somerset's tactics be to try and dig in or to dominate the bowling by scoring runs. Would the target be to get to 250 ahead before having their second go at Yorkshire? Abell, again, and Hildreth needed to keep Maharaj at bay. I watched pleasantly on the livestream, but wished that Somerset had a back-up camera across the pitch just to supplement the down-the-pitch cameras. At lunch they were 49-2, and an hour later were 107-2, while Warwickshire were now on 401-6. If Somerset were to win their game and Essex lose theirs, Somerset would surely come back into contention for winning the title. At the close of play they were 269-5, bad light having ended play early, while Warwickshire, having been all out for 517, had several overs to bowl at Essex, a situation tailor-made for a big Alastair Cook score. It was not to be when he succumbed to Jeetan Patel for 7 runs. So, Essex had a big fight on their hands: they had 2 days to bat out and 19 wickets to preserve, while rival Somerset were likely to be eyeing victory by the end of the day.

On Thursday 12 September the Fifth Test had started, so my eye was off the county championship ball. At lunchtime Somerset had been 329 all out, with another 5 wickets for Maharaj, but this time at the expense of 122 runs. Yorkshire were 2 wickets down, with the crucial wicket of Ballance falling just before lunch. For their part, Essex were playing the long game and had lost only 2 wickets for 120 runs.

The Yorkshire innings quickly eroded: wickets fell after lunch with the score on 54, 71, 94, 94, 94, 103 and 127 all out. A win by Somerset of 298 runs. Beat that, Essex! The next day Paul Edwards on Cricinfo was so lyrical that he quoted the hymn writer William C Dix and the closing lines of Clifford Bax's 'Cricket Days', and mused on the prospect of the county championship coming to Somerset for the first time.

At 5.15 on the third day Essex were 278-6, with the aim of avoiding the follow-on at 367 runs. The match was delayed by bad light, which will have helped Essex with their eye on a draw. Westley was on 123 not out off 266 balls, and hopes must have largely rested with him. The next day saw the loss of Wheater and Harmer with the score on 288, and then Westley fell at 320. Essex were all out for 324, well short of the 367 target to avoid the follow-on. So, Essex to bat again, and on the fourth ball of the innings Browne, having scored 65 in the first innings, was out for nought. Alastair Cook, on the other hand, having gone for 7 in the first innings, now had to play a saving role for Essex. In conjunction with Tom Westley, he did so, and at the end of the game he had reached 57 off 164 balls, while Westley, carrying on where he left off, was out for 97 off 161 balls. The game finished with Essex on 158-2, giving them five points for the draw, plus four batting and bowling points. Somerset may have been straining to run ahead, but Essex were just keeping a hand on their shoulder, on 197 points to Somerset's 205. In their first innings they had needed 22 from 9 overs for a third batting point, and in the last of those overs they needed 2 runs but Essex could only score one so missed out on the point. This esoteric fact will be chewed over in the event of a very tight conclusion to the season, but if not it will remain esoteric, not even a footnote.

Division Two seemed to be sorting itself out. After their round of matches, Lancashire were still well out in front on 204 points, while Northamptonshire (161 points) and Gloucestershire (156 points) were to the fore. Durham were on 147, and Sussex on 145, with Labuschagneless Glamorgan fading on 136. Since 3 teams would be going up, there was a big prize here, but it could still be very tight for that second and third place. Being eyed up was the game in the final round between Gloucs and Northants at Bristol.

*

The penultimate **thirteenth round** was to be played on Monday 16 to Thursday 19 September, with the absorbing Ashes series finally over. When I checked in at 10.45 on the first day, I learnt that the Essex-Surrey start had been delayed by bad light, and Hampshire, playing Somerset at Southampton, were 3-1 after 3 overs, having won the toss and elected to bat. The Somerset Titanic had sailed at dawn with a natural optimism, helped by the fact that the weather forecast for the 4 days was pretty good, despite some rain being expected on the first day. At Chelmsford there was some rain in the morning, which was then reducing, and again the weather forecast was reasonable. It was a blessing that it was not weather that was going to determine this round of matches. At lunch Hampshire were 75-6, with Essex unable to play so sat watching, possibly unable to watch – but then no one knew of the iceberg waiting to sink Somerset.

Proceedings got underway at Chelmsford at 2.15. Surrey won the toss and elected to bat. Unfortunately the Essex livestream started to misbehave, while that at Southampton was a bit squashed and with imperfect definition. Then the Essex livestream went off-line, a bit like being at a lecture when the PowerPoint breaks down. And then a livestream on YouTube popped up showing Scotland as 72-0 off 6 overs playing the Netherlands, courtesy of Cricket Ireland which had 56,000 subscribers. Then the Essex livestream returned, and Pope was struggling against Harmer, including one of those balls that hits the base of the stumps but the bails then fail to fall off. This is a good batting education for a prospective Test player. At 4.59 Surrey were 111-4, and it was commented that there was a 'terrific' crowd in attendance. And then at 5.37 the Surrey batsmen were spotted returning to the pavilion on 137-4, bad light again playing its part. The weather may be good in September but then at the end of the afternoon the light is not so good.

At Southampton Hampshire were rescued from complete destruction when Dawson and Barker took them from 88-7 to 180-8. Hampshire were soon all out for 196 but conditions were clearly tricky, since Somerset were 30-2 at close of play.

Deprived of a magic last hour of cricket, I idly turned up details of proceedings at Malahide, which was the second match of an Ireland tri-nation T20I series, arranged in place of the cancelled Euro T20 Slam. Scotland made 252-3, in which George Munsey scored the third fastest hundred in all T20Is, and Netherlands did very well but far from well enough in getting to 194-7.

The next day, Tuesday 17 September, and an hour into play, Surrey had moved to 170-9. Until Essex batted there was no way of knowing whether a real contest was going to ensue. But at Southampton Somerset were in deep trouble at 59-7 with the prospect of being over 100 runs behind in a low-scoring game and having to bat last. The top order had quite collapsed against the bowling of Kyle Abbott, and unless the tailenders turned the innings around very significantly, it was hard to see Somerset getting any batting points at all from this match. A draw looked very unlikely, so only a victory snatched miraculously would bring them any result points. Might this spoil the last round when ideally you would want the winner taking all?

Just after noon Surrey were all out for 174, and Essex had started their innings, no doubt greatly encouraged by the news from Southampton. A good win would put them in significant control for the last game at Taunton. However, Bess and van der Merwe had now put on 22 for the ninth wicket and the game was not feeling so hopeless for Somerset, especially when some wild overthrows from a single hit by Bess enabled the pair to run a five. At lunch Somerset were 103-8, and at 1.50, Bess (37 off 96) and van der Merwe (25 off 45) were still there fighting. Although they were 68 runs behind, they had the example of Dawson's century in the first innings to inspire them. But then they were all out for 142, 54 big runs behind. The cause of their destruction was Abbott who finished the innings with figures of 18.4-9-40-9. He must have been drawing great motivation from not just destroying the Somerset innings, but also ruining their chances of winning the title. How were Somerset to get out of this one? Nor was the news from Chelmsford particularly helpful since at tea Essex were still 53 runs behind but with 7 wickets in hand. Somerset had soon got Hampshire 4 wickets down for 34 runs, but this still left Hampshire 88 runs ahead.

I started watching the livestream at Southampton because Somerset had taken 6 wickets and I thought they would pick up the remaining 4 quickly, but not so. They were not making the breakthrough, and James Vince, who had been absent from the final of the one-day cup in May because of England duty, was chipping in with a win-securing innings for Hampshire. His eighth-wicket partnership with Abbott took the score from 103-8 to 222-9. Vince's fear would have been of being stranded, but by sticking around, Abbott was able to sustain Vince's innings in yet another example of a stroke-maker teaming with a batsman with a good defensive technique, and Vince being good enough to farm the strike.

Amidst these excitements, a quick study of Division Two scores showed Sussex's chances were slipping away, Glamorgan was hanging in, Northants seemed to be in control against Durham, and Gloucestershire now needed only 108 to win.

At 5.23 Essex had their first batting point, and it was commented that the pitch would not deteriorate massively. They would want to secure some decent bonus points by batting on. At Southampton, Hampshire's lead was now 183, and Somerset were not threatening the necessary breakthrough. They badly needed to finish the innings and bat at the end of the day when Abbott might be tired. Instead Vince and Abbott were still there at close of play.

At Chelmsford Essex had extended their lead to more than 100 runs, with 2 days to go in the match. Would Essex want to extend this to 250 runs, even 300, beyond Surrey and then bowl them out to win by an innings? There was also the bonus of batting points to consider. At close of play they led by 128 runs with four wickets remaining. The Surrey player Amar Virdi's figures of 24-4-79-0 suggested spin was not a great threat, at least not yet. Essex would want another 70 to 80 runs, leaving time to bowl Surrey out and bat to hit the winning runs.

In Division Two, Gloucestershire chasing 115 were 54-4, so seemed likely to win, while Northamptonshire were dominating Durham and also likely to win. The oddity was the game at Lord's between Lancashire and Middlesex. Lancashire had virtually sealed the Division Two title, and made 259 on the first innings, and then

Middlesex wickets fell at 15, 15, 15, 23, 23, 34, 141, 217, 311, finally all out on 337. John Simpson, batting at number seven, made 167 not out.

The third day began with Somerset on 208 points and Essex on 200. Dan Lawrence's 147 for Essex could well be the platform for their victory and enable them to leapfrog Somerset in the points table. He was still only 22, and must be an England prospect of some kind. As it happened, on this day I was in the car but still able to listen to the Hampshire-Somerset game on the radio. Vince and Abbott were still going for Hampshire, when Vince, having been assured for 20 minutes, suddenly started looking scratchy. Overton was back on and at 11.15 finally snared him caught behind for 142, and Abbott fell soon after. Hampshire were all out for 226, 280 runs ahead: a massive task faced Somerset while in Hampshire hearts they were thinking:

Whatever happens we have got
the lethal Abbott and they have not.
They'll never make it.

Somerset had to get their thinking in confidence mode. Get through the first hour and go on to get the runs. There were plenty of batsmen who could chip in and get them over the line.

And so it seemed at the beginning. Murali Vijay started to score, and Steve Davies likewise. They saw off Abbott's first spell (had all that batting got to him?), but after lunch, Vijay miscued a hook off Abbott and fell for 29 runs. Had Abbott appeared to have found how to bowl again? If there was any steel in the Somerset dressing room, it was of the most bendy kind. From 86-1, they went to 100-7, all wickets except one falling to Abbott. He was apparently moving the ball startlingly off the seam while hammering away at a good length. Abell was bowled shouldering arms; Hildreth feathered behind; Bartlett was trapped lbw in front of his stumps. Somerset now had to get 150 or so runs with three wickets remaining. Impossible, surely. Ben Stokes was otherwise engaged. And then Lewis Gregory and Overton started to make a stand. Abbott's second spell finished. Meanwhile, Essex were looking to overwhelm Surrey, having gone well beyond them on the first innings, and then having Harmer getting among the wickets. But at tea they must have been toasting Abbott with whatever they were drinking. Gregory and Overton were hanging on, but at 3.28 Overton was out for 10 (off 56 balls), making him Abbott's sixteenth wicket. Gregory was 32 not out scoring in more cavalier fashion, but Somerset still required a lot more. What is more, Surrey were still 111 runs behind Essex with only 5 wickets remaining. In the first innings, Porter and Sam Cook had shared the wickets between them but in the second innings Harmer already had figures of 29-5. The livestream was still stuttering away with no sound. The settings read '240p' and the speed was normal – except that the resulting picture was fuzzy, and there was a camera at one end only, unfortunately not over Harmer's arm so he bowled into the camera and the ball got obscured by both wicket-keeper and batsmen. Constant interruptions did not help either. It felt regrettable that at this important moment in Essex's season when the team was firing on all cylinders, the camera was not. At 4.35 Harmer was into his 26th over, having bowled without a break since lunch. Jordan Clark was facing the quicks while Morkel stuck to Harmer, using his height to good defensive effect. A lot of singles were declined in an admirable if bloody-minded, pointless even, tactic to delay Essex's victory – or bloody-minded on its own. But then some great cricket has resulted from bloody-mindedness. At 4.52 I learnt that 11 runs had come from the last 10 overs. But all things must pass: with the score on 161 Clark fell to Bopara, and at 181 Harmer finally bowled Morkel for 21 off 80 balls in 102 minutes, last man out, so that Essex won by an innings and 40 runs. Harmer's figures were 34.2-14-58-7.

At Southampton, Somerset had finished at 144 all out, a defeat by 136 runs. What had fired Hampshire? Although Somerset and Hampshire are not adjacent counties topographically, in sporting terms they are, and nothing fires competition to win than beating your neighbours, especially if they look as if they might be winning the championship. That is a simple explanation, perhaps simplistic since it does not account for Abbott producing a very great bowling performance. Of his 17 wickets in the game, 10 were bowled or lbw, 4 were caught behind, and 1 each held at slip, short leg and mid-on. Seam, swing, reverse swing, overall unplayable. The performance can be watched on the ECB highlights of the game [Jan 2020] on https://

www.youtube.com/watch?v=n_69dw8wZkQ, or search 'Hampshire v Somerset 2019'.

Hampshire had thrashed Essex in the first game of the season, winning by an innings and 87 runs, from which pit Essex had travelled from nadir to zenith. All in all, an excellentissimo result for Essex, a dirissimo one for Somerset; pretty satisfying for Hampshire; and the question kept returning: what had happened to Surrey this season? It is as if they had been unglued.

In Division Two Sussex had fallen to Derbyshire so that they were out of the equation, Gloucestershire had beaten Worcestershire, with one crucial match to go, Gloucs v Northants, and Northamptonshire were on the verge of beating Durham, again with a crucial match to go, Northants v Gloucs. Northants only needed 4 points from the match to go up, and while Glamorgan have an outside chance, Gloucestershire needed at least a draw.

*

Trevor Bayliss, the Australian who had been managing England since 2015, on his retirement from the position took the opportunity, or the invitation, to offer on Cricinfo some thoughtful and incisive reflections, direct in the Australian way, regarding county cricket. He started by admitting that "these conversations had been going on for twenty-five years and nothing changes." He thought that England should really grasp the nettle (whose sting he did not appear to recognize) and reduce the number of teams in the county game from 18 to 10. He then had a swipe at the quality of county pitches as too soft and damp. He described the gap between county and Test cricket as 'huge' and commented: "Top players come back from county cricket and they are not complimentary about the standard. They don't think it helps prepare them for international cricket." Batsmen were not in the habit of building long innings (something for which contrary evidence I felt could be found), and better pitches would help develop fast bowlers. He then added something arresting to my mind. "You might even see better slip catchers because I think the big problem in English cricket is concentration. Players have forgotten how to concentrate for long periods of time." But then added a wry note that part of the reason may be because society conducts itself so much more quickly now. As it so happened the dilemma was apparent when England played New Zealand in November at Mount Manganui. New Zealand won easily by grinding out a long innings, whereas England, despite attempting to do so, could not. But at the same time more than one journalist commented on how soporific the game got at certain points.

While I find the commentariat on both TMS and on Sky generally excellent, every now and again they hint at a patronising mindset towards the county championship, echoing Bayliss, who had made clear at the beginning of his tenure that he had limited interest in watching county cricket, as if he found it irrelevant to his job. It is not irrelevant since the link between it and Test cricket in this country needs to be made of steel if the latter is to survive. It has all its own merits: teams with illustrious histories, lovely grounds, the capacity to provide absorbing cricket, and one of high-quality too, *pace* Bayliss and Atherton (see below). To go from there to Tests is a step up, a difference in degree but not of kind, but the commentariat risks giving the impression that county cricketers are second class if they cannot do it.

As it turned out, the county championship had had a crucial role in 2019. Witness Broad bowling for Nottinghamshire. Witness the Australians Siddle, Pattinson, Labuschagne and Bancroft playing county cricket prior to the Ashes. It is the training ground for Ollie Pope for him to make the step up. Root had two games for Yorkshire early in the season. The point has applied especially to Burns, who learnt his basic technique at Surrey of how to bat according to the situation and how to lead as captain. The Test matches were a step up, but so far he seemed to be making it, witness his adjustment to short-pitched bowling. And the man without airs but with 630 Test matches to his name, Alastair Cook, has chosen to score a pile of runs for Essex. However, on Tuesday 24 September, Mike Atherton in The Times was blunt: "The standard of first-class, as opposed to one-day, batting in the English county game has probably never been lower." He even talked of 'mediocrity'. Normally a measured and generous journalist, Atherton on this occasion had not quite found the right words – and thrown his wicket away.

Despite not watching county cricket, Bayliss had a shrewd close up of the game in this country, and so his comments are important. Much less convincing was his criticism of the ECB for letting Australians play county cricket before the Ashes series. "There was no way Australia would allow England players to acclimatise in the [Sheffield] Shield ahead of an Ashes series. And quite right too." Spoken like a true Australian I thought. Very much in the Australian character that they have more of a 'win at all costs' mentality. Would the ECB really introduce a rule specifically excluding overseas players from a country due to play Tests in England, not just Australians, but Indians, Pakistanis, Sri Lankans, West Indians, New Zealanders, others? Cricket is a global game, and the lightly-regulated trade in players, and indeed managers, should not be stopped.

More attractive by far was a comment made in an interview with Morné Morkel, the fine South African quick bowler who had made a big mark with Surrey on the first-class circuit. In praising county cricket, he made the memorable comment, "One day you can be the peacock, the next day you're the feather duster." This quality, more marked in slow cricket than in its fast form since moments have more time to marinate in the mind, is not to be undervalued.

*

The force was with peacock Essex. For their win at Chelmsford they had probably had their best crowd of the season, boosted by non-members, an aggregate of 7000 over the 3 days. Essex would be taking a 12-point lead into the last game.

21 . . . and more endgame

The rains came, not a monsoon but soggy persistent drizzle, conducive to melancholy in Somerset if not in Essex. A draw was being heralded as the most likely result, in the **fourteenth CC round**, i.e. last game of the season, due to start on Monday 23 September. This would suit Essex nicely. The weather helped in another way. They had been involved in the high-octane Blast final 2 days before, so they would be tired, physically and mentally, would they not? Bad weather would allow them to sit in the pavilion twiddling their thumbs and their smartphones in satisfactory recuperation mode. Their team was virtually unchanged from Saturday's so clearly they were not concerned, except to make one change that would suit anyone, bringing in Alastair Cook to strengthen the spine of the batting.

Somerset, on the other hand, had to mend an Abbott-sized hole punched in their self-belief the week before. A spin pitch would be prepared to assist Messrs Leach (back from England duty), Bess and van der Merwe, but then it would also help Harmer and Nijjar (in the team in place of the fast-medium Beard). One was duly provided but a different sort of grenade blew up on it: in mid-November it was discreetly announced by the ECB, well after the captains and the kings had departed, that Somerset were found guilty of "preparing a pitch for the game against Essex marked poor for its 'excessive unevenness of bounce'." A penalty was imposed of starting the 2020 county championship with a 12-point handicap. This was no doubt justice but with the weather likely to be poor, at least some sort of game ensued thanks to spin and bounce.

In ideal September weather, one might expect 80 overs at least in a day, i.e. 320 in four days. What we got was 137 overs in total, only enlivened by a spin-fest, and still not enough to spark a real contest. All the other competitions had finished, so the cricket fraternity duly descended on Taunton, but not even their best efforts could squeeze the moisture from this damp squib. All that remained was to enjoy the play that did occur, careless of the result. For me, the prime attraction was Harmer versus Leach, a contest whose honours were in the event even.

Somerset opened the batting, and Harmer bowled virtually half the 62 overs, his figures being 27-5-105-5, with 118 out of the 162 balls being dot balls. Leach bowled 25-9-32-5 with 130 out of his 150 being dot balls. Only their economy rate differed: Leach's was 1.28 an over (exemplary), Harmer's 3.88 (hardly earning a reprimand).

The other contest in my mind was focussed on how the two captains fared. Tom Abell for Somerset, still only 25, had led through the season by example, with both bat and ball, and by a growing shrewdness. Ryan ten Doeschate (Tendo), 14 years older at 39, had first played for Essex in 2003, becoming a cornerstone of the team and then a key leader of their success, with to my eyes, whether seated on the boundary or in front of a screen, a wonderfully underplayed style. Abell will be a cornerstone of county cricket in general; Tendo has become one. I wanted them both to have prizes for good character. Somerset won the toss, elected to bat, lost a wicket in their second over, and so Abell at number three was in as an opener. He needed to be cool and concentrated, while Tendo came into short leg, eyeball to eyeball as it were.

We only got 1¾ hours of play, but it turned out as absorbing as I could wish, as if the result was quite unpredictable. The floodlights were on, and it was darkening, then there were a few drops in the mind, and at 12.15 the rain was heavy enough to drive the players from the field. In that time, Somerset had lost 4 wickets to Sam Cook's and Harmer's excellent bowling. Abell was concentrating mightily, and cleverly batting out of his crease to the pace bowlers.

In Division Two things were not much better: in fact the place to be was Chester-le-Street in the north of England, where only the Durham-Glamorgan game was still going at 5.30 pm.

The next day, Tuesday 24 September, only saw play restarted at noon, but conditions looked better. Somerset were on 75-4, so could they get to 200 and a bonus batting point? With difficulty. When Bartlett went (75-5), Gregory took a shine to Harmer and hit 16 off an over. It couldn't last, nor did it. He padded up to Cook and was lbw for 17 off 13 balls. A cameo, but only a cameo when a main performance was needed: red-ball mode, not white-ball. Bess, in at number eight, joined

Abell in being circumspect, and at lunch Somerset were 126-6. However-er straight after lunch, Harmer trapped Abell lbw. He went back in-stead of forward, but could he have got to the pitch of it? Had lunch caused a loss of concentration? And then in the same over Craig Over-ton succumbed in the same way so Somerset were 130-8 and the 200 target looked very distant. The situation was tailor-made for cavalier batting, but where Gregory had failed, van der Merwe succeeded. Harmer's first ball to him he swept for a six, and in due course reverse-swept him for another six. When Sam Cook bowled Bess with move-ment off the seam that took him by surprise, that brought Leach on to partner van der Merwe, in his case as had been learnt over the summer defence being the best form of attack. The attacking proper was left to van der Merwe, although it did not stop Leach taking boundaries off Cook's first two balls including a nicely judged drive. And then he played his part: singles were declined; van der Merwe took on Harm-er. Somerset reached 170, only 30 off a batting point when Leach sur-vived an lbw decision that hawkeye showed as out. No matter since hawkeye was irrelevant to the county championship. At 2.35 Tendo tried the 'Paine option': bowl a leg spinner to the left-handed Leach and snaffle him that way. Thus Nijjar came on, only to be hit for a six by van der Merwe, taking the partnership to 50 and 6 runs off a bat-ting point. Not content with that, he repeated it: Harmer went for a six also and the 200 was attained. And then we had one of those mysteri-ous ball-changing rituals, which, in reverse-sweeping Nijjar, may or may not have accounted for van der Merwe being bowled for 60 off 51 balls. Somerset were 203 all out, giving 1 batting point to them and 3 bowling points to Essex, so Somerset were now 14 points behind the leaders. Like at the start of the game only a win would do: 16 points would take them to 228 points against Essex's 223. If the weather were to co-operate a meaningful struggle could be permitted to take place.

Essex made a reasonable start to the innings, Browne and Alastair Cook taking them to 25 off 67 balls. Then it was tea, then rain, then stumps. I grumbled but I needed to be grateful because I learnt that several county matches around the country had been rained off all day. At least we had had some play at Taunton.

Yet time had run out. Rain prevented any play on the third day, so, on the last day, Somerset had to knock Essex over for 100, hit 100 quickly to get a lead of 200, and then knock them over again – before bad light stopped play. It was not going to happen. Just as likely was that Cook and Browne would dig in, so that Somerset would stumble on their obduracy.

The cricket was frustrating in a slough of inactivity, but it was as nothing compared to the goings-on in Parliament. On the second day of the match, the news came through that the Supreme Court had ruled the government's prorogation of Parliament as illegal. Of all the damaging developments in our governance this year, this was the most dismaying, emphatically the slough of despond.

I got to the fourth day of the Somerset-Essex game, Thursday 26 September, therefore, in a mood of no expectation. Why then was I so annoyed at the news that there would be an inspection at 11.30, with a probable start at 12 noon. Why be annoyed? It was all pointless, was it not? Already there was a dark cloud over to the west, and the floodlights were revving up. Elsewhere the cricket season had ended with a whimper, although one thing had been decided: in Division Two Northamptonshire and Gloucestershire were promoted.

Play then started up at 12 noon and for one last time in this epic season I was hooked. Leach took the second over and almost had Alastair Cook first ball, then with the third ball almost had him lbw, and replays showed the ball actually hitting the stumps. Never mind the umbrellas going up, never mind the players going off, at 12.15 they were back on. It was Bess's turn, drifting the ball into the left-hander. His third and fourth ball almost did for Cook, and the fifth elicited a shout for lbw. There was plenty to observe: Leach's good turn and good bounce; Cook's long reach with his bat; Overton fielding at second slip on his knees, the 'Trescothick gambit'.

And then in the eleventh over of the morning Browne pushed Bess into Hildreth's midriff at silly mid-off for 18 off 71 balls. Essex were 35-1, 168 runs behind. At 12.42 the players went off for rain, so they had lunch and were able to restart at 1.21. Cook walked back out obliged to restart his innings for the nth time. At 1.45, after 32 overs, Essex were 50-1 – at an economy rate of 1.56 an over – so the game was drifting away. After one maiden over it was commented, "That'll do well for Essex." Then it rained, then it stopped. And then at 2.55, 3 wickets had gone: Cook for 53 (off 148 balls), and Lawrence for nought 2 balls later, both to Leach who had tracked down something discomfiting in the pitch hitherto coyly hidden. He now had 6 fielders plus the wicket-keeper round the bat.

Now it was pure spectacle, pure absorption. Wickets had fallen at 35 (Browne), 102 (Cook), 102 (Lawrence) and 111 (Bopara).

After tea, the television switched to golf and, deprived of watching the cricket, deemed by Sky to be purely an academic exercise – right in the head but somehow wrong in the heart – I stepped backwards in time to listen to Vic Marks and Dan Norcross on the radio, mouth agape at Essex's demise. Wickets fell on 126, 126, 126, 137, 137. This last was Sam Cook out first ball for nought at the hands of Leach, his fifth wicket. For the hat-trick ball to Porter, there were seven men in his face. But he survived. And then at 4.13 Essex were all out for 141, trailing by 62 runs. Somerset had done well, except that it had taken them 68.2 overs, when it needed to be 20 overs less. For that Essex could thank Alastair Cook. Jack Leach, what were you doing? 25 overs, 9 maidens, 32 runs, 5 wickets. You needed to do all that in 15 overs.

What next? In fact an intriguing question came next: would Somerset bat at all? The umpires were telling them to do so, and then the answer came over the public address system that Somerset had forfeited their second innings. All Essex had to do was score 63 to win! All Somerset had to do was get 10 wickets for less than 63 to win! More prosaically all Essex had to do was bat out the day, of which there were only about 20 overs left. Cook and Browne, get in that zone, you're on again. To rub salt in the wound, the sun came out as Somerset took the field.

At 4.28 I found the game on TV again, Sky canny enough to know the grand finale was taking place. Like Cook, the opener Nick Browne was now taking a stride to the ball; Abell for his part was geeing up Somerset. Bess's speed was creeping up: was he too tense, striving too hard? Cook padded up to Leach but the lbw appeal was turned down. While there was Cook there was hope (for Essex), I reflected. Then Cook hit a boundary off Leach, his patience paying off, and then two boundaries off van der Merwe. Essex only needed 35 to win. The result seemed obvious, but the drama of it somehow carried you with it.

Then the drama gave way to ceremony. Much play was rightly made of the fact that Trescothick was retiring at the end of the season. He felt like an exemplar of some kind. Of Englishness? That was being too nationalistic. Of professionalism? After all he had played 76 Tests and 123 One-Day Internationals for England, and 391 first-class games for Somerset, nor had he been a mercenary elsewhere. But his age – 44, allowing him 26 years in first-class cricket with Somerset – suggested a career in cricket above the call of professionalism. Of grit? He had battled through self-doubt, had never "ceased from mental strife", and yet had come through, a great survivor. What he truly exemplified was how cricket, in all its global aspirations, could still be played by local heroes.

Putting aside the justified protests from other counties, I felt warmly, sentimentally perhaps, that no two clubs exemplified this better than Somerset and Essex. Trescothick ran on to bring the drinks. Then Browne hit a four off van der Merwe: only 26 was needed to win. At 5.13 Overton retired from the field and Tres took his place in the slips, fielding on his knees since it was his second nature to do so. He had after all invented this ploy.

Bess then had Browne caught by Vijay. The script had missed a trick here, since it would have been better theatre if it had gone to Trescothick. Then Cook was reprieved on a lbw that may well have been out. All diversions. At 5.20 diplomatic manoeuvres started to take place on the field. Somerset's plenipotentiary, His Excellence Thomas Abell, offered a draw to Essex's, His Serene Magnificence Sir Alastair Cook, which he duly accepted. Hostilities, in reality terminated for several overs now, were terminated formally, Essex choosing in magnanimous fashion not to humiliate their opponents by winning the game. Hats off to Browne and Cook grinding out 98 balls. Hats in the air to the county championship, ending not with a bang, not with a damp squib as I had anticipated, but with something to match the Christmas truce in 1914. Yet the fact remained that the dampness did rule events: in both divisions of the county championship, extended into the fourth week of September, all 9 games had ended in a draw as the bad weather and shorter days had prevented any finishes.

22 2019: the year of 'The Hundred' war

The new Hundred competition had been first proposed in 2016, with further decisions and clarifications in 2017 and 2018. Cue enthusiasm? Some. Cue outrage? Certainly. It meant that the cricketing world in England and Wales entered 2019 with a sense not just of battle lines drawn, but also of battle joined. The difficulty for those opposed to The Hundred was that they had little resources, especially after the counties signed up to it. Arguments were deployed throughout 2018, but when the season started in April 2019, The Hundred juggernaut was moving forward, finalising details and spending its marketing budget. Rearguard actions in opposition were not crushed, merely circumvented, leaving isolated pockets of resistance.

In the cricket bubble, three items caught my attention, all notable in their different ways. The first was Huw Turbervill's assessment in 'The Cricketer' (summer edition) of where the new competition had got to, both overview and micro-investigation spread over 8 pages, the unusual length of the coverage an indication of the passion The Hundred had aroused in that bubble.

This was prose. The approach of 'Wisden Cricket Monthly' was more poetic. In October, an anonymous piece by a professional county cricketer poignantly unpicked some of the tensions the new competition was creating in the counties. There are some 400 professional cricketers in this country: not more than 90 (8 squads of 15) will be involved in The Hundred so some are chosen to step into the stellar and lucrative world on offer, but the majority are not. Not everyone will be taken into the future. Some will be saved, some damned: in cricket as in life we all have come to terms with this.

The third item was sheer mockery. In its November/December News Bulletin, the Cricket Society published the names of the eight teams and beside them choice specimens of the marketeers' craft. The names were not a scoop but the verbal dross was. There were 8 samples of this and it seems invidious to quote only one since my choice is anything but objective. Here it is though: "Southern Brave: follow Southern Brave and go boldly where others shy away. Endlessly curious, with an insatiable appetite for adventure, what's over the horizon?" Reflection on these words, although they were not written to be subject to it, concludes that this team may be useless but that is of no significance, provided that innovation and a Star-Trek-like optimism are being cherished in themselves regardless. I worry too about what people will say when the Oval Invincibles are defeated. I do like the title 'Manchester Originals' and have wondered whether London Spirit, based at the home of cricket, might have been titled 'Lord's Lords' (while the women's team could be called 'Lord's Ladies'). Perish the idea.

It is clear that some tectonic plates on the cricketing globe are grinding away. The new 8 teams are based on big cities, since urban success and a big urban fan-base are perceived as measures of progress. In this country – possibly not in other cricketing nations – this is producing a 'tension in the soul' for some people. Cricket's origins are in the rusticity of the village green, where players played cricket for itself as a release from the humdrum, and even the grind of the social hierarchy. Spectators could watch as they wished, and the game was not assessed by whether they did so or not. 'Quiet enjoyment' was the order of the day.

Another friction was an alleged divide between the generations: many cricket aficionados are 50+, white, male (*mea culpa*). The ECB want to charge up a new audience that is young, diverse, male and female. It is their most powerful argument for the radical approach they are taking. On the other hand, cheerleaders for The Hundred sometimes paint a new kind of *homo sapiens*, addicted to speed, alert to a quite different version of society, digitally wired in the senses and in the workings of the brain. Old Believers (*mea culpa*, again) remain sceptical of this divide in the evolutionary fork. What is more since they do still have a hand on some of the levers of opinion-making, their view has felt to be not only louder but more articulate in 2019. (Better arguments for The Hundred are needed than that supplied by Captain Morgan, CBE, who was mischievous in 2018 when he said that some of his friends liked The Hundred "because it's upsetting people that already come to a game and that is the point of the product". Premeditated disruption seems an unsound basis for initiating it.)

The success of The Hundred will not be judged by who wins or loses the argument, but by attendance at the cricket, by the size of the TV audience, by the enthusiastic adoption of cricket as a 'favourite sport'. And there is one sub-criterion as well. The World Cup in 2019 brought teams from South Asia: Afghanistan, Bangladesh, India, Pakistan, Sri Lanka. Some fans flew in to support them, but they were particularly cheered by UK citizens of South Asian origin. Yet those same fans melt away from cricket when their teams or players are not involved. Leicestershire County Cricket Club is sometimes quoted: 52% of Leicester's population is South Asian in origin, but on the whole they do not go to Leicestershire's games. So success will also be judged by whether the new competition is attractive to them.

It seems likely that The Hundred will gather a new audience since it will be a new and hence fashionable product – until the novelty wears off. People will come to see individuals as much as, perhaps more than teams, a formula which works in football's Premier League. They may respond with enthusiasm to celebrity presenters, except for this to work those presenters will need to know something about cricket. But is a point being missed? The ECB want cricket to be 'cool', but when I summon up remembrance of my youth, a necessary condition of 'coolness' was that the older generation did not like it; if they did like it, ipso facto it could no longer be called cool. Yet to be successful the Hundred is going to have to attract all ages, including the older generation, so it is never going to be cool in its purest sense. The search for coolness should be abandoned; uncomplicated popularity should be the aim.

The most pragmatic argument to emerge against the newcomer is that 5 competitions are now scheduled for 2020: The Hundred, the Blast, the one-day (50 overs per side) competition, the dear old dowager county championship, and the small matter of 5-day Test matches. A 4-format season barely looks feasible; one of 5 formats is still messier – and even impossible.

23   The end of an epic year or of an era?

What a season for Essex! They had won their second county championship in three years and what with their mixture of well-seasoned cricketers with battle-hardened youth, to which combination Simon Harmer
and Alastair Cook have been added, Test cricketers in all but name,
they can look forward to the 2020 season in the Championship with un-
diminished enthusiasm. And Essex had won the Blast too. Done the
double. What a moment to be an Essex supporter!

And what a season for Somerset! Founded in 1875, 144 years ago,
and still going strong. They had won the one-day cup, no mean feat,
and while a first county championship title still eluded them they had
acquitted themselves in red-ball cricket more than well. The white-ball
Blast contributed £500k to total gate income in 2019 of £750k, with every
Blast game sold out. Their membership is 6500, their debt is low and
under control. Three clouds loom: first, their players are now being chosen to play for England, which is a testament to their strength. (When is
this going to happen to Essex, I wondered as the season wore on?) Second, they start the 2020 county championship 12 points in arrears.
Third, next year they will lose 8 of their players or thereabouts for the
duration of The Hundred. Another testament to their strength? Or a
fatal undermining of the club, and perhaps not just the club but the loy-
alties of the players? It will take some maturity for both parties to cope
with this.

So, definitely the end of an epic, but was 2019 also the end of an
era? Trescothick was retiring – would we ever see his like again? The
Blast had had its best season ever – pessimists thought it could not be
repeated. England had won the World Cup – when would that happen
again? Australia had retained the Ashes in England for the first time in
18 years – oh England, weep! The standard of cricket in the county
championship had, I learnt, "never been so low" – so, had a tipping
point been reached, with the consequence that those standards would
never recover? And next year, a dragon was waiting to devour all this,
The Hundred.

Television is key to how cricket develops in the future, hence the significance being attached to the fact that some of The Hundred will be on free-to-air TV. Some optimism may be in order too from the fact that counties are developing livestreaming of games. In 2019 Somerset boasted 2.1 million viewers of their livestream, while Surrey streamed over 70,000 hours to viewers this season. Results are crude at present but in 20 years it is possible to imagine livestreamed coverage as reasonably sophisticated, with images still linked to the present high-quality coverage on local radio.

Even more encouragingly, cricket culture continues to spring surprises amidst – and behind – all the big-noise cricket. One or two lowly but enterprising clubs started in 2019 to put clips on YouTube of their own champagne moments and in the YouTube manner suddenly lots of curious outsiders started looking at them, so much so that the ECB trialled its own video initiative under the title 'Play-Cricket'. This enables teams to livestream matches and create a highlights reel using a camera placed on a sight screen or by the side of the ground. This will be rolled out to the wider club network in 2020.

For livestreaming to develop, money will have to flow to the counties, and for that to happen The Hundred will have to be a success. But if it is a success it will erode county cricket. . . The round hole will have to accommodate the square peg. Is this possible? This leads to larger speculations about how the players themselves will adapt to the changing landscape. At present, all countries have players who can perform well in both red-ball and white-ball cricket. But is a trend emerging of younger players choosing one over the other – and choosing the white ball over the red, since the financial rewards are so much higher?

And yet on several occasions this season players struck me as not just professionals but as 'amateurs' – in no pejorative sense but as connoisseurs of the game. As such it is far from impossible that, provided there is some financial reward, even if it is not commensurate, they will choose to play slow cricket instead of, or as well as, the fast form, for the more protracted and deeper pleasures it can give.

A more immediate problem from 2020 onwards is accommodating the Hundred as well as the Blast, a conflict that masks the wrestling match being set up between the old 18 counties and the 8 new city-based teams. The Hundred will make more money because of the television rights involved, but the Blast may find itself attracting more spectators in aggregate. As a result will one of them have to go?

In the end, since The Hundred is here, one might as well be reluctantly in favour of it, not least because cricket, both English and global, will carry on regardless. England will go on playing Tests winning and losing them in timeworn fashion; Australia are no doubt already licking their lips for the next Ashes series in Australia in 2021; India are top nation Test-cricketwise, and that is not about to change, so no end of an era there. Somehow, the Blast, one-day cricket, four-day cricket, plus Test matches, One-Day Internationals, T20 Internationals and the Premier Leagues (India PL, Caribbean PL, the Big Bash in Australia, and so on) will all carry on. Alongside The Hundred, of course. Secondly, if there is no Hundred, there will be less central-contract money, so that some counties will become even more insolvent with an increased risk of going under altogether, and possibly triggering the contraction in the number of first-class counties from 18 to 10. Development programmes and grassroots funding will be at risk. The Chairman of the Professional Cricketers' Association, Daryl Mitchell, said bluntly that if The Hundred fails, "We are all in trouble." So in assessing its worth it will be necessary to take a five-year view from 2020 to 2024, the length of the new TV contract. The jury will need to be out for at least the next two years, hard as that is to imagine.

I suspect that what will attract the least comment is what the anonymous player in 'Wisden Cricket Monthly' drew attention to, namely the tensions created in the dressing room. Some young professionals chosen for the new competition's draft of players "haven't stopped talking about it since", while another drafted player will be "gutted" to be absent from the club halfway through the season. Then there are the older players thinking that if they had been a bit younger they would have had a chance of sharing in this loot. A gap will continue to grow between the well-paid and the bottom of the ladder. The only response can be that of a foot soldier, 'I am here to obey orders.' But these destabilisers and their tensions will require shrewd handling by those in command.

In all this uncertainty, there will still be plenty of cricket to watch in the future quite as pleasurable as the variety of cricket encountered in 2019. What had been most striking with the contrasts: between cricket played in a full stadium and in a two-thirds empty ground; between a crowd quietly absorbed, and one whipped into raucousness by huge screens; between the pleasant, detached warblings on the radio and the close-up, eye-grabbing visual detail of cricket on the screen, both being incisive in their way; between the professionalism of Sky's coverage and the endearing amateurism of livestream as currently delivered; between the high intensity of top players arm-wrestling for an advantage ball by ball, over by over, hour by hour, and in the County championship bubble the days of attrition, of striving, and of personal glory.

It is not therefore that all is for the worse in the worst of all possible worlds. It will still be a cricket season, with all its glories, its champagne moments and wormwood disappointments, its sunlight, shadow and rain stopped play. Where there are problems, old-style *homo sapiens* will have to try and fix them. Yet at the same time, players of all ages and spectators of all ages are going to have to adopt a blithe optimism, that this is the best of all possible worlds.

And where there is optimism, there is its opposite, since autumnal melancholy induced by 'no more cricket' can bring out your inner pessimist. The freneticism of all these fixtures exemplifies the globalisation of the game, and globalisation has difficulties with slow cricket; somehow there is a cultural mismatch. Slow cricket needs to accommodate soporific cricket to allow for high-intensity conclusions: to appreciate it will require a cultural adjustment for the expanding cricketing population.

Can the county championship survive and develop? Or must it, like empire, pass? To cling to it is to be unreformed, unreconstructed, dead from the neck down – and yet those convictions refuse to be shaken off. The dustbin of history beckons, but Old Aficionados still make 'The Grand Refusal', magnificent in their obstinacy, preferring to die in a ditch than give up long-form red-ball cricket. Finally we shall all die off leaving only a fading echo.

It is not the end of an era, yet you can imagine it, and what is imagined can be proved.

*

And also disproved. The year could not just end on a question mark. In the New Year, pessimism turned to optimism. The parliamentary impasse had unjammed itself as a result of a General Election with a decisive result. In a hard-fought series in December 2019 and January 2020 between England and South Africa, England won 3-1, a victory away from home and marked by the fact that a handful of young players hatched in county cricket took flight at Test level, namely Bess, Crawley, Curran, Pope, Sibley, thus affirming the importance of the link between the two levels.

To adapt the words of Edmund Burke, cricket is a partnership between the dead, the living and the unborn. Living cricketers are with us constantly, in the press, on YouTube, on social media. It is not reckless optimism to think that the unborn will be as entertained by this as generations living now. That leaves the dead. By a perfect symmetry, exactly 12 months on from playing family cricket in New Zealand on

Christmas Day in 2018, I found myself walking by the sea at Sidmouth. And there was a cricket ground, pavilion and all, and on the pavilion was a blue plaque informing me that in 1875, Somerset played a Devon team on this ground, and from that match the decision was taken to form Somerset County Cricket Club. They still await their first cricket championship, but I could hear all those long-gone cricketers speaking in 2019, the epic year.

ACKNOWLEDGEMENTS

In writing this book I have relied principally on my own observations and on my own notes. However, it is undeniable I have also made use of the reports on Cricinfo, in The Times, in The Cricketer, in Wisden Cricket Monthly, and in the bulletins of the Cricket Society, not to mention off-the-cuff comments picked up from both radio, national and local, and television. Overall coverage, for those who wish to follow it, is well-informed, stimulating, and capable of provoking disagreement without being disagreeable. I am therefore grateful to cricket journalists. In this book, none of the faults are theirs; all of the errors are mine.

One missing ingredient is following the game on social media. I have lacked the time to do this, and have probably missed some gems as a result, but in addition I have lacked the inclination to do so for fear of encountering the disagreeable. Why should one give it the oxygen of one's attention?

I am grateful to Harriet Monkhouse for the *capax umpirii* story (page 25) and to Emma Roebuck for the cover design.

The interest in cricket of my daughter's family has been an encouragement: if the game of cricket is to survive as an institution then the newly born generation needs to develop an interest, and judging by their enthusiasm and by their involvement in the big games of the summer it will be. Finally, I acknowledge again the fact of Maggie's attachment to the game, a willingness to listen to me on the subject, and her own judicious comments as a reader; this is another manifestation of the fruitfulness of our union over 50 years.

ABOUT THE AUTHOR

Tim Cawkwell is a freelance writer on cricket. *Cricket on the Edge* is his fourth book on the subject. Sforzinda Books is the name of his self-publishing venture.

He also writes on film and other subjects, having launched in 2008 his own website for writing about the cinema, later adding to it a Wordpress blog.

See www.timcawkwell.co.uk and www.cawkwell200.com.

From 1968 to the 1980s he was a film-maker working initially in 8mm and then in 16mm. His dvd LIGHT YEARS – THE FILM DIARIES OF TIM CAWKWELL 1968 TO 1987 was released in 2018.

He is the author of several books:

- *The World Encyclopaedia of Film* (co-editor, 1972)
- *Temenos 2012*, a diary about the Temenos film festival in Greece in 2012 (digital only)
- *From Neuralgistan to the Elated Kingdom: a personal journey inside Sicily* (2013, digital only)
- *Between Wee Free and Wi Fi: Scotland and the UK belong surely?* (2013, digital only)
- *The New Filmgoer's Guide to God* (2014, Troubador Press)
- *A Tivoli Companion* (2015, Sforzinda Books)
- **Cricket's Pure Pleasure: the story of an extraordinary match – Middlesex v. Yorkshire, September 2015** (2016, Sforzinda Books)
- **The Tale of Two Terriers and the Somerset Cat: the County Championship 2016** (2017, Sforzinda Books)
- *Belaboured. Bats Broken. Britain Shaken – a personal account of the 2017 General Election* (2017, Sforzinda Books)
- **Compleat Cricket: eight days in September** [about the CC relegation battle in 2017] (2018, Sforzinda Books)
- *Film Past, Film Future: an enquiry into cinema and the imagination* (2019, Sforzinda Books)

He was born in 1948 and lives in Norwich in the United Kingdom.

Essex slips in line ahead: Alastair Cook,
Simon Harmer, Tom Westley

Printed in Poland
by Amazon Fulfillment
Poland Sp. z o.o., Wrocław

58893762R00129